INTERNET PROPHETS

INTERNET PROPHETS

The World's Leading Experts Reveal
How to Profit Online

STEVE OLSHER

NEW YORK

INTERNET PROPHETS
The World's Leading Experts Reveal How to Profit Online

ISBN 978-1-61448-232-1 paperback
ISBN 978-1-61448-233-8 eBook
Library of Congress Control Number: 2012931094

Morgan James Publishing
The Entrepreneurial Publisher
5 Penn Plaza, 23rd Floor,
New York City, New York 10001
(212) 655-5470 office • (516) 908-4496 fax
www.MorganJamesPublishing.com

Cover Design by:
Rachel Lopez
www.r2cdesign.com

Interior Design by:
Bonnie Bushman
bonnie@caboodlegraphics.com

In an effort to support local communities, raise awareness and funds, Morgan James Publishing donates a percentage of all book sales for the life of each book to Habitat for Humanity Peninsula and Greater Williamsburg.

Get involved today, visit
www.MorganJamesBuilds.com.

ACKNOWLEDGMENTS

To Janet Bray Attwood, Christopher (Kit) Codik, Dean DeLisle, Mike Filsaime, Pat Flynn, Kathleen Gage, Steve Harrison, Dan Hollings, Pam Ivey, Mike Koenigs, John Kremer, Armand Morin, Mike Muhney, Marc Ostrofsky, Christian Pankhurst, Leslie Rohde, David Riklan, Riel Roussopoulos, Callan Rush, Jennifer Sheahan, Yanik Silver, Kristin Thompson, Jeff Vacek, Christopher Van Buren, and Jason Van Orden for graciously sharing your time and wisdom.

To Rick Frishman and David Hancock for believing in my vision. To Seth Czerepak for making the interviews easier to process. To Hy Bender for continuing to teach me the difference between writing and being a writer. To Candi Parker and LeAura Alderson for your eagle eyes and brilliant suggestions.

To Lori Gordon, for running the craziness known as Bold Enterprises and freeing me up to write this book. To Bobby, Isaiah, and Xavier for helping me to recognize that being a father is a journey of love. To Gail, Al, Harvey, Barbara, Irv, and Sylvia for helping me become the man I am. And to Lena, the love of my life, who makes the world a better place to be, and who always keeps me on point with her guidance, support, and compassion.

I love and appreciate each of you, and could not have taken this project on without you. You forever have my gratitude.

CONTENTS

FOREWORD

Steve Olsher's *Internet Prophets: The World's Leading Experts Reveal How to Profit Online* is like a dictionary in a world where language has just been discovered. The language is meaningless unless you know the meaning of each word.

Rather than attempting to teach you the language and its nuances, Steve has enlisted the help of those who have created and mastered it. Their fluency is your combination to the vault. Without their guidance, you are destined to wander in the wilderness—an evolving terrain which is being discovered and explored every day.

Although Steve himself is an Internet pioneer, the experts who contribute to this revealing and oftentimes shocking book are what make it the breakthrough manual it has become. Attempting to make heads or tails of the online world without the information they put at your disposal in this incredibly valuable volume is like traversing a foreign land without a map, with blinders on, and relying on instinct in a place where instinct has become extinct.

I congratulate you first on your discovery of this treasury of wisdom, and next on the success that is sure to be yours as a result of learning and implementing what Steve and these prophets so willingly impart to you.

Jay Conrad Levinson
"The Father of Guerrilla Marketing"
Author, *Guerrilla Marketing* Series

INTRODUCTION

Have you ever wondered how certain people make millions every year leveraging the power of the Internet? Does it frustrate you that everyone seemingly has access to the same information, tools, and technology, but only a select few fully realize the benefits of the Internet's extraordinary reach and massive profit potential?

Consider these facts:

- Millions of dollars are spent annually on video tutorials, webinars, membership sites, workshops, books, and seminars that promise to explain how to best market products and services online and via mobile. Yet, seldom do these materials deliver the specific, step-by-step answers needed to exponentially grow one's business.
- There are more than *2 billion* Internet users worldwide and over *5 billion* mobile device users with both audiences increasing daily. This means a staggering number of potential customers exist for your products and services.
- It has never been easier to launch or improve an Internet-based business without spending significant capital to do so than right now.

It would be nice if all you needed to do to profit online was create an attractive website, offer products for sale, and set sail on your luxury vessel "Yacht Com" as cash accumulated in your Swiss bank account. Unfortunately, it's not that easy.

So, how do you take advantage of all the Internet offers to become the next millionaire success story? With so many options, what's the best use of your time, energy, and resources? To lay the groundwork for answering these potentially life-altering questions, let's begin with a look back at 1993.

Dial-Up Days

In 1993, my colleagues and I were sitting around a rectangular table in one of Chicago's venerable West Loop diners discussing who would end up king of computer communications: CompuServe or America Online. My company, Liquor by Wire, provided worldwide delivery of wine, champagne, spirits, and gift baskets through a network of licensed retailers. We'd recently launched the first wine and spirits store to be hosted on CompuServe's Electronic Mall, so I was an avid CompuServe proponent.

Even though it took roughly a minute to download a picture of a single bottle of wine that was no bigger than 1" x 2", I was confident nothing would stand in the way of CompuServe dominating the online game. My friends were pro-AOL. Led by Craig Goldwyn, founder of the Beverage Tasting Institute who would subsequently manage AOL's Food and Drink channel for nine years, they were huge fans of AOL's growing platform and proud of their affiliation with the company.

After numerous visits to Columbus, Ohio to meet with the CompuServe team and hear directly from CEO Bob Massey, I was sure Craig was delusional. It would be far from the last time I was wrong.

The Entrepreneur Within

As a lifetime entrepreneur, my DNA is wired to try to turn a quarter into a dollar. From a young age, I raked leaves and shoveled snow. When I was older, I waited tables, pumped gas, stuffed envelopes, and even sold speakers out of a van. In my late teens, I made exceptional money as a headline DJ (under the name Mr. Bold) and built a significant following. This led to my opening and running a nightclub called The Funky Pickle!

I then went on to build four multimillion-dollar companies in four different industries: catalog, real estate, dot com, and personal development. My first multimillion-dollar business was Liquor by Wire. Together with my mom, we steadily built it into a profitable company. Just as we were pioneers during the dial-up days, we didn't sit idly by as the Internet took over. In 1995 we launched one of the web's first fully functional eCommerce sites, LiquorByWire.com.

In 1998, we acquired Liquor.com and Bourbon.com for $7,500 from a smart young man who was squatting on the domains. Liquor by Wire subsequently became Liquor.com and online sales flourished as we benefited from direct type-in traffic. By late 1999, the height of "irrational exuberance" had kicked in and we sought to take full advantage of the free-flowing capital. As a company with a killer domain and nearly $3 million in annual sales, we felt confident about attracting investors to help us grow. Most of the heavy lifting was completed and we simply needed funds to ramp up marketing efforts and hire a staff to handle the increased sales.

At the time, dot com companies with little more than outlines were being bankrolled. I remember thinking, "If companies with just ideas on a napkin can raise millions, shouldn't a company with a high value domain that's already grossing millions be able to raise capital to achieve additional millions?" (I was a bit obsessed with the word *millions* back then.) Blinded by the dot com light, we brought in investment bankers to take us to the promised land. These highly paid advisors quickly convinced my mother and me to:

- Cut off a huge piece of the company to hire the lettermen Wall Street likes to see: CEO, CFO, and CTO.
- Sign away our management rights to allow the experts to take over.
- Sit quietly in the back playing *Mad Libs* as they cultivated investor interest.

We bought in hook, line, and sinker. Convinced they knew how to maximize the opportunity better than we possibly could, we readily signed on the dotted line and turned the reigns over to those more "capable." This was Mistake #1. As fate would have it, the S-1 was filed in early March of 2000. On March 10, the stock market collapse began as NASDAQ intraday trading peaked at 5,132.52 and closed at 5,048.62. On October 4, 2002, the NASDAQ closed at 1,139.90.

Needless to say, we were unsuccessful in our attempt to raise public funds. Further, it became increasingly apparent our lettered saviors had no clue how to run a business. It didn't help that the company was based in Chicago and they were in New York. This was Mistake #2. Six months later I quit and walked away from everything, including the domains. After nine years busting my tail to create a viable enterprise, my net proceeds totaled exactly…zero.

When I returned home early that day, I sat on our front porch trying to decide how to break the news to my wife. I also analyzed my family's financial position…which wasn't pretty. Mom and I had continually reinvested our profits into the business and, as our family's primary breadwinner, we sat on the verge of bankruptcy. Drawing in my breath, I climbed what seemed like an endless flight of stairs to enter the second-floor apartment of our three-flat. When I saw my wife's beautiful smile, reality sunk in hard. With a family to support, I needed to get to work… immediately.

And For My Next Act…

With no time to waste, I reviewed available options. Opening the Sunday *Chicago Tribune*, two things struck me:

- I was far too stubborn to get a job.
- The real estate section was massive.

Shortly before the Internet's peak, nearly everyone had begun looking at the tremendous opportunities in real estate. Tens of thousands of apartments were being converted to condominiums, decent-sized single-family homes were torn down to make room for McMansions, and ground-up development was bourgeoning. I knew a tiny bit about real estate, as we owned our three-flat and the monthly rental income helped offset a significant share of our expenses. A few days later, I overheard a taxi driver at a convenience store telling the clerk how he'd just made $50,000 flipping a condominium. I took this as a sign.

I immediately began looking for an apartment building to convert to condos. Within a week, I found a nice seven-unit in Chicago's Palmer Square neighborhood. Knowing little about the process, I spoke to a few people and, within a week, wrote a 36-page business plan, began negotiating the purchase, and raised investment capital. After securing a construction loan (which was amazingly easy to come by given the loose lending practices of the day), I hired and fired a general contractor, scrambled to find another one, and opened our model unit on September 10, 2001.

Timing really is everything. Though the economy was in temporary free-fall due to 9/11, the market quickly recovered. Within seven months, all of the units were sold. After paying the investors, I cleared $50,000. In retrospect, it would have been a lot less work to flip a single condominium unit. Nevertheless, a ton was learned. I've since gone on to develop over $50 million in commercial and residential properties. As I write this my company, Bold Development, owns and manages $25 million in property.

Some projects have exceeded expectations. Others haven't. Two of my properties are currently in foreclosure. Overall values have plummeted. What I wouldn't do for a crystal ball.

Another Round

In 2006, I spotted this headline in *The Wall Street Journal:* "Domain Name Prices Approaching 1999 Values." I immediately thought of Liquor.com. For more than six years, it was out of sight and out of mind. I had buried all emotional connection to it. However, having never relinquished my right to the domain, I was suddenly curious what had happened to it. After digging around, I tracked it down to a gentleman in the country of Panama. We exchanged emails. When I asked how he gained ownership of the domain, he was highly evasive.

Whether it was his conscience or a desire to avoid trouble, the day before Christmas 2006 he asked for my account information so he could transfer the domain to me. I scrambled to quickly set up an account at DomainSite.com. Having never received a domain before, I needed a bit of technical assistance and provided him with my account information (including my password!). He obliged me. On Christmas Eve, he emailed to say the domain had been transferred.

A bit skeptical, I checked my account—and sure enough, there it was. I expressed gratitude to the universe...and reset my password. Within days, I posted a simple page indicating the domain was for sale. I received numerous offers. Some were a bit humorous, such as the person who suggested I trade the domain for her car (a 2003 Honda Accord). Another suggested I donate the domain to his charity. Other offers better reflected its actual value: $1 million, $1.5 million, and $2 million.

Eventually, I accepted $4.25 million. The company made the first two payments, but bailed on the third. I kept the domain...and the cash. With startup capital in hand, I contemplated launching Liquor.com V2.0. While I understood business in general, I'd been out of the Internet game for too long to jump in without help. Recognizing that much of the world's top Internet talent was based in Silicon Valley, I brought in a partner, Warren Yamakoshi, to help write a detailed business plan and headed to Sand Hill Road together to raise venture capital. No one wrote us a check.

I learned that while having a great domain is important, having an experienced team is even more so. Though I had run Liquor.com in the late 1990s, in Internet time that was ages ago. Warren and I therefore entered the Demo Pit of Michael Arrington's *TechCrunch 40* in search of operational partners. It was there we met Christopher (Kit) Codik and Nicolas Darveau-Garneau, who'd recently created a new venture advisory firm focused on helping entrepreneurs build and grow their businesses. As they traversed the event in search of possible clients and emerging companies, we discussed our plans.

Several months later, an agreement was executed to collaboratively build a substantive business around the high value domain. Leading the charge, Kit and Nick reworked the model, established compelling metrics, and raised angel funds. In late 2009, Liquor.com V2.0 went live. Within two short years, Liquor.com became its category leader.

With more than 280,000 Facebook fans, over 18,000 Twitter followers, nearly one million monthly visitors, and partnerships with every major alcohol beverage conglomerate, Liquor.com's growth was nothing short of remarkable.

Since the launch, Kit has been fully responsible for the company's operations. I remain its co-founder and chairman, and own a substantial share.

My Wake-Up Call

In 2008, everything shifted. My stepfather, who'd raised me since I was 10, lay in bed at home dying. The illness he'd fought tooth-and-nail for years was finally winning the war. As we sat together, I held his hand. Though he could no longer verbally express himself, I believe he spoke to me through our physical connection.

A vision of my funeral flashed before my eyes. As I was being lowered into the earth in the dark, damp casket, I could hear the words spoken graveside: "Here lies Steve Olsher. He dedicated his life to chasing the almighty dollar."

That's all that was said. It was a huge wake-up call that slammed me with the force of a kick to the head. I began to think about how to best use the years I had left and started wondering what accomplishments I could look back on toward the end of my life that would make me feel proud. Interestingly, none of them involved making money.

I've always had a nagging feeling I was meant and made to do something extraordinary. However, it was clear to my stepfather that the path I had forged was leading me away from my natural talents. By providing a vision of my inevitable fate, he was imploring me to change course. I faced what I now call a *YāNo* (pronounced Yay-No) moment. It's a pivotal moment of truth that can lead you in either of two directions:

- Away from honoring who you truly are.
- Towards a path that best aligns with your core being, and allows the *You* of tomorrow to look back and give thanks to the *You* of today.

I've since learned there's a significant difference between living well and living for the sake of making money. Don't get me wrong; each of us is entitled to make a phenomenal living. I'm not one to suggest you resign yourself to life as a starving artist simply because you're compelled to draw. If you can sell your paintings for $1 million a pop, why shouldn't you accept what the market will bear? And, if money is not your bag, then give it away and support your favorite charity. What I am saying is that we're all obligated by our common bond of humanity to not only pursue what brings us financial success, but also what can make a positive impact on our community, our environment, and our world.

In the years since beginning my transition, I've come to understand I have a unique gift for helping people discover their *WHAT*—that is, the one thing they were born to do. Following this path has led me to:

- Co-starring in the groundbreaking film *The Keeper of the Keys* with Jack Canfield, John Gray, and Marci Shimoff.
- Creating *The Reinvention Workshop* (TheReinventionWorkshop. com), which many describe as the pivotal event in their lives.
- Developing and hosting *Reinvention Radio* (ReinventionRadio. com), the show dedicated to "creating empowered leaders driven to make a monumental difference."
- Writing the Amazon bestseller and USA Book News' Self-Help Book of the Year, *Journey To You: A Step-by-Step Guide to Becoming Who You Were Born to Be.*
- Being featured on ABC TV, FOX TV, CNBC.com, and more than 200 radio shows including national programs hosted by Lou Dobbs, Jim Bohannon, and Mancow Muller.

Perhaps most fulfilling, I now have the opportunity to speak to people of all ages and see the light in their eyes as they envision creating a life filled with fulfillment, success, and happiness.

The How
I don't provide the history of my life to boast, but to help explain the motivation for creating this book. As I've continued on my journey

and realized the power of discovering one's *WHAT*, I've found that discovering your purpose is not always enough. To attain your objectives, you often also need the right tools and skills. In other words, you need to have the *HOW.*

Today, there's typically no easier way to achieve your goals than by leveraging the extraordinary power of the Internet. After nearly two decades online, I realized I knew very little about how to fully grasp even a small fraction of the Internet's potential. This had to change, so I began searching for answers. Consulting my good friend Google, I found a number of wizards who, for thousands of dollars, could teach me the ropes. But I sought more than just one person's perspective. I kept digging.

I asked my associates who they knew and liked. Their answers were consistent. I also explored online forums, product reviews, and other resources. The same names kept coming up over and over. With a list of top gurus, I began looking at each of their offerings. With so much incredible content to choose from, it was difficult to make a choice.

I really wanted to work with all of them, as each covered topics pertinent to my business. But at a cost of $2,000 or more to train with each one individually, this was not a possibility. I then exhaustively searched for a single product that provided specific how-to information from a variety of experts. My search came up empty for an all-encompassing product.

What to do? I could spend hundreds of thousands of dollars to learn from each on an individual basis. Or maybe I could create an interview series that provided the answers every small business owner, entrepreneur, IT professional, and Internet marketer needs. I chose the latter. Then I wondered, "Who am I to ask these experts to participate?" I was far from a celebrity and had never spoken to a single one of them before. Regardless, I pressed on. I searched online and networked until I found their contact information or someone who knew them, and started typing and calling. In my correspondence, I explained my rationale for wanting to help others learn precisely how to profit online and asked if they'd be willing to:

- Pull back the curtains to reveal their process.
- Define step-by-step details for exactly what to do.
- Provide valuable resources for getting started.

To my delighted amazement, 25 said they'd be happy to participate. Over the next four months, I had the privilege of sitting down with many of the world's leading experts and asking questions that cut straight to the bone. As a no-nonsense interviewer, I wanted answers that could be immediately applied to my business…and yours.

None of them batted an eye. Each delivered advice, knowledge, and specific *HOW-TO* instructions to assist you in bringing your unique *WHAT* to the world regardless of whether you're an experienced or novice marketer. The people with whom I'm honored to have conducted interviews include a virtual who's who of the online world:

- **Janet Bray Attwood:** An alliance expert, and co-author of *The New York Times* bestseller, *The Passion Test: The Effortless Path to Discovering Your Life Purpose.*
- **Christopher (Kit) Codik:** Co-founder and CEO of Liquor.com.
- **Dean DeLisle:** Marketing and business development expert with 30 years of experience and an extensive focus on social networking.
- **Mike Filsaime:** Internet marketing legend, and creator of Butterfly Marketing—which grossed over $1 million within the first five days of its release.
- **Pat Flynn:** Blogging expert and founder of SmartPassiveIncome. com.
- **Kathleen Gage:** Internationally recognized Internet marketing advisor.
- **Steve Harrison:** Publicity expert and co-owner of Bradley Communications, Inc.
- **Dan Hollings:** Online, offline, and mobile marketing specialist who headed the Internet launch strategy team for *The Secret.*
- **Pam Ivey:** Expert on virtual assistants and outsourcing.

- **Mike Koenigs:** Video expert who created the bestselling Internet products Traffic Geyser and Cross-Channel Mojo, and is largely credited with inventing Internet infomercials.
- **John Kremer:** Marketing expert and author of *1001 Ways to Market Your Books.*
- **Armand Morin:** Well-known Internet marketer since 1996 whose online business has generated over $85 million in revenue.
- **Mike Muhney:** Co-creator of ACT!, which began the Contact Management industry, and an app expert.
- **Marc Ostrofsky:** Bestselling author of *Get Rich Click!*, speaker, venture capitalist, and serial entrepreneur. Perhaps best known for his $7.5 million sale of Business.com.
- **Christian Pankhurst:** Coach, speaker, author, and 2009 winner of Britain's Next Top Coach competition.
- **David Riklan:** President and founder of Self-Improvement Online Inc., which owns SelfGrowth.com.
- **Leslie Rohde:** Internationally recognized SEO strategist.
- **Riel Roussopoulos:** Creative professional, technology strategist, and QR Code evangelist.
- **Callan Rush:** Leader to Luminary Training CEO and top-notch sales and marketing expert.
- **Jennifer Sheahan:** Facebook advertising expert and founder of FBAdsLab.
- **Yanik Silver:** Maverick marketing expert and serial entrepreneur with eight different million-dollar products and services.
- **Kristin Thompson:** Presentation expert and offline conversion specialist.
- **Jeff Vacek:** Information marketing expert, online specialist, and co-creator of Blueprint to Financial Freedom.
- **Christopher Van Buren:** Launch development expert and author.
- **Jason Van Orden:** Internet marketing and online media strategist. Co-founder of Internet Business Mastery, the top-rated Internet business and marketing-related podcast.

Each chapter features a single expert, is based on their expertise, and derived from an hour-long video interview. The content has been condensed into the most pertinent information and delves extensively into the respective expert's subject matter. Whether you're an entrepreneur, Internet virgin, executive, business owner, or IT pro, *Internet Prophets* will teach you proven strategies for:

- Using cutting-edge marketing tactics to add millions to your bottom line.
- Profiting with teleseminars and webinars.
- Harnessing the power of Joint Ventures and Alliances.
- Recruiting the industry "big dogs" to promote your products and services.
- Creating multimillion-dollar product launches.
- Growing your list to over 100,000 people.
- Leveraging the next huge wave: mobile.
- Creating community and having millions spread your message.
- Identifying and profiting from your niche.
- Attracting tens of thousands of people each month to your blog and podcasts.
- Powerfully executing business ideas most likely to succeed.
- Efficiently using outsourcing to exponentially increase annual sales.
- Implementing video to garner substantial traffic.
- Building a personal or business brand that is instantly recognized.
- Powering up your presentations to massively increase conversions.
- Creating a meaningful app that attracts attention and sells.
- Using SEO to boost your search ranking.
- Generating offline and online publicity.
- Securing the right domain to build your multimillion-dollar endeavor.

- Taking advantage of social media for sales, networking, and brand building.
- And, much more.

This book is a comprehensive resource. Never before has so much wide-ranging Internet marketing knowledge been gathered that you can apply immediately to your business. As the online landscape grows increasingly complicated, *Internet Prophets* cuts straight to the chase and provides the precise answers you need to create your ideal lifestyle in expedited fashion.

The time to take advantage of all the Internet offers is *now*. I look forward to our *propheting* together.

Steve Olsher

For more information and to access the
video interviews, please visit **InternetProphets.com.**

1
0
1
1
0
0
0
0
0
0
1
0
0
1
0
1
1
1
0
1
0
1
0
0
1
1
0
0

PART I

MASTERING THE PRODUCT CYCLE

CHAPTER 1

GREAT IDEAS AND GREAT EXECUTION

D amn Tim Ferriss. His bestselling book, *The 4-Hour Workweek*, popularized the idea of being your own boss, avoiding the rat race, shooting the alarm clock, and watching zeroes accumulate in your bank account. While this lifestyle is certainly appealing, most business owners know that making it happen isn't nearly as simple as setting up a shopping cart on your homepage. If an entrepreneur doesn't need to wake up to an alarm, it's probably because he never went to sleep.

Creating, and operating, a profitable business takes significant effort and dedication. That said, Tim provided a real service in spreading the word that it's not nearly as complicated to pull off as most people assume. Armand Morin is living proof that it's possible and is a self-made multimillionaire. His company, which has only eight people on staff, has grossed over $85 million to date.

His secret: Simplicity, and capitalizing on what's next. These two powerful pillars have been Armand's mantra throughout his stellar business career.

Armand Morin: Perpetual Pioneer

In 1995, telecommunications was red-hot, especially pre-paid phone cards and long-distance aggregators. Seizing the opportunity, Armand created a telecom company that provided long-distance discount services. Within 10 months his business grossed almost $2 million in sales. While impressive, Armand heard gold jingling in the beeps and hisses of his 14.4 modem and sold his telecom venture to concentrate on the forthcoming Internet wave.

Armand's first online venture reinvented the traditional advertising structure. As he was surfing the web he stumbled upon a site that provided links from a directory-based page to other sites. Site owners paid $20 to have the link created and no performance guarantee or representation of traffic was provided. The idea intrigued him and he sought to replicate the model. Using an AOL website builder to launch his first page, he began to market his service online.

The year was 1996 and, at the time, there were few options for driving traffic to one's site. Given that thousands of pages were being created daily, the opportunity to provide low cost exposure was appealing. In his first week, Armand earned more than $8,000. Unfortunately, current automation technologies and financial tools didn't exist. For instance, he couldn't accept credit cards. When customers wanted to buy advertising, they'd have to send him a check. He'd then have to wait for the check to clear before undertaking the arduous process of entering each link by hand.

Given the significant volume of business Armand had generated, this took a great deal of time. Armand responded by hiring data entry workers and also by developing proprietary software to simplify the process. As traffic online increased, sites that offered free products such as calendars and business-related reports gained in popularity. Search engines, however, were just in their infancy. During Armand's detailed study of the Internet, he'd created more than 600 bookmarks for sites that offered customers free products and resources. After organizing the sites into categories, he offered the list for sale... for $110.

He sold 100 in the first week. Traffic spiked from there. Eventually, the site attracted over two million visitors per month. In just 12 weeks, his company grossed over $4 million.

Tools Equal Jewels

Sometimes when things are going most smoothly, life puts a speed bump in front of you. While Armand was driving traffic and sales online with breathtaking success, trouble was brewing.

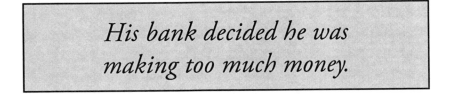

His bank decided he was making too much money.

As funds poured in, Armand's bank shut him down and froze access to his accounts. Why? Because they assumed such a massive flow of cash must be the result of illegal activities. Nothing, however, was even remotely illegal about Armand's operation. Regardless, they wouldn't listen and put millions into deep freeze. At this point, some might have thrown in the towel while crying about grossly unfair treatment. Not Armand. He immediately sought to create effective tools to help others avoid the same fate. There were two glaring issues that needed to be addressed:

- Accepting credit cards.
- Gaining access to a merchant processing service that would release funds earned.

Armand started devouring as much information as he could find on the subjects. From white papers on merchant accounts and credit card processing to industry reports on available software and forthcoming technologies, he absorbed a huge amount of knowledge, and boiled down the most critical facts into an easy to understand report.

Armand recognized many site owners and IT professionals would directly benefit from his research. Believing he had a potentially lucrative product, he next sought a streamlined way to deliver it. Printing and mailing paper-based books was expensive and time-consuming. It was also difficult to create interim updates for information that might change over time. Nowadays, Armand could have simply used a PDF. In 1996, the format did not yet have mainstream acceptance.

The solution? He developed software that opened an .exe file containing several HTML documents. In other words, he created a browser that was built specifically for the purpose of reading his report. It was one of the first ebooks ever released.

These endeavors marked the start of Armand's online empire. By leveraging the knowledge gained through his early experiences, he was in strong position to propel his company forward. He remains front and center.

Ideation Is Priority #1

Product creation is paramount to achieving massive success and, while execution is important, you first need an idea. Armand is a master at creating products *that sell.* Those last two words are especially important. People are often struck by bouts of inspiration and spend significant time and resources bringing their ideas to fruition. Unfortunately, most ideas aren't commercially viable and many have wasted thousands of dollars creating products that collect dust in a garage.

The key is to create a product that meets an existing need. Armand's ebook accomplished this. It taught site owners and IT professionals how to accept credit cards, streamline payment processing, and identify merchant servicers who won't freeze their accounts.

Further, when he sought to distribute the ebook and found there was no simple way for doing so, he created his own software to solve the problem. That meant he had *two* products to sell which fulfilled specific market needs—the ebook, and the program to deliver it. Both ended up selling well, taking the sting out of Armand's problem with his bank.

Armand concentrates on satisfying market demand by creating products that:

- Makes tasks easier.
- Or, automates existing tasks.

This formula consistently provides above-average returns. If you keep these two goals in mind, you can continually generate winning product ideas.

Mo' Problems, Mo' Money

When evaluating ideas, consider the correlation between the size of the problem your product solves and the amount you can charge for it. The bigger the problem, the higher the price tag. Too many companies price a product based on operational and marketing costs, and the desired return. That can create a substantial disconnect insofar as what that product is actually worth to its target audience.

The overriding factor to consider is how much the market is willing to pay for the product or service. Regardless of whether you spent millions on research and development or pennies, your potential customers don't care about your costs. They just care about getting what they perceive as substantial value for their investment.

> *Create products that solve existing problems at what your target audience considers a great price.*

Successful Internet marketers begin with addressing small problems and creating low-priced products. In fact, many argue the first touch-point should be providing valuable *free* content in exchange for a customer's contact information. The objective is to entice a customer to enter your *sales funnel,* whereby a meaningful relationship is developed over time, and you proactively inspire her to purchase higher-priced products and services. Industry leaders recognize the first sale represents merely the beginning of the relationship, not the end.

Armand's funnel is structured as follows:

- **Free:** An example is Armand's *Internet Marketing Newsletter,* which has no subscription fee; you simply provide your name and email address.
- **$27-$47:** An entry-level product that solves a specific problem or provides information that can be leveraged for profit. Examples include an hour-long MP3 in which Armand reveals a game-changing process or a social media "white paper" delivered via PDF.
- **$97:** A low-end offering that adds value. Examples include many of Armand's simple, yet effective software products.
- **$197:** This is Armand's magic price point. The beauty of $197 is that it's affordable for most, converts about as well as lower-priced options (e.g., $97), and huge numbers aren't required to generate significant revenue. Examples of $197 offerings include live events and training products.
- **$497-$9,997+:** As the Internet has grown in popularity, so has a customer's willingness to explore untraditional classroom environments and purchase high-end learning tools. To satisfy this market, Armand offers a wide-range of premium products and services. These range from home-study courses and coaching programs, to private three-day training at his home.

Armand prides himself on both his creativity and consistently delivering value that far exceeds the cost of his products. The beauty of the Internet is that you can easily launch new products, test the waters, and modify pricing as necessary. Having the courage to try something new and remain flexible enough to make adjustments on the fly are critical to your overall success.

Don't Go The Extra Mile, Go The Extra Marathon

Product creation and pricing are challenging, but an even greater hurdle is differentiation. Most companies in the same field offer comparable products and services at about the same prices. Achieving major success requires standing apart from the crowd. Armand does this by maintaining excellence throughout his organization. From product development to customer service, he sets Six Sigma standards.

We've all experienced One Sigma service—you have a problem, call customer service for help, and have to deal with a maze of menu options, after which you're placed on hold for 30 minutes. And when a human being finally answers your call, the person lacks the training to be of genuine help.

When was the last time you called or emailed customer service and had your issue resolved immediately, without a supervisor being involved—and received an extra product, discount, or bonus because **you** were inconvenienced? That's the level of customer service Armand's company delivers—and it's what you should strive for too. It creates loyal customers for life.

> *Regardless of whether someone purchases a product for $29 or $2,999, give that customer top support. You're likely to be rewarded with years of repeat business.*

Most companies don't do this. They fail to pay for adequate customer service, choosing short-term profit margins over long-term customer satisfaction. This is a foolish strategy as it costs them word of mouth recommendations and repeat business.

A related issue is that companies rush products to market before putting them through adequate quality analysis. This results in a flood of calls to customer service. Armand tries to anticipate all possible issues before a product is ever sold. And by spending so much time on the front-end, end-user issues seldom occur. Specifically, Armand's company has grossed over $85 million, but it typically receives less than 20 customer service-related questions each day. His products are so well designed, vetted, and tested that customers rarely need support.

Despite best efforts, occasionally a product will slip through Armand's rigorous tests for quality. When this happens, customers are notified and his team immediately focuses on finding solutions. When the problem is fixed, the new version is offered to product owners for free. Machiavelli said, "A prudent man must always follow in the footsteps of great men and imitate those who have been outstanding." Consider following Armand's strategies. There is much to be learned from a true master of his craft.

⏻ TAKEAWAYS

Great Ideas and Great Execution

- Keep up with current trends and capitalize on what's next.
- Recognize adversity as opportunity. Every trouble carries the seeds of triumph.
- Create products that make existing tasks easier or automate existing tasks.
- The bigger the problem, the higher the price tag. There is a direct correlation between the size of the problem your product solves and the amount you can charge for it.
- The market determines price. Customers don't care about your costs. They care about how much value you deliver for their investment.
- Encourage customers to enter your sales funnel with free and inexpensive products, and then inspire them to purchase higher-priced products and services.
- Deliver value that far exceeds the price of your products.
- Strive for Six Sigma standards. Sell only outstanding products, and provide a level of service that cultivates loyalty and keeps them coming back for life.

CHAPTER 2

DOMAIN DOMINANCE

Over time, technology and business practices evolve in a predictable manner. With each revolution, new opportunity is created. This process is defined by four distinct phases:

- **Research and Development:** New technologies and business practices emerge. Uncertainty is prevalent and adaptation is unclear.
- **Ascent:** Awareness and implementation expands.
- **Maturity:** Widespread acceptance is commonplace and the threat of over saturation exists.
- **Decline:** Demand is met, sales and adaption declines, and new technologies and business practices emerge.

This circle of transition has existed for centuries. To illustrate the power of leveraging the inherent inertia found within this cycle, let's discuss the Internet. In its infancy, the World Wide Web held significant promise. However, bandwidth and related issues were met with uncertainty as to the Internet's viability and mainstream appeal. (Phase 1)

New companies emerged to dramatically increase the Internet's functionality and both businesses and customers slowly began to take notice. Once stability and utility were in place, usage spiked. (Phase 2) Today, virtually everyone is connected to the Internet, has a website, and even your 85-year-old aunt is offering products for sale. (We are currently in Phase 3)

With the rare exception of the millennium's turn when the implosion was in full-swing, dot com millionaires are created every day. Marc Ostrofsky—now a bestselling author and multimillionaire—was one of the first.

The Life And Times Of Marc Ostrofsky

We are each wired to excel in very specific ways. Marc's DNA is stacked with an entrepreneur's fire and, at just seven years old, he opened his first business: a lemonade stand. After selling countless cups, he graduated to selling "darn near anything he could get his hands on." During the 1980's and early 90's, Marc created niche-oriented magazines and trade shows, leveraging the synergy between the businesses. Because he had access to customers and businesses who wanted specific information (the magazine subscribers) and vendors who wanted access to them (the advertisers), trade shows were a natural next step. Phone calls, face-to-face meetings, and personalized direct mail were (and still are) time-consuming and expensive options. Current technologies, such as teleconferencing and videoconferencing, did not exist at the time.

Trade shows, however, provided a cost-effective solution for both buyers and sellers. Marc stood at the precipice of an incredibly lucrative opportunity. Given his business acumen, he took full advantage. His trade show and magazine businesses exploded, and by the time he sought to acquire Business.com as the domain name for a new magazine he sought to launch in 1995 he had already amassed considerable wealth. For this reason, the $150,000 price tag did not present a meaningful barrier.

Before buying Business.com, he asked his father for his thoughts. His father was a tenured university business professor and Marc often sought his wisdom before making big decisions. When asked if he should buy the domain, his father responded: "Will you make more money owning the domain or keeping $150,000 in the bank collecting interest?" Marc pulled the trigger. This turned out to be a brilliant move. In 1999, after a heated bidding war ensued between two rival companies, he sold the domain for *$7.5 million.*

> *Marc's Business.com deal landed him in the Guinness Book of World Records for the most money received from the sale of a single domain name.*

At around the same time he purchased Business.com, he also secured the rights to eBusiness.com. After the sale of Business.com was finalized, he contacted the other company to see if they had an interest in the second domain. They did. He then sold eBusiness.com for **$10 million.** (Terms of this sale were kept confidential, which is why it's not in *Guinness.*) Marc grossed $17.5 million on the sale of the two domains. Not a bad return on his investment. However, he wasn't done yet.

With the sale of Business.com, he demanded "put rights" which allowed him to buy stock in the firm at a later date or keep the cash, whichever was larger. In 2004, Marc exercised his "put" rights and received stock in the newly formed Business.com entity. In 2007, the company was sold to RH Donnelley for $345 million, netting Marc an additional windfall.

Today, he continues down his entrepreneurial path and is involved with numerous online ventures. He is a partner in Blinds.com (which generates $80 million a year), owns CuffLinks.com, and other valuable domains, and is the bestselling author of the book *Get Rich Click!* To learn more and/or purchase *Get Rich Click!*, visit EZ.com/getrichclick or use your mobile device to scan the QR code to the right.

Over the years, Marc has learned invaluable business lessons. If you want to dramatically increase your chances for success, heed his wisdom.

Know What You Don't Know

One person cannot possibly know *everything* and be good at all things. Unfortunately, far too many are reluctant to release the reigns and unable to admit they may not be the best person for the job. Recognize your weaknesses and leverage the strengths of others to propel your business forward. Beginning to understand what you don't know is the first step toward achieving this goal.

For example, if you want to open a restaurant and have never done so before, there's more you don't know than you do. Yes, you could buy myriad how-to books, go behind the scenes at other venues, and attempt to learn how to do everything, but this will take valuable energy and resources away from your key focus—launching your business—and are a poor investment of time.

By understanding what you don't know, you can become clear on whom you need to hire and what holes exist in your game plan. This can only happen if you're willing to be brutally honest...and avoid being so cheap, you'll never accumulate wealth. Numerous low-cost and free options exist in virtually every field. For example:

- Fiverr.com: An awesome site where you can find someone to do darn near anything for $5.
- Weebly.com: Free website builder.
- KnowEm.com: Profile builder.
- Wix.com: Free Flash websites.
- PageModo.com: Free Facebook Fan Pages.

By outsourcing specific strategies, you've taken an important first step. Hold something too tight and it dies. Let it go and it evolves.

Recognize that there are literally millions of people who can help you get to where you want to go.

> ## *The days of lengthy trial-and-error processes and learning from your mistakes, while still beneficial, are over.*

Today, there are free video tutorials, newsletters, seminars, podcasts and more that provide the tools you need and direct access to valuable resources. Sure, you can do it all yourself, but you can also build your own car from scratch if you'd like. While it might be fun, and eventually get done, you'll have already lost the race...twice.

Knowledge really is power. Concentrate on what you do well and leave literally everything else alone. Once you know what you don't know, move to Lesson #2.

Surround Yourself With Intelligent People

Hands down, this is one of the most important concepts. Successful people don't create formidable organizations alone. Yes, they provide the vision, direction, and ideas, but other people execute. Let's return to the example of building an Internet business. Creating a successful online venture is very difficult.

The "all we need is a website to make millions" mentality leaves would-be high rollers scratching their heads wondering what happened. A successful Internet company requires substantial effort from a multitude of experts.

A smart businessperson stands on the shoulders of giants and allows those who understand their area of expertise to flourish. A control freak who feels it's more important to cross every *t* and dot every *i* will eventually go broke.

> *Meaningful growth is a result of concerted effort by talented people.*

This is the equation to model for success. In the words of Michael E. Gerber, the author of *The E-Myth Revisited*, you want to "work on your business, not in your business." To purchase *The E-Myth Revisited* or for more information, please visit EZ.com/emyth or scan the QR code to the right.

Of course, not everyone can afford to hire experts right out of the gate. However, there are multiple ways to accomplish your desired objectives:

- **Ask an expert for help.** Be advised, however, that you're more likely to elicit a positive response if you first offer to promote their work, submit an article for their blog, volunteer at a live event, etc. and *then* ask for what you'd like. People will go to bat for those they know and trust far before they'll help those they don't. And, while it's commonplace to be intimidated by other's success, keep in mind that, other than those born with silver spoons and trust funds, they're just like you. They started out with a dream, worked the plan, and accomplished their objectives. Most decent entrepreneurs will lend an ear to a fellow soldier. Worst case—they say "no." More often than not, though, they'll offer invaluable words of wisdom.

- **Cut off a piece of equity, or partner with someone who has cash and resources.** Money only makes money when it's invested. An incredible number of high net-worth individuals are sitting on the sidelines waiting for the right opportunity. While you may have to give up a significant piece of the pie, 30% of a million-dollar company is far better than 100% of a company that is valueless. Craft a plan and pitch it until you're blue in the face. If you knock on enough doors, someone will answer.

- **Hire interns.** Universities are stacked with talented students who need work experience and a place to implement their abilities. Many will work for free while others require only a small stipend to help offset living expenses. By providing an inspiring environment where they can implement tangible application of their knowledge and skills, you'll end up with plenty of takers.

- **Bring on performance-based employees.** In other words, pay them only when their actions result in sales. And, when they make rain, be willing to pay them a huge commission. If they're good, you'll eventually have flexibility to bring them on as salaried employees.

Surrounding yourself with intelligent people has numerous benefits. Perhaps the greatest of which is being able to incorporate different philosophies and perspectives into your business. With rare exception, multiple solutions to problems and obstacles exist. Having intelligent, capable people on your side empowers you to move beyond your self-imposed limitations and achieve remarkable results.

Learn More, Earn More™

Contrary to popular belief, education is a lifetime endeavor and exists outside of the classroom. As a matter of fact, college may be the single worst investment a parent can make, but we'll save that discussion for another book. Too often, people attend grade school, graduate from college, and consider their education complete. Ultra-successful people like Marc never stop learning.

> *Creating and maintaining wealth goes hand-in-hand with education and knowledge. The amount of money you earn is a direct reflection of how much you learn.*

Fortunately, there are more ways to learn now than ever before—and much of the content is free. From newsletters and substantive videos, to seminars, books, DVD's, and podcasts, you could spend a lifetime trying to consume all of the available information without coming close to doing so. The successful understand that you must continually be a student. No matter the degree of success achieved, true masters never stop learning. From private coaching to mastermind groups, the world's best subscribe to the notion that there is always someone to learn from.

Think about those you know. Everyone is an expert at something. Whether it's building model trains, throwing a curve ball, or cooking rack of lamb, they have knowledge to impart. Whether or not you choose to heed their knowledge ultimately spells the difference between success and failure. When you cut yourself off from learning, the awakening is coming. Before you know it, you'll lose grasp on the position of prominence you once held. It may not happen in a year or even a decade but, eventually, it will.

Study people who are successful and seek to replicate their strategies. A key component is to continually sharpen the blade. Stand close enough to an expert and, eventually, you'll get cut—a cut of the profits that is.

The Riches Are In The Niches

Sean Rich is the president and CEO of Tortuga Trading in Carlsbad, California. The company specializes in antique arms and armament from all over the world, concentrating on the 16th through the 19th centuries.

Sean's love for the past began at age 10 when he acquired his first antique weapon. Over the years he's participated in numerous archaeological digs; was designated as New Jersey's state representative

for Gulf Coast Rare Coins and Investments where he specialized in treasure recovered from the Spanish Galleon Atocha and 1715 Plate Fleet; and underwent a master five-year apprenticeship for antique gun restoration while attending Salve Regina University in Newport, Rhode Island.

His expertise led to a three-year stint as a weapons consultant for Second Mate Productions, which helped develop the second and third *Pirates of the Caribbean* movies. In 2009, Sean began working as an antique arms and armament specialist for Leftfield Productions, the producers of The History Channel's *Pawn Stars*. Whenever rare arms or armament from the 16th through 19th centuries show up at the pawnshop, Sean is the guy the owners call before making their purchase decision.

By becoming an expert in a specific field, Sean has created his own market, is able to charge a premium for it, and has the world knocking down his door to pay for what comes most naturally to him…that is, his *WHAT*, the one thing he was born to do. Sean is a perfect example of Marc's contention that the "riches are in the niches." Though often difficult to imagine, no matter your area of expertise, there is someone who will pay you for it. If you don't think this is true, check eBay. Even a stale piece of bread can find a buyer.

> *Do one thing, do it better than anyone else, and get paid extraordinarily well for your talent.*

But to achieve this level of game-changing impact, you'll need to become intently cued in to what most appeals to your soul, then concentrate on the precise activities that drive you to make an inordinate difference. By recognizing that a broad-stroke approach results in career suicide, you'll begin to ask yourself the right questions and hone in on your niche. Think about the most successful or happiest people you know—the lawyer who only takes on fathers' rights cases, the dentist who specializes in pediatric root canals, or the teacher who focuses on troubled teens.

They've all become experts in one specific arena, dedicated their lives to it, and are compensated at levels far superior to those of their counterparts. Getting to this point, however, is a journey. Many doctors begin as general practitioners before deciding on their specialty. The majority of successful entrepreneurs endured multiple business failures before creating ventures that make the most of their passion. Thanks to Google and the power of the Internet, people can now easily find you and leverage your talents—whatever they may be. And, while it may seem counter-intuitive, the more targeted your niche is, the more you'll be able to charge for your services.

Consider Marc's company CuffLinks.com. Here, people buy cuff links of all shapes and sizes. From cuff links shaped like martini glasses to a pair that doubles as thumb drives, there is an incredible assortment that represents the gamut of tastes and interests. While it's true that not everyone wears cuff links, or needs a pair in the form of dollar signs, enough do to sustain a high-margin business. And, when Marc reflects on his success and has pursued specific niche opportunities, dollar signs are, more often than not, what he sees.

Connect Buyers And Sellers

With Marc's trade show and magazine businesses, he found lucrative ways to connect buyers and sellers. Often, income generating opportunities are no more complex than emulating this model. Perhaps the most appealing aspect of this structure is that you do not need a significant understanding of the industry you serve, nor specific skills related to it, in order to create a cash-flow positive endeavor. You simply need to be an effective conduit.

For example, you don't need to know anything about cars to profit from connecting buyers and sellers. Choose a niche (e.g., 1960's Mustangs) and then create a simple site and post related products and services. The easiest way to do this is to contact existing sellers (e.g., car dealers, parts manufacturers/distributors, etc.), negotiate a percentage of each sale consummated to be paid to you as a commission, and utilize their existing content.

Though set-up will take time and effort, your overhead is virtually non-existent. You own zero inventory and, if the site is properly optimized (SEO), you'll begin to receive traffic and, hopefully, subsequent sales. While it may not be "easy" money, it's as close as you can get to it. Marc is a master of the middleman model and has taken this concept to new heights.

Blinds.com is one of Marc's most lucrative ventures. The company grosses over $80 million a year and is a formidable entity in the window coverings market. One would think the company must have a tremendous number of employees, huge inventory, and substantial overhead to generate almost nine figures per year. This couldn't be farther from the truth. Blinds.com carries no inventory, has relatively few employees, and its overhead is nominal. How can this be? Every single order received is drop-shipped directly from the manufacturer to the customer. That's right; Blinds.com doesn't stock *any* of the merchandise sold.

It's a true win-win-win model. Blinds.com handles the marketing, customers are able to select from a wide range of products, and the manufacturers receive additional business. This is a fantastic example of how to create a well-organized, well-presented middleman structure. When done correctly, customers experience the same seamless process they'd enjoy dealing directly with the manufacturers, and all sides benefit. In other words, Marc makes millions annually by providing quality products while keeping customers in the dark about how their orders are being processed. The intent isn't to *blind* customers to what's going on so much as shield them from unnecessary light.

Domains = Online Real Estate

In 1995, Marc crafted the slogan "Domain names are Internet Real Estate™." Sought-after domains routinely sell for over $1 million and prices continue to rise. Marc believes a domain name is the equivalent of online land and can prove to be invaluable as it's the location where a business is built and conducted. Just as there's a strong competitive advantage to owning real estate at the corner of Main and Main, you're likely to do much better with Liquor.com than 312Liquor.com.

Of course, there are exceptions. Google.com, Yahoo.com, Amazon.com, and eBay.com are examples of domains that have enjoyed phenomenal success without the benefit of an industry-specific domain. But these companies had to spend millions of dollars to market and promote their brands. In general, a domain name that describes the business you're in will be more effective, and more likely to appear in search results, than one that doesn't. The latter is especially important, as 85-88% of all traffic is generated via search engines and direct marketing.

At the same time, an estimated 12-15% of all traffic is a result of direct navigation (e.g., typing a URL directly into your browser's address bar). That makes short, easy to spell one-word domains especially valuable. A huge market has emerged for buying and selling domains. If the domain you want is already taken, you may find it to be prohibitively expensive to purchase.

Marc recommends limiting your .com domain investment budget and considering other domains such as .biz, .info, .net, and .org. He believes a domain such as Cars.info is of much greater value than a less relevant .com domain such as 213Cars.com. Sites such as JustDropped. com, and domain brokers Sedo.com and BuyDomains.com, offer thousands of domains for sale. You can also Google "domain names dropped," "new domains," and "domain name buy and sell" to find domains that may work well for you.

Domains are here to stay, and so is the demand for them. You may not make millions buying and selling domains; but you'll never know unless you get into the game.

Final Advice

In the words of Marc Ostrofsky, "just get started." While it's easy to get overwhelmed by the idea of starting a business, the stars will never align to provide the exact moment in time with which to begin. There will always be reasons not to do something. From kids and work obligations to health issues and lack of investment funds, it is inevitably easier to focus on all of the reasons why you can't bring your ideas to fruition, as opposed to why you can.

For that reason alone, don't let years pass and opportunity disappear. Once you have the wheels in motion, you'll be like a locomotive on a downhill track, only you can step on the brakes. Success is the direct result of a focused investment of time, effort, and resources. Marc is the personification of someone who has mastered this equation and, by following his example, you can absolutely learn to *Get Rich Click!*

⏻ TAKEAWAYS

Domain Dominance

- Know what you don't know. The path to freedom requires you to gain an understanding of your strengths and weaknesses, choose what to do with this understanding, and powerfully move forward based on your conscious choices.
- Hire your weaknesses. There are extremely capable people who want to help bring your vision to reality. Let go of the reigns. You can't possibly do it all.
- Ask for help and opinions. The smartest people continually put themselves in position to be the dumbest person in the room. While counter-intuitive, remember Enron.
- The riches are in the niches. Do one thing, do it better than anyone else, and get paid extraordinarily well for your specific talent.
- Connect buyers and sellers. You can make a substantial income doing so. Blinds.com grosses $80 million annually a year and doesn't inventory a single product.
- The right domain is important. However, you don't have to own an industry-leading, category-defining domain. Google, Yahoo, and many other companies have built significant brands around meaningless words. That said, owning Liquor.com is certainly better than owning 312Liquor.com.
- Learn More, Earn More™. Continuing education is not an option, it's a necessity. Hire a coach, attend seminars, buy DVD's, and become a part of a mastermind group. Learning is a lifelong process.
- Get started. This is the key. The stars will never align and provide the perfect time to do something. Now is the time. Tomorrow may be too late.

CHAPTER 3

TEST THE WATERS, THEN JUMP IN

Yanik Silver is an Internet marketing pioneer. Unfamiliar with the name? You will find it consistently near the top of the GuruDAQ (GuruDAQ.com). A child of Russian immigrants, Yanik came to the U.S. when he was 2 and began working in his father's medical equipment sales and service business at the age of 14. In 1995, when he was 21, one of Yanik's customers suggested he listen to a tape by Jay Abraham on direct response marketing. This was a life-altering event.

Yanik applied Abraham's principles to his father's business and sales skyrocketed. The company morphed from a small regional business to a large, nationwide player. His initial direct marketing success led to a new idea: Instant Sales Letters. The year was 2000 and the Internet was fast approaching mainstream status. Yanik began to think that, if he could sell report-style information via hard-copy advertisements and phone orders, the potential for selling this same information online could be significant. He compiled many of the ads and letters he'd written for his dad, as well as information from consultations he'd been involved with over the years, and created a downloadable package priced at $29.95. By the end of the year, sales for Instant Sales Letters had reached six figures.

Today Yanik's business-to-business consulting services come with a five-figure price tag, and entrepreneurs are standing in line. In this chapter, Yanik outlines the key steps you can use to also realize online marketing success.

The Keys To The Kingdom

Direct Response Marketing existed long before the Internet. It's a method of targeting clients directly through various media by offering a specialized product or service along with a discounted rate or perk, coupled with a deadline for action. In 1995, Yanik started down this path by placing an ad in a dermatologic journal offering a free educational report to teach dermatologists and cosmetic/plastic surgeons how to increase patient volume. To receive the report, the doctors simply needed to call an 800 number.

Though the report itself was free, it included an order form to purchase additional materials further outlining the process of increasing patient volume and a deadline to respond. After cultivating several leads and sending the free reports, Yanik still had no orders. Finally, the first order for the additional material came through. The rub? Yanik hadn't written it yet. While he didn't have the product in hand, he had something even more valuable: The knowledge there was a market for it.

He contacted the client to inform him the document was being "republished" and would be available in 30 days. He then got to work creating the material. In other words, this was Yanik's marketing strategy:

- Test the waters to determine if there's a market for a particular idea.
- Offer a meaningful discount or perk to generate initial interest (in this case, a free report).
- Wait until you have an order.
- Create the product.

Yanik had all the knowledge he needed to write the additional material and his instincts told him a market existed for it. But before investing time and energy, he confirmed his instincts were on target. Once he had validation, the game was on. Today, there are a number of Internet resources that can help you do what Yanik could accomplish only through placing hard-copy ads and waiting. They include:

- KickStarter (<u>KickStarter.com</u>): Funding site that allows you to dream up an idea, post it online, and ask visitors to provide money for product development in return for something you'll deliver once the project is completed.
- IndieGoGo (<u>IndieGoGo.com</u>): Like KickStarter, a popular funding site.
- WordPress (<u>WordPress.com</u>): Free, easy-to-use site that lets you create and run as many blogs as you want.
- PreOrderific (<u>PreOrderific.com</u>): A site Yanik created that focuses on pre-ordering products.

Each of these tools allows you to create an online presence and test the market before investing significant time and money.

Set Yourself Apart: Differentiate Your Brand

Yanik didn't achieve the level of success he enjoys today through direct response marketing alone. He also follows three crucial strategies:

- Generate new ideas, tied to value and marketplace constraints.
- Create unique experiences.
- Connect to others in an authentic way.

Yanik's *Maverick* brand is a perfect example of how blending these concepts can create profits. Maverick grew out of Yanik's passion for adventure and his desire to guide entrepreneurs to achieve great results. For Maverick's first event, Yanik orchestrated an off-road Baja racing trip. With little more than an idea and a date, it developed into an event boasting 24 eager entrepreneurs who make up the nucleus of Maverick today. Yanik even managed to get Jesse James on board for the five-day adventure.

Yanik realizes that sharing a unique experience creates a much greater bond than, say, a cocktail party. Maverick hosts multiple epic events each year such as the Baja race. It also hosts special interactive dinners, memorable networking opportunities, and more. These events help teach entrepreneurs how to leverage their talents, passions, and ideas so they can find success and financial freedom through creative Internet marketing. In recent years there's been a huge increase in online entrepreneurs seeking market share and sales. To surpass these other players, you must:

- Identify, and then leverage, your unique talents and passions.
- Differentiate yourself.
- Capture your target audience's attention.
- Connect authentically with your audience and develop trusting relationships.

Yanik has demonstrated that if you incorporate these ideas into your marketing plan, you can establish a meaningful competitive advantage.

Leverage Affiliate Marketing

Like other successful Internet marketers, Yanik takes full advantage of affiliate opportunities. In his own words: "In affiliate marketing, you're the merchant selling a product. You then go out and recruit dozens, hundreds, or even thousands of people with websites who are looking for interesting products to offer their clients. They put a link on their site or send out an email with a special code attached to it. If their customers purchase your product, they receive commissions and you make additional sales. It's a nice win-win for everyone."

Yanik leveraged the affiliate concept to further boost sales of his already lucrative Instant Sales Letters. Googling "sales letters," he quickly found those with the top rankings for that search term. Presumably they enjoyed heavy traffic due to their high search position. Once he identified a viable list of potential partners, he wrote a personalized email to the top 20 ranked sites, described his product, and included an access code so they could review it. With a bit of perseverance, Yanik converted 35% of those 20 leads into participating affiliates. He now had the pieces in place to gain momentum.

Part of the reason for his success was his personalized, one-on-one approach to cultivating a genuine relationship. He avoided the often repeated, and highly insulting, faux pas of sending out generic spam solicitations.

> *Good business always comes down to the strength of your connections.*

The more someone trusts and respects you, the more that affiliate will want to promote your product. A key factor in growing any businesses is developing positive, mutually beneficial relationships. Reaching out to potential affiliates is similar to connecting with any other type of client:

- Offer a useful product that greatly benefits customers.
- Identify your target audience (e.g., via a focused search).
- Connect in a genuine way, be it by phone or personalized email.
- Inspire trust in the relationship.

However, if a product or its accompanying message doesn't resonate with your target audience, you'll never convert them into paying customers. To combat this possibility, Yanik strives to create what he refers to as "fish" products. We've all heard the adage about giving a man a fish and he'll eat for a day. However, if you teach a man to fish, he'll eat for a lifetime. Yanik doesn't agree. He believes that people want fish handed to them on a silver platter…and, garnished nicely. It is this belief that helped make "Instant Sales Letters" one of the most successful products ever sold online.

Instant Sales Letters provides proven, promotional text that can be modified for virtually any business. The owner simply needs to adapt the language for her clientele and watch the magic happen.

Yanik's templates convert over and over again, regardless of the business one is in. This is a perfect example of offering "ready-to-eat fish" that remove the guesswork, time, and frustration usually associated with most products. Think about the IKEA desk that took six hours to build (not including the two hours you spent returning to the store *twice* to grab missing parts). Would you have paid a premium for the desk to be assembled, delivered, and installed? Of course, you would.

In today's instant-gratification society, time is our single most-precious commodity and customers will gladly pay a premium to "plug and play." If your product can make their lives easier, streamlines productivity, or addresses a specific problem, they'll be interested.

A key component of effective conversion is positioning. *8 Minute Abs* sells tremendously well. However, a product named *Abdominal Exercises* likely wouldn't. Likewise, Instant Sales Letters is very successful. However, a product named *Learn How to Write Your Own Sales Letters* would fall flat.

Marketing success entails:

- Creating a product that fills a known, or unknown, hole in the market.
- Speaking to benefits, results, and/or timing in the product's title.

And, your website better be good. This is your face to the world—your full-time salesperson. An effective website introduces your product or service and, ultimately, sells what you have to offer. The layout and design must reflect your message, create a pleasant customer experience, and have a clear call-to-action.

Yanik believes far too many people get caught up in the notion that their site has to have bells and whistles that detail their life story. While it may be interesting to see how you and Mickey Mouse shared a laugh, unfortunately, this style of site often fails to convert visitors to paying customers. Reality is, only one of two things should happen when someone visits your site:

- Email/contact information is captured.
- A purchase is made.

Period.

Rather than creating a fancy site that doesn't convert, design a specific landing page that easily moves visitors through the sales process. And, while it's okay to include a few extras on the site, video for example, the extras must enhance your message, product or service in a powerful way and not confuse or turn off visitors. Here are the keys to making money online and successfully converting browsers into buyers:

- Create a ready-to-go "fish" product that addresses a specific problem or makes the customer's life easier in a tangible manner.
- Make sure the product name and/or marketing message resonates and evokes emotion (think *8 Minute Abs*).
- Your site is there for one reason—to move visitors easily though the sales process.
- Use "extras" on the site, ONLY if they help to enhance the marketing message or product.

The 2x2 Matrix Marketing Approach

A potential pitfall for any businessperson is losing focus or taking on simultaneous, differing projects that fall too far outside the realm of one's expertise. Though Yanik oversees multiple endeavors, he remains focused on building from his existing product foundation and client type. Taking advantage of his knowledge of the medical industry, he started with an informational report, which was then revamped into a downloadable, sales letter package and further leveraged through affiliate marketing.

This is known as Yanik's "2x2 Matrix." The Matrix involves either creating a new, or enhanced, product for existing clients, or introducing an existing product to new clients. This way, at least one factor remains under your control. It's a much safer approach to building your business and greatly reduces risk. No matter your field, product, or service, if you target loyal, existing clients, it will be much easier to exponentially grow your business. Start with people who already love and respect you and create an exclusive product for them to purchase.

Make the product more expensive than prior offerings, unique in scope, and initially available only to existing clients. This will make the client feel special about having the first opportunity to benefit from their relationship with you and is an integral component of the sales process. Most importantly, be clear about your motives. If you're transparent about your intentions, odds are good a few will bite and you'll know you have something worth offering. If it doesn't sell, then it's not the right product. To massively increase revenue, take the process a step further by parsing your products into individual offerings or modules. Consider selling each one separately, rather than as a complete unit.

For instance, a $2,500 course can be broken down into 25 modules that sell for $150 apiece. The same material is now available to a wider audience (as the individual components are more affordable) and the same content grosses $3,750 versus $2,500—a 50% premium. Incredible profit potential exists by following the 2x2 Matrix. Here are the steps to take:

- Develop a product based on personal knowledge or expertise.
- Start by making it available to your existing clients.
- Expand your business in focused steps, finding ways to enhance or build from your existing product or client list.
- Introduce either a new product to existing clients, or approach new clients with an existing product. (The key is to avoid creating brand new products for new, or "unsecured," customers.)
- Parse your product into individual modules so each can be sold separately.

Stay Current: Follow The Trends...And Yanik

You must stay in touch with the latest trends. Consider the current generation of youth who will likely never read a newspaper or open a phone book. While you have a choice for what to embrace on a personal level, if you want your business to remain relevant, heeding what's here and what's next is an absolute necessity. There are countless examples of obsolete companies who denied the inevitable. While this is an option, it's certainly not recommended. Yanik constantly looks for future marketing opportunities and knows his products must be available on the various platforms.

Whether a customer chooses to get information from Facebook, iTunes, Mobile, or somewhere else isn't up to you. You can't have your head in the sand and expect to outrun the storm. Make sure to offer your products through every popular medium your customers are likely to use. If you want to profit online:

- Read industry publications such as *Wired, Technorati, TechCrunch,* and *Shop.org.*
- Keep up with current trends, and embrace them.
- Make your products available on all popular sites.
- Be willing to ask experts questions about new technology that will help your business.

There are countless opportunities for making money online. Yanik found his niche in Direct Response Marketing and has taken it to impressive heights. However, he didn't get there by remaining stagnant. If you want to excel, you must continue to grow, take risks, and face insurmountable challenges. The online population continues to expand and, every day, new customers seek better, faster, and more effective products that can enrich their lives. Remember, Direct Response is just one of the available avenues that lead to financial independence. The key is picking a path and taking the first step.

⏻ TAKEAWAYS

Test The Waters, Then Jump In

- Generate an idea for a product or service based on personal knowledge, expertise, interest or passion. Focus on something that will make the customer's life easier and/or solve a specific problem.
- Test the waters to make sure there's a market for your product. Take advantage of helpful resources such as KickStarter, IndieGoGo, WordPress, and PreOrderific.
- Target your customers in a personalized way. Quality relationships matter and don't forget to include a perk and strong call to action.
- Differentiate your brand by focusing on ways to leverage your unique talent or expertise. Grab the customer's attention and make an authentic connection that inspires trust.
- Incorporate affiliate marketing into your business plan. Affiliates offer meaningful opportunities for creating significant revenues.
- Convert visitors to clients by optimizing your website. Keep in mind the appeal of a "ready to go" product and be sure your landing page easily moves visitors through the sales process. "Extras" should only serve to enhance your message or product.
- Reduce your risk and incorporate the "2x2 Matrix" model by either introducing a new, or enhanced, product to existing customers or market an existing product to new customers. Avoid developing new products for "unsecured" or non-existent customers.
- Stay within your area of expertise and consider breaking an existing product into modules for individual sale.
- Stay current with the latest technologies and make sure your business leverages what's available to directly benefit your clientele.

CHAPTER 4

NAILING YOUR NICHE

Harris Interactive recently polled 1,215 full and part-time workers and asked an interesting question: "If your job were a living, breathing person, would you marry it?" The results were quite telling:

- Only 9% of respondents said "yes."
- 34% agreed they liked their job enough to "date it seriously."
- 43% stated they'd "date it casually."
- 9% said the relationship "won't last long."
- 5% said they "want to break up immediately."

This doesn't exactly scream job satisfaction; and there's little wonder why. The average annual salary of full-time employees in the United States is $30,000 and nearly 87% of college graduates don't work in their field of study within five years. Couple this disconnect with ill-suited career choices and an average student loan debt of $20,000 and it becomes apparent something's amiss.

Jim Rohn, the author and motivational speaker largely credited with launching the careers of Tony Robbins, Mark Victor Hansen, and others gurus said, "A formal education will make you a living. A self-education will make you a fortune." Far too many people end up as wage slaves, stuck in the vicious cycle of needing to work in jobs they loathe to pay off debt related to education they don't use. If this applies to you, it may be time to seek viable alternatives and create a *career* that cultivates satisfaction, fulfillment, and contentment as opposed to having a *job* that perpetuates your living at the juncture of bankruptcy.

To achieve your ideal career, you must identify and pursue the sweet spot where something you love to do, are good at, and will be paid for all overlap. Like the legs of a tripod, each component is necessary to establish a solid foundation. For example, if there's something you love to do and are good at, but hardly anyone will pay you for it, basing a career on this activity or skill inevitably leads straight to the poor house. Conversely, if there's something you're good at and others will pay for it, but you have no love for the activity or skill, you'll always be operating with one foot out the door.

There is a tremendous difference between being good at something and achieving fulfillment doing it. You could spend 20 years filing stacks of paper in alphabetic, numeric, and subject order while blindfolded and become expert at it. However, this reflects an acquired ability, not something you're necessarily compelled to do. When societal expectations or financial pressures lead you to continue serving others via performing a skill or service that fails to resonate, you're living from an inauthentic frame of mind.

The secret to life is finding your personal sweet spot where you're able to pursue a career getting paid for what you love to do **and** what you're good at. Once found, everything will take on new meaning. You'll greet each morning with vigor, there won't be enough hours in the day to accomplish all that you want to, and things that used to worry you no longer will. To make a real difference in our world, tap the inherent blueprint that exists within and pursue your calling with reckless abandon.

Kathleen Gage has identified her calling. She teaches her clients how to leverage their natural gifts and make an extraordinary living sharing their expertise. An award-winning author and speaker, and creator of the Street Smarts Marketing VIP Club, Kathleen consistently generates multiple streams of income. To achieve similar results, follow her step-by-step program.

Making The Shift

Far too frequently, you can get caught up in *emotional bureaucracy*, in which making a decision becomes a decision-making process itself. By the time you transition out of this state of paralysis, the opportunity has passed you by. This can sometimes happen as a result of being overly conservative. But more often it stems from the fear of losing a perceived safety net. If you let yourself be ruled by a fear of failure, when will you give yourself the opportunity to succeed? Just as importantly, when will you allow yourself the chance to learn and grow from your mistakes? What is *failure,* anyway?

> *Failure is success with an unintended ending.*

Bringing an idea to fruition takes courage. Whether or not everything goes according to plan isn't nearly as important as your daring to try to make something new happen. Most people fail to take action because of fear. But you should think of fear as an acronym: *Forget Everything About Reality*. The truth is you can seldom predict what will happen when you embark on a new path. No matter how many scenarios you envision, chances are things won't go as well as hoped for or as poorly as feared.

You must be willing to expose yourself to both the accolades and the ridicule that accompany taking risks. You don't buy tickets to amusement park rides to go three miles an hour around a flat track. You pay for the unexpected thrills—the ups, downs, corkscrews, and loops.

You should have the same attitude about how you live your life. By putting something forth for the world to judge, you'll feel a similar kind of excitement. The question is: Do you want to exclusively consume the creations of others, or will you dare to become a creator? Anyone can be a critic. Kathleen has happily endured the bumps and bruises associated with being a creator.

Becoming A Creator

The first step on the path to creation is to nail your niche. Many aspiring entrepreneurs make the mistake of trying to cover too broad a market. This seldom works. For example, someone might love dogs and decide to try to serve everyone who owns one. This approach is unrealistic for three reasons:

- **Competition**: There are hundreds of companies vying for the dollars of dog owners. While a bit of competition is acceptable, it's very difficult to dethrone companies that have significantly more experience, capital, and traffic.
- **Non-targeted approach:** Attempting to provide value for all dog owners is an overwhelming task. However, focusing on a particular breed (e.g., German Shepherds) can make sense. A core component of building online wealth is to be as specific as possible, while avoiding being so laser-focused you limit the potential audience.
- **Establishing categorical expert status**: Unless you're Jack Hanna, being perceived as an expert on all animals is very difficult. However, establishing expert status is paramount to developing a meaningful following. The solution is to establish a leadership position in a specific niche. For example, if you've raised German Shepherds since you were 10 and have an innate love for the breed, you'll have a much easier time portraying yourself as an expert on German Shepherds than as an overall dog expert. Remember, people don't want advice on dogs; they want advice on *their* dog.

To identify your niche, Kathleen recommends looking at areas of your life where time stands still when you're engaged in a specific activity. For example, maybe you love playing with model trains. After dinner, you head to the basement and begin building tracks. Before you know it, the clock reads midnight, and you'd love to keep going for another few hours.

At various times in your life, you experienced an incredible feeling of lightness. It's as if the world melts away and nothing remains but you and your soul. Some feel this profound sense of stillness when meditating. Some feel it when participating in sports. Others tap into it when playing with their children. When time stands still, you have achieved *emotional nirvana*. You simply "are," and have zero conscious thought.

Try to identify as many of these moments as possible. Here you'll begin to find clues to how you're innately wired to excel. Look for subjects and activities that make your being sing. Use them as a starting point for identifying what you love and you'll lay the initial foundation for creating a formidable career and highly successful business.

Creating Your Product

Once you've identified your niche, you're ready to dream up products and/or services you can sell. Too many wonderful ideas, however, die on the vine. People become stuck in the Catch-22 of not yet being an official expert, and having difficulty feeling confident they can add value for others until they've actually done it. Consider borrowing credibility. The easiest way to do so is to enroll established industry leaders the public recognizes.

First, use Google and/or web directories (e.g., Technorati.com) to identify experts in your niche. Ideal partners will appear in your search results. Identify those you feel are most likely to help your audience reduce their learning curve. Then, contact them and ask to conduct an interview. Your goal will be to ask questions you know from experience your potential customers most want answered. When reaching out to the identified experts, you'll find many will gladly participate and allow you to record the interview. Established experts understand their participation further enhances credibility and visibility in the marketplace.

The easiest way to record the interview is by phone. A recommended resource is AudioAcrobat.com. However, it's suggested you conduct the interview via video as this provides greater flexibility and empowers you to create multiple products. Services such as Skype or Oovoo work well. When the interview is complete, send a transcriptionist the video; or first create an audio file and send that instead. In either case, the file will be large. Free file-transferring services such as WeTransfer.com and YouSendIt.com make it easy to share larger files.

Your transcriptionist can then create a Microsoft Word file that accurately represents each word spoken. And once those words have been captured as text, they can be edited. Each hour of video or audio will cost $40-$50 per hour to transcribe. If you sent video, you can also pay for the creation of an MP3 audio file. After spending $40-$200 (depending on how many hours of conversation you recorded), you're the proud owner of three valuable products:

- Interview transcript.
- Interview audio file.
- Interview video file.

After editing the files, you can make each of these products available for sale. Once you do, you'll have begun establishing yourself as an expert in your niche. Best of all, you'll be a step closer to monetizing your expertise on a large scale.

Makin' Bacon

With your three products in hand, you're ready to generate income. A proven formula for converting interviews into dollars is to create free *telesummits* or *videosummits*, in which customers call a designated phone number (for audio only) or visit a website (for both audio and visual) to tune in for the expert's provision of pertinent information. To attract a large audience, telesummits and videosummits are often structured as synergistic ventures between the host and experts. Everyone involved invites their tribe to attend and word is spread through low-cost tools such as email and social media. This structure benefits each contributor as they receive exposure to the other experts' customers and vice versa.

The most common format is to schedule a specific day and time for customers to listen to and/or watch the interviews for free in exchange for their contact information. This accomplishes two key objectives:

- You receive valuable exposure and credibility as the host of the event.
- You capture a significant number of prospects to whom you can market in the future.

Summits are usually provided once every few days over the course of weeks, or once every week over the course of months, with each session devoted to a particular expert. If a customer tunes in at each specified day and time, she can access all of the free content. Because customers have other commitments in their lives, few will manage to hear each interview. Therefore, the complete series can be bundled and sold. Summit pricing varies depending on the subject matter, notoriety of guests, and number of interviews. For example, a 12-person series is typically priced as follows:

- Standard package that offers only the transcriptions: $97
- Mid-grade package that offers the transcriptions + audio: $197
- Premium package that offers transcriptions + audio + video + bonuses: $297

There is little additional cost for providing all three versions of the interviews. However, you're able to charge a substantial markup on the mid-grade and premium packages because audio and video are perceived by customers as adding meaningful value that are worth a substantially higher price than text alone. One of the great things about this business model is that once you create the transcripts, audios, and videos, your work is virtually done. You can repeatedly sell the series so long as the content remains relevant to customers. Another appealing aspect of this model is that, as additional products are added, you can charge substantially more. For example, an effective way to encourage customers to choose the most expensive version is to offer bonuses only for those who purchase the highest-priced package.

With rare exceptions, the experts you interview will have for-sale items they'll be happy to throw in the mix at no charge. These can range from videos and white papers, to interviews they conducted with other experts, to discounts on products and services. You simply need to request them. One of the most popular freebies many contributors offer is a limited-time enrollment opportunity to join their membership program. Such programs provide weekly, biweekly, or monthly content, and take a customer's learning and ability to implement the information provided to a higher level.

Eventually, you may want to create your own membership program. When first starting out, however, it's much easier to offer someone else's. A common price point is $27 per month; and it's not unusual for experts to provide your customers with the first three or six months for free. Why would they do this? For two key reasons:

- They've already sunk the money into creating the program and content. Adding additional members is easy and cost-effective.
- They're hoping that after the trial period expires, customers will sign up as paid members. Even one sign-up can make it all worthwhile, since little expense is involved in creating the free trial.

Further, many experts will pay you an affiliate fee for new sign-ups. That means if enough of your audience becomes paid members of their programs, you can reap solid residual income. As your knowledge and following develops, you'll eventually create proprietary products that best serve your clientele and will likely be asked to contribute as an expert to other's events. When this happens not only will you be ready, you'll be well armed to include your summit as a value-add bonus.

Transparency

People are continually bombarded with physical junk mail, email spam, web pop-up ads, slimy sales offers, and more. As a result, our B.S. meters are set to high alert. Reaching potential customers with valuable content that can transform their lives is difficult. Too many crappy products and shady operators have damaged the trust of customers. It has never been more important to be transparent. People need to know who you are, what you're about, and what your intentions are. No one will hold it against you if they're told point blank you receive an affiliate fee for selling someone else's product or make money on yours. As a matter of fact, it's expected.

Attempting to hide the obvious will only work to your detriment. People expect to pay for knowledge and, in many businesses, a finder's fee is commonplace. Online, finder's fees are paid every second. Receiving payment for an introduction is normal. So don't beat around the bush. Tell your prospects straight away that if they sign up to receive a free product, for-sale products and services will be introduced down the line. They'll understand and it will be their choice whether to take your free content and walk away or stick around for more.

People respect honesty. Few will work with those who are two-faced or knowingly omit relevant details. This is how Internet marketing works today. Flashy sales pages with loads of unnecessary content are dead. Cut right to the chase, be transparent, and provide value. You'll be amply rewarded for it.

Sometimes the road to success traverses the path previously traveled. Kathleen has provided a glimpse of the map. Tune your GPS to her guidance.

 TAKEAWAYS

Nailing Your Niche

- Don't just work a job. Cultivate a career.
- Failure can be viewed as success with an unintended ending.
- To nail your niche, be aware of competition, take a targeted approach, and establish yourself as an expert in your field.
- Borrow credibility from others. It's a lot easier than you might think.
- Create for-sale products and services. These can often be created at low cost, but must be packed with value.
- Be transparent. People respect honesty.

CHAPTER 5

F.A.S.T. COMPANY

As the successful will attest, seldom does creating a flourishing business happen without the combination of both incredibly hard work and a bit of luck. Luck, however, is not about finding a four-leaf clover and making a wish—it is the byproduct of preparedness, execution, and fruitful timing. Of these variables, many argue that timing is the most important factor. Having the necessary message reach the right person at the correct time often spells the difference between massive success and being two minutes late for the ferry.

Internet legend Mike Filsaime is clear on the importance of timing. While the Internet has seen exponential growth in usage since its initial penetration, acceptance and leverage of the medium began hitting its stride in 2004—the same year Mike began building his online empire. According to Internet World Stats, in 2004, there were 745 million Internet users. This number reflected 11.4% of the world's population. By June 2011, the number of users had grown to over 2.1 billion, or 30.4% of the world's population.

> *At this point, Mike already had 7+ years under his belt.*

Over this period, he became the second person to create a million dollar product launch and the innovator behind many of the most recognized and widely used tools such as Butterfly Marketing and Traffic Fusion. Today, his company generates over $10 million annually. As founder of the Marketers Cruise (MarketersCruise.com) which sails every January with a packed house of notable guests from around the world, Mike not only makes darn well sure he catches the ferry before it sets sail, he determines when it leaves the dock. Get your life vest on; this ride takes us into deep waters.

Pick A Car, Any Car

Few people can legitimately carry the title of guru. Mike's track record of helping thousands reach new levels of success certainly places him in this very rare air. Things weren't always this way. His early years were spent with Pathmark Supermarkets where he worked in the frozen foods department. After attending school at New York's Institute of Technology, he shifted focus to pursue a career in the automotive field. For 14+ years he managed some of the largest auto dealers in North America. At the turn of the millennium, he began dabbling on the web and in August 2004, pursued Internet marketing as his full-time profession after receiving an ultimatum from his boss to choose car sales or the Internet.

In just three short years, Mike went from a virtual unknown and operating out of the spare bedroom in his house, to a staff of 36 that operates 50+ sites. Since his shift, he has grossed over $35 million in sales. From a distance, it's easy to look at Mike and say he had it easy. This couldn't be farther from the truth. At one point, things were so bad he had to sell his wife's ring to pay the mortgage. At another, they had to burn his father's set of encyclopedias to keep warm.

However, with a singular purpose, creativity, and laser-like focus, Mike eventually reached his goal of becoming financially secure. Although his story might be disappointing if the preferred route to wealth is via the road known as "get rich quick," it's actually encouraging news. Why? Because, his story demonstrates that *anyone* can achieve his or her desired level of success regardless of circumstance.

> *History has repeatedly shown that initiative combined with incentive begets undeniable results.*

There's simply no denying the facts. Millionaires are made every day. According to the 2010 World Wealth Report, 2,466 to be exact. (Note: Millionaire status does not include the value of one's principal residence or lifestyle assets, such as cars, jewelry, and furniture.) That's correct—while most suffered through The Great Recession, 900,000 people worldwide achieved millionaire status.

Realizing your career objectives often begins with understanding the motivating factors for taking action. Whether it's watching your father's possessions go up in flames or answering the burning desire in your soul, everyone has their trigger...one simply needs to make sure their gun is locked and loaded when the volcano erupts.

Spam

Say the word...*spam!* For most, it conjures up either questionable sustenance on a Ritz substitute or an email inbox chock full of ED pills and wires from Nigeria. For Mike, dollar signs come to mind. It's hard to believe but, yes, Mike's foray into profiting online began by sending spam. Back in the early days of AOL, when email hit the inbox, your sweet, strangely excitable, funny, but not ha-ha uncle would cheerfully let you know, "You've got mail!" At this point, email was viewed as a welcome present. People weren't yet sick of, or significantly aware about, spam.

If someone was kind enough to send an email, well by-golly, it was our responsibility to open it. And, open them we did. Consider the 2004 statistics from *Spam Filter Review*:

Spam Statistics 2004	
Email considered Spam	40% of all email
Daily Spam emails sent	12.4 billion
Daily Spam received per person	6
Annual Spam received per person	2,200
Spam cost to all non-corp Internet users	$255 million
Spam cost to all US Corporations	$8.9 billion
States with Anti-Spam Laws	26
Email address changes due to Spam	16%
Estimated Spam increase by 2007	63%
Annual Spam in 1,000 employee company	2.1 million
Users who reply to Spam email	28%
Users who purchased from Spam email	8%
Corporate email that is considered Spam	15-20%
Wasted corporate time per Spam email	4-5 seconds

As shown, 12.4 billion spam emails were sent *daily*. Perhaps, most interestingly, 8% of Internet users reported *buying* something via spam solicitation. The numbers are still frightening. A March 2010 report conducted and released by MAAWG (Messaging Anti-Abuse Working Group) Email Security Awareness and Usage Report revealed the following:

- 43% of respondents "Opened an email I suspected was spam."
- 11% "Clicked on a link in an email I suspected was spam."
- 8% "Opened an attachment in an email I suspected was spam."
- 4% "Replied to an email I suspected was spam."
- 4% "Forwarded an email I suspected was spam."

Yikes. People's willingness to open unsolicited emails provided Mike with a window of opportunity. Though not nearly as lucrative as his current above-board initiatives, he did realize marginal success finding decent response rates to, of all things, pumpkin pie recipes.

Eventually, these actions caught the attention of his ISP (Internet Service Provider) and they made clear that, should he continue to distribute spam, he would be permanently banned from sending email. He heeded their warning. Shifting to legitimate activities, he began focusing on creating active lists of customers interested in various products. In his words, "I made squeeze pages before they had a name."

He'd build a topic-specific, search-friendly static page and offer visitors a free product (typically an ebook or report) in exchange for their email address. Concurrently, he formed partnerships with existing marketers and frequently promoted their products to his list and received a commission on each sale. He quickly discovered there was a 1:1 correlation between the number of subscribers and monthly income. In other words, a list of 1,000 people translated to $1,000 in monthly income. As Mike's list grew, income accelerated, as did his knowledge. Deciding it was time to create, market, and find affiliates to sell his own product, he created Carbon Copy Marketing.

Carbon Copy Marketing translated Mike's Internet marketing process into an easy-to-replicate blueprint that empowered others to emulate his success. The kit provided squeeze page templates, directions for cultivating free traffic, affiliate products to promote, etc.—essentially, everything needed to profit online. It was during this period that Mike began testing the power of a one-time offer. By providing opt-ins with a limited opportunity to purchase products at a steep discount within a finite period of time, conversion rates soared. The strategy was fairly straightforward:

- Drive traffic to a squeeze page.
- Offer value in exchange for contact details.
- Once signed on, deliver promised value.
- Within a specific window of time, offer an incredible deal on a for-sale item.

Because people naturally associate free, valuable content with for-sale product that *must* be worth so much more, they'll be sufficiently motivated to purchase if proper incentive is provided. Therefore, within days of opt-in, a one-time offer to buy a proven next-level product at an unbeatable price is provided. Today, this model is common practice. At the time, however, no one had seen, or been willing to test, such unorthodox measures.

And therein you'll find the single biggest distinction between those who lead and those who follow. Leaders, in calculated fashion, throw caution to the wind and honor their instincts. Followers consistently allow themselves to be blown around by the whims of others. Mike clearly chose to lead. There's no shame following in his footsteps.

The Elevator Effect

The one-time offer is extremely powerful. Most people, however, are unclear as to how it works and, as a result, fail to effectively implement the strategy in their marketing efforts. Think of a one-time offer in the context of an elevator. When an elevator's doors are open and people file in, there's no sense of urgency to secure their space. However, when the doors start to close, there's a rush to get on. What inevitably happens is people quicken their pace to catch it. If they're farther away, they may engage in a full-on sprint to get their hand between the doors. Creating scarcity consistently works as a sales tactic. And, today's technology can help make it happen.

For example, an auto responder can be structured to deliver an offer for a $197 product four days after opt-in and the free product is sent. This is an ideal time to target prospects as they have, hopefully, had time to review the added-value materials and are primed to learn more about additional products and services. However, instead of being $197 for the next 24-hours, the price is reduced to only $47. After that time, the offer is pulled and the product will only be available in the future at the original price.

Fortunately, this is simple to enforce as cookies and IP addresses can be collected, thereby preventing existing clients from accessing the one-time offer outside of the 24-hour period. Best of all, the call-to-action moves people to take immediate advantage of the pending opportunity. When executed properly, a limited-time offer can create unlimited profits.

Multi-Level Love

By leveraging the one-time deal format, Mike was able to drastically increase conversion rates. As a result, monthly income was now consistent. A larger concern, however, loomed that prevented him from exponentially growing his business—generating considerable traffic. He needed a mechanism that could quickly ramp up monthly visitors. Going back to the drawing board, he created Don't Touch My Ads, a next-generation product for taking advantage of the Internet's innate social protocol...viral marketing. Building off the traditional Multi-Level Marketing structure, Don't Touch My Ads provided incentive for participants to share the concept with others and rewarded those who actively recruited "down-line" partners.

The basic premise, though a tad complex, enabled an ad to be shown on a fellow participant's computer after 10 to 30 seconds of no activity. For every five ads shown, and subsequently, clicked to close, someone in the network would see one of your ads. Credits were received based on the number of ads shown in one's distributor network. Therefore, the higher up on the pyramid one stood, the more their ad would appear. As a result, participants were very active in promoting involvement to others. For Mike, as creator of the hierarchy, exposure for his ads piled up quick. On the first day the network went live, he grossed *$19,000*.

Though Don't Touch My Ads no longer accepts new members, due to the pervasiveness of social media, the opportunity to go "viral" and receive massive exposure is easier than ever. And, thankfully for the rest of us, one no longer needs to *expose* parts of who they are in order to garner significant attention.

Living The Dream

When many think about those they believe are "living the dream," fat bank accounts, pimped-out rides, 24-karat gold mansions, designer clothes, and the world's best food and drink come to mind. However, if you ask someone with an abundance of cash what he or she would define as living the dream, often the answer is they'd greatly prefer an abundance of time. Boatloads of cash seldom equates to satisfaction, especially if one is working 80+ hours a week to support their chosen lifestyle. Therefore, balance is required.

Early on, Mike did everything in his power to build wealth while freeing up time to enjoy it. He developed a powerful mantra upon which he bases his career and lifestyle choices. In a word, his philosophy can be summed up as *F.A.S.T.*:

- **F = Fun:** Without fun and excitement, work quickly becomes stale. People tend to spend more time at work than anywhere else. Mike insists on creating not only profitable endeavors, but also an environment where both he and his employees relish working because it gives them satisfaction, fulfillment, contentment, and happiness.
- **A = Automation:** Technology has made it much easier to create products and deliver them to customers. Mike is a huge proponent of taking full advantage of available tools, ranging from automated webinars and teleseminars to pre-loaded social media messages and press releases. If your business isn't

structured to churn cash while you sleep, you're doing yourself and your company a disservice.

- **S = Scalability:** You want to create products and services that have the ability to serve the masses without needing to engage in customization. Mike develops each new offer with this in mind. Doing so enables him to sell the same item to thousands of people. This is one of the key tenets the successful use to create wealth.

- **T = Time-Freeing Ability:** One of the tremendous strengths of the Internet is its ability to make things happen in the blink of an eye. If a product is downloadable, it can be provided within seconds of a customer ordering it. And if the product is physical, the confirmation and details of the order can be delivered to the customer within moments...and the automated process of fulfilling an order may begin just as quickly.

Yes, a considerable amount of time goes into development and implementation. This should go without saying. Ultimately, though, creating your ideal life is infinitely possible and the formula for doing so is spelled *F.A.S.T.* Unlike baking a cake, once your products, marketing, and supportive tools are in place, not only is it unnecessary to go back into the kitchen and start from scratch for the next customer, you won't even need to be in the building. And, if you do, it's possible you won't find Mike behind the desk.

⏻ TAKEAWAYS

F.A.S.T. Company

- Luck is the byproduct of preparedness, execution, and fruitful timing.
- One-time offers convert extraordinarily well. Remember the elevator.
- History has repeatedly shown that initiative combined with incentive begets undeniable results.
- Driving traffic requires significant creativity. Look to create your own mechanism when necessary.
- Leverage, and apply, available technology to your business.
- Mike's formula for success can be spelled F.A.S.T.

CHAPTER 6

MARKETING MAGIC

For many entrepreneurs, marketing is simply one of many components required to operate a business and is primarily viewed as a necessary promotional tool. The successful subscribe to the notion that marketing *is* business. For example, consider the following ad campaigns:

"When E.F. Hutton talks..."

"Where's the...?"

"Plop, plop, fizz, fizz..."

The large majority of people born from the 40's through the 70's can easily recall that, "When E.F. Hutton talks, *people listen.*" Wendy's put itself on the map by asking, "Where's the *beef?*" And, "Plop, plop, fizz, fizz" ends with, "*oh, what a relief it is.*"

When implemented correctly, marketing not only tells a company's story, it serves to establish bonds with customers, differentiates their product from the competition, and secures brand commitment. Effective marketing is the combination of three distinct elements:

- **Partnerships:** Building a profitable entity requires partnering both with those who directly serve one's specific niche and others who can benefit from forging a mutually beneficial relationship.
- **Presence:** Online or off, via social media or mobile, creating a formidable business presence is an important factor of the success equation. Without brand recognition, developing a sustainable business is almost impossible.
- **Products:** This is arguably the most important. After generating interest, deliver high-value products. Failing to do so will lead to customer dissatisfaction, massive rates of return, and securing few, if any, repeat customers.

One of the world's foremost marketers is John Kremer. An Internet authority and award-winning author he understands, and consistently implements, cutting-edge strategies. Seldom does one have the privilege to learn from a living legend. Fortunately, John not only shares his knowledge, he provides the exact map needed to locate a massive bounty.

A Look Back

Today, John is well known among marketers and authors across the globe. By constantly delivering value and building relationships with influential people, his online and offline presence is considerable. It wasn't always this way. John started his career handling marketing for a friend who owned a toy company. Though he knew little about the subject, he dove in headfirst. Over many years, he honed his skills and eventually left the company to become a writer. Given his marketing expertise, he opted to self-publish his titles.

He was soon selling 5,000-10,000 copies of each of his books.

Due to his noticeable success (the average self-published title sells less than 100 copies), others contacted him to learn more about replicating his process. As a result, he wrote the now-famous industry bible, *1001 Ways To Market Your Books,* which Jack Canfield and Mark Victor Hansen largely credit with helping them sell more than 200 million copies of the massively successful *Chicken Soup for the Soul* series.

To learn more and/or purchase *1001 Ways To Market Your Books,* please visit <u>EZ.com/1001ways</u> or use your mobile device to scan the QR code to the left.

In addition to writing, John has become a leading voice for cultivating inexpensive online traffic. He currently operates dozens of sites, including <u>BookMarket.com</u> which is ranked #1 on Google for virtually every keyword it targets. John's methods are simple: provide pertinent information, build optimized sites, and establish relationships with as many of the top people in your niche as possible. Let's dig deeper.

The Value Proposition

When John released *1001 Ways to Market Your Books,* it cost $27.95. If you were to ask the authors of *Chicken Soup* if the price was fair, they'd likely say they would've gladly paid 100x that amount for the results realized. Creating happy customers leads to long-term profitability. This process begins with over-delivering for clients. One of the easiest ways to over-deliver is to provide beneficial products or services without cost. Providing free merchandise, learning materials, ebooks, and other products not only attracts attention, it helps ingrain your brand into the customer's mind.

People love a bargain (think about the mayhem created on Black Friday and the stratospheric rise of Groupon*).* Nothing, however, is a better bargain than free. So why do the majority of business owners fail to implement this simple yet highly effective marketing technique? This could be due to their misguided concern for devaluing for-sale items.

Fact is, however, this correlation is an illusion. Providing free product only serves to enhance the value of what is sold.

Provided that the free products are well produced, contain valuable information, and help to serve the reader in meaningful ways, the customer will naturally make the assumption "if they're giving this away for free, the for-sale materials must be incredible." Thus, the opportunity is created to not only sell a substantial amount of product, but to do so at premium prices.

Further, in order to receive the free product, contact information is provided. This data has immense value (for example, Daily Candy, which sold to Comcast for $250 million, or $50 per subscriber), as does entering the sales cycle. Though metrics vary wildly, consider Internet marketing standards:

- Marketing response rates hover around 2%. As an example, for every 1 million impressions, approximately 20,000 visits are generated.
- Of the 20,000 visits, 11.5% opt-in to join a mailing list or receive a free product.
- In addition, 3.5% convert to paying customers within three months.

Therefore, for every 20,000 visitors or 1 million impressions:

- 700 customers are secured.
- 2,300 potential clients are added to one's database.

The chart shown on the next page from comScore Ad Metrix details the typical Cost per Thousand Impressions across various Internet categories.

As indicated, assuming a median cost of $2.52/CPM, a typical expenditure will be $2,520 for one million impressions. Based on the above metrics, the lifetime value of a single customer must be $3.60 to break even ($2,520 per 700 customers). This is certainly a viable proposition if $24.95 books, $97 workshops, and other items are being sold with reasonable profit margins. However, if the ultimate goal is to sell high-end coaching services (e.g. $300/hour with a 3 hour minimum) or multi-session workshops (e.g. $10,000 for six weeks of training) the metrics look pretty darn appealing.

Top Display Advertising Site Categories
April 2010
Total US—Home & Work Locations
Source: comScore Ad Metrix

Publisher	Total Display Ad Impressions (MM)	Share of Impressions	Estimated Spending ($ 000)	Cost per Thousand Impressions (CPM)
Total Internet : Total Audience	354,636	100.0%	893,681	$2.52
Social Networking	98,176	27.7%	54,684	$0.56
Portals	69,664	19.6%	181,266	$2.60
Entertainment	38,104	10.7%	181,147	$4.75
e-mail	34,327	9.7%	32,370	$0.94
Community	15,884	4.5%	33,435	$2.10
General News	12,542	3.5%	77,055	$6.14
Sports	10,850	3.1%	68,214	$6.29
Newspapers	8,506	2.4%	59,441	$6.99
Online Gaming	7,929	2.2%	21,234	$2.68
Photos	7,391	2.1%	7,953	$1.08

That said, conversion is a byproduct of multiple tangible and intangible factors and there's no guarantee things will happen as planned. Further, many Internet marketers simply cannot afford pay-for-placement/performance marketing and must pursue other options. If this is the case, low-cost or free traffic must be generated to sustain one's operation *if* online sales are the primary component of revenue. Providing free, high-value products and driving traffic through synergistic partnerships leads directly to the second step of the equation, bypassing the upfront investment required in step one.

Given no out-of-pocket expense, this equates to an immeasurable ROI as each opt-in costs nothing to secure. Even if less than 1% of the 11.5% of visitors who opt-in become paying customers, the metrics are phenomenal. Best of all, the customer views the relationship as a favorable exchange of value: "For providing my name and email address, I receive valuable content. That's more than worth it."

And should one choose to give nearly everything away for free (e.g. books, white papers, presentations, etc.), it is absolutely possible to still make an extraordinary income. How? Most people want someone to hold their hand and show them precisely what to do, even if the information provided defines the exact process to follow and does so in alphabetical order using the Dewey decimal system.

This desire opens the door to membership programs, live events, consulting services, etc. Therefore, the value proposition must be viewed as an initial investment whereby sacrificing a small percentage of immediate cash flow provides access to clients and allows for the realization of significantly more income down the line.

Guerilla Traffic

There are three proven strategies for generating traffic online:

- Spend millions on traditional and online media.
- Create a site that Google and other search engines love.
- Create an interactive forum that promotes stickiness and contribution.

Assuming the first choice is out of the question, let's move to the engines. For simplicity's sake, we'll focus on Google. Google, like any other company, seeks to best serve its customers. Their business model requires the provision of relevant results that addresses the user's specific inquiry. While there are a multitude of SEO techniques that can be leveraged to land on page one, the easiest way to make this happen is to establish authority in your niche and feature massive amounts of content related to the subject matter. One of the most powerful ways to accomplish this feat is to build a directory.

> *A directory features scores of related providers. Google loves directories.*

Say, for instance, you're a dentist based in Atlanta. A Guerilla marketer will create a directory that features as many Atlanta dentists and as much detailed information about them as possible. Why do this? For one simple reason: When someone searches for "Atlanta Dentist," the directory will likely appear at the top of the results page.

A Cornell University study performed by Laura A. Granka, Thorsten Joachims, and Geri Cay analyzed eye-tracking and click through behavior of search engine users. By examining the results, one can clearly understand the importance of not just landing on page one, but of being one of the first three listings. The first three listings account for almost 80% of all clicks on the chosen subject matter. Further, the first three listings also account for slightly over 68% of the total time spent exploring the subject from every search result provided.

In other words, forget about page two...and the bottom of page one. Everything after the third search result is nearly invisible. At this point, you're likely thinking, "Okay, that's interesting, but why on Earth would I want to promote other practices?" Great question. By creating the directory, you now ostensibly own the category. And, you have complete control over the order in which the practices appear, the ads are displayed, and the content is featured.

Any guess as to whose practice and value-add content is going to appear first? If it's not yours, we need to chat. Further, you've now created a powerful online resource that can provide significant ad, CPC, affiliate, and content revenue. While it may not be your primary business, there's little reason not to take full advantage of the income-generating opportunity created. This model clearly flies in the face of how many think about dealing with the competition. And, while the directory may drive traffic to others, if your practice is positioned as the "Preferred Provider," and you back that up with outstanding service, a few pennies lost will pale in comparison to the overall wealth gained.

Interaction = Transaction

Building a community of followers, content providers, and visitors is crucially important. Today's most successful online marketers look for ways to start discussions, open up message boards, create user groups, and involve their audience. The theory is by jumpstarting participation and encouraging a free-flowing, interactive dialogue, traffic will be generated. TripAdvisor (TripAdvisor.com) is a prime example of a site that plays this concept to the hilt.

Described as "the world's largest travel site, enabling travelers to plan and have the perfect trip, TripAdvisor offers trusted advice from real travelers and a wide variety of travel choices and planning features with seamless links to booking tools." The site, and its 18 other travel-related brands attracts more than 65 million unique monthly visitors, has 20 million members, and features over 50 million reviews and opinions.

A search for "Travel Advice" on Google demonstrates the power of content. While TripAdvisor has paid for placement at the top of the page, it is likely done as a preventative measure and clearly doesn't need to. The sheer mass of feedback, photos, and advice propels the company to the top of all travel advice site listings. By cultivating user-generated content, they have built one of the industry's largest businesses. Monetization is realized through brand placement, booking fees, and pay per click revenue.

In 2010, TripAdvisor grossed $486 million, an increase of 13% over 2009, and earned $260 million. Not bad for a site that largely aggregates available information and profits from its visitors' contributions. And, TripAdvisor is *sticky* as the average visitor spends around four minutes on the site. While not nearly as impressive as Facebook (24 minutes per visit), Yahoo (eight minutes per visit), or eBay (14 minutes per visit), it far exceeds the average time spent on a web page—which is 58 seconds, as reported by Nielsen.

Ultimately, fostering longer visits and encouraging visitors to participate by contributing content establishes brand loyalty and a sense of commitment. This, in turn, results in fulfilling perhaps the most important component of the business equation…profits.

Relational Currency

As discussed, traffic is the lifeblood of any online business and the Internet's highest valued commodity. A site with a large number of visitors is ostensibly a sale waiting to happen as eyeballs equate to dollars. Developing an in-demand site not only takes significant resources, but also ingenuity. One of the best ways to build traffic is to develop substantive relationships with others. These relationships can be nurtured to provide meaningful dividends for both parties and seldom requires the allocation of funds. Like traffic, relationships have immense value and provide a solid barrier to entry for the competition.

John is a master at aligning with others and offers two, no-cost, proven strategies for developing relationships that anyone can easily implement: post to blogs, and become a columnist.

Contribute To Blogs You Admire

Leaving thoughtful comments or interesting information under your signature not only contributes solid content for their readership, it has the potential for driving traffic to your site and opens the door for future collaboration. Bloggers live for feedback and appreciate those who provide constructive criticism, share opinions that further other's understanding of the topic, or offer new ways of thinking.

The most popular bloggers generally receive hundreds (if not thousands) of comments per post. As a result, they may not read more than the first 10 or 20. To grab their attention, post early. An easy way to be alerted to new posts is to sign up for their RSS feed or alert services such as those offered by Google and Twitter. All are simple, yet powerful tools that provide email updates of posts relevant to your desired topics. These alerts allow you to easily keep track of industry leaders and their activities. And, if a particular topic really hits home, reach out for them.

Putting something forth for the world to judge is not easy. Demonstrating your support for their efforts will separate you from the pack and sets the stage for developing rapport.

Write A Column

Online, content rules. website owners desperately need fresh, quality material that keeps their audience engaged. A powerful way to build your brand and add value to others is to create your own column. Columns vary from interviews with industry experts to original posts or a Q&A format. Written daily, weekly, biweekly, or monthly, columns achieve four objectives:

- Adds value and no-cost, high-quality content for the site that features it.
- Drives traffic to your site/business.
- Establishes credibility and increases search results.
- Can often be sponsored, which provides revenue based on the size of the audience.

One of the more popular columns is a Q&A. Devoted to providing answers to commonly asked questions it is an easy plug-and-play option for industry participants. For example, the Atlanta dentist could write a Q&A column. A common question might be "How do I naturally whiten my teeth?" The columnist would then provide detailed answers applicable to any dentist's practice and suitable for placement on their site. At the end of the column, the writer may feature an ad from a sponsor (e.g., Crest Whitestrips), and contact information.

It's a win for everyone involved. The site featuring the column receives traffic and provides information their clientele seeks; the columnist receives click through traffic from customers and income from the sponsor; and, the sponsor receives desired exposure. In one fell swoop, the columnist has established position as an expert, developed new relationships, monetized their expertise, and increased their online presence. This is a simple, yet incredibly effective technique.

Ultimately, creating a profitable business requires a pinch of luck, a handful of focus, and a ton of effort. John has provided the recipe for creating magical results. Time to get the apron on.

⏻ TAKEAWAYS

Marketing Magic

- Marketing *is* business, not just a necessary promotional tool.
- Effective marketing is built on three proven fundamentals: Partnerships, Presence, and Products.
- Don't underestimate the value of providing information for **free**. Data, and entering potential customers into the sales cycle, is worth big money.
- Consider creating a directory and drive traffic to others. While counterintuitive, it can generate huge traffic, both online and off, and easily be monetized.
- Appear in the top three of Google listings. Everything else is virtually invisible.
- Create a **sticky** site that fosters user participation and content contribution.
- Leverage the value of relationships and model John's two no-cost, proven strategies for driving traffic.

1
0
1
1
0
0
0
0
0
0
1
0
1
0
1
0
1
1
1
1
0
1
0
1
0
1
0
0
1
1
0
0
0

PART II

DOMINATING
POPULAR MARKETS

CHAPTER 7

PRESENTATION PROWESS

One of the fastest ways to grow your business online and off is to share your message and mission in high-visibility venues. The hottest trends among top experts and online marketers today include video marketing, teleseminars, webinars, and the big kahuna of profit, live events. But, how can you stand up and stand out in a competitive marketplace? Oren Klaff, author of *Pitch Anything: An Innovative Method for Presenting, Persuading, and Winning the Deal*, says:

> *"A great pitch is not about procedure. It's about getting and keeping attention."*

Knowing how to grab people's attention, share your message, and close the deal is a skill that allows you to secure expert status, shine at local networking events, speak to groups, and build your marketing platform. Be forewarned—studies show that people make approximately 11 assumptions in the first 11 seconds…and, those first impressions are long lasting and hard to overcome. Make a great first impression and people will be forgiving of later missteps. Start off on the wrong foot, and it's a continuous uphill battle. Whether online or in person, it is important to secure a strong first impression that accurately reflects who you are, what your message is, and how you want to be perceived. To make a name for yourself and attract leads, clients, cash, and referrals, you need to know how to capitalize on the opportunity of speaking and selling to groups both large and small.

Kristin Thompson of SpeakServeGrow.com believes that many presenters shy away from developing persuasion-based presentation skills in fear of being perceived as slick, sales-driven, or pushy. This inevitably works to their detriment.

In her words, "It is the presenter's responsibility to solidify expert status, command the room, and generate an emotional charge. If this is not accomplished, the message will be lost and sales will be left on the table." Consider the following quote from Dr. David C. Funder of Stanford University: "Positive self-presentation is clearly not the deceptive tendency it may at first appear to be. Instead, by capturing others' attention, self-presentation facilitates more accurate first impressions." In other words, by focusing on presenting yourself in natural fashion, the audience subsequently forges an authentic opinion about you. This is your goal—to expediently reveal your truest self.

Entrepreneurs simply cannot escape the necessity of honing presentation skills. Virtually every action, conversation, and promotional effort represents your personal brand and can potentially make, or break, a positive purchase decision. Like it or not, in business, you're continuously selling. And, while many factors are outside of your control, nailing your first impression and learning how to powerfully present products and services are not.

Few elements affect the likelihood of creating a thriving endeavor in a greater manner as does effectively presenting your message.

Fortunately, one of the world's best, Kristin Thompson, will provide us with a guided tour for realizing extraordinary presentation results.

Making The Shift

Raised in Southern California, Kristin received her degree in psychology from Loyola Marymount University in Los Angeles. When she moved north to Monterey, she convinced a local radio station to hire her in their sales department.

> *She thought she'd won the lottery, but all she really won was a telephone and a phone book. That's how her career in sales began.*

She learned everything she could about sales, marketing, and advertising and attended numerous seminars, read books, and listened to audiotapes on the subject. Shortly after picking up steam at the radio station, she was recruited by a top-rated NBC television station to be part of their sales team. There she became a top seller, winning awards for new business development. But, something major was about to disrupt the smooth course of her career.

Kristin and her husband were ready to start a family. Given that a sales position is far from part-time work, they made the conscious decision for her to resign. It was the best choice she could have made. Her success in sales opened her eyes to her innate love for speaking. Pursuing her natural talent, Kristin began speaking on various subjects and dedicated herself to honing the craft. Speaking every day of the week *(while pregnant)*, she quickly learned what resonated with audiences and led to profits versus what generated glazed-over stares and left her empty-handed.

She quickly developed proven techniques for cultivating a rush of new clients, income, and referrals. This enabled her to create full-time income on a part-time schedule. Over the years, her focus has evolved organically and it is now clear that her passion is to help entrepreneurs, coaches, and consultants turn their mission and message into a virtual ATM. Her powerful strategies, while simple to implement, can produce extraordinary results.

Please join me as I welcome Kristin Thompson to the stage.

Is Content Really King?

A common challenge for entrepreneurs, coaches, and consultants speaking to groups, is focusing too strongly on content. And, while content is crucial, it's <u>not</u> what motivates people to take action or what someone is actually buying. Kristin believes moving prospects to take action is the direct result of implementing the compelling combination of content, connection, *and* inspiration. This is what drives someone to open her wallet and take the next step.

Each element carries equal weight and ALL are needed to realize desired results. For example, if your content is outstanding and you're an inspiring presenter, but fail to connect with the prospect in a meaningful way, the sale won't happen. Further, if you're an inspiring presenter and people connect with you, but your content is essentially worthless, that doesn't work either. As Oren Klaff says, "The better you are at keeping someone's attention, the more likely that person will be to go for your idea." He explains that our brains are designed to filter information into one of three categories and make choices accordingly:

- If it's not dangerous, it is largely ignored.
- If it's not new and exciting, it is largely ignored.
- If it's new, it is summarized quickly and an immediate choice is made for what to do with the information provided.

People today are The Flash-like quick in making decisions. While not every presenter can use pyrotechnics and a celebrity spokesman to position their product, you must introduce new material that excites the senses and will be remembered. In the words of Simon Cowell, the last thing you want to be is "forgettable."

Command Any Room

Many who pursue their calling position themselves as an industry expert. Being recognized as an expert typically carries significant cache and greatly improves one's ability to monetize their abilities. Becoming an expert is not terribly difficult. Here are the steps:

1. Choose a subject that aligns with your purpose.
2. Study existing industry experts.
3. Gain a meaningful degree of knowledge.
4. Identify your niche.
5. Position yourself to be highly visible.
6. Declare yourself an expert.
7. Become a creator.

So easy, even a caveman can do it. Very few experts, however, make enough money to avoid needing government subsidies. Why? Only a handful of experts know how to truly leverage their knowledge to both add value to others and sufficiently monetize their expertise. Most create a signature talk, fill the presentation with their best content, and then are left to wonder why no one buys their products or services.

They fall into the trap of becoming what Kristin calls "the accidental philanthropist"—they share their message, educate people, but never profit from it. Conversely, other presenters go straight for the jugular and try to close the sale before they've barely said hello. Successful experts properly position the sale by combining meaningful value with offering next-level products and services for purchase. The key is balance—something far too few get right. For example, Kristin shares how most experts approach positioning.

They'll begin their presentation with, "Hello, **I'm** Expert X. **I've** been in business since 'X' and here are **my** products and services. **Our** product does this and is made like that… etc, etc." Focusing on you is a big temptation and should be avoided. People don't care about the presenter or their products. They care about solving *their* problems and finding easy-to-implement solutions.

Instead, Kristin suggests a presenter develops a simple "before and after" formula whereby the presentation first addresses the pain or problems a potential client is experiencing now and then shifts to how their expertise can transform the client's life. Including stories of those whose lives have changed as a result of using the item being sold adds immediate credibility. Here's an example of a typical presentation, i.e., one we want to avoid. Notice the focus on the presenter and his company:

DON'T:

"Hello! **My** name is Expert, and **I'm** the owner of **Expert Yoga. I** have been a student of yoga for 10 years, traveling all across the globe to learn from the masters. **Expert Yoga** is one of the most comfortable yoga studios in the world. You just have to try **our** new state-of-the-art mats!"

While typical, Kristin suggests a slightly different approach. Using a simple "before and after" formula, the problem is addressed and solution provided. Note how the presenter engages the attendee.

DO:

"Do **you** suffer from debilitating back pain? For those of **us** over 40, back pain is a very real problem. Yet, **we've** found that practicing yoga just two times per week can quickly and easily erase **your** lower back pain and reduce stress immediately. In fact, many of **our** clients are here today and, in a moment, we'll share with **you** their stories of how yoga has transformed **their** lives."

By targeting a specific problem or challenge (in this case, back pain), and including the audience in the conversation, an immediate connection is formed and a glimpse of their problem-free future is provided. This opening immediately engages. To create interaction, Kristin suggests incorporating the subtle, yet effective skill of asking "gathering questions." The goal is to ask two questions that get nearly everyone in the room to respond. For instance, one might say, "How many of you have tried yoga?" Typically half or more of the room will raise their hand. The follow up question is, "And how many of you have never tried yoga before?" While, theoretically, this should capture the rest of the room, there may be a few holdouts.

Although 100% of the room isn't a necessity, it's nice to get everyone involved. At this point, you could inject some humor, "And how many of you couldn't care less about yoga or his friend Boo-Boo?" (*insert laughter*)

When speaking to groups, gathering questions are critical as they immediately create interaction and shift the audience into a "Hey, she's talking to me" mode. Regardless of which question is answered, you've gained their attention and they'll be more likely to listen to the balance of the presentation.

To Close Or Not To Close

Most people are fairly comfortable speaking about their area of expertise and end up providing far too much content, failing to create a craving for more. A well-structured presentation entertains and provides a taste of information, without overwhelming attendees or quenching their thirst for further knowledge on the subject matter. It is a delicate balance of adding value while leaving unanswered questions. Few get this equation right and when it's time to close the deal, most presenters quickly become tongue-tied. Torn between a desire to secure clients and their fear of being pushy or aggressive, many opt to do nothing.

They thank everyone in the room for their attention and expect those who are interested in learning more to approach them. It's not that simple. While attendees may have an interest in the subject matter, unless they're told specifically what to do, most won't take the direct initiative. Yes, it's nice to improve the lives of others however, if you're unable to profit from your efforts, it won't be long before they're no longer able to hear your message.

People will gladly pay for knowledge and to work with someone who can help them accomplish their objectives. Never be ashamed to ask for what you're worth and you should be paid extraordinarily well for your unique gifts. Converting knowledge into profits is an acquired skill. Let's look at Kristin's strategy for closing the room.

The Big Close Made Simple

Returning to our yoga example—the audience is engaged, solid content has been shared, and enough has been held back so people are ready to learn more. You're now ready to close. Kristin suggests this simple mind-shift:

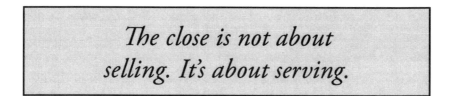

The close is not about selling. It's about serving.

Every element of a strong close is designed to help someone who needs your products or services feel an overwhelming compulsion to say, "Yes!" It's important to remember you're not intruding into their personal space or asking them to commit to something they don't want to do. You're simply providing clear direction for moving forward with purpose and conviction and showing those who are ready the exact steps to take. Here is Kristin's recommended step-by-step close:

1. Review the main takeaways of your presentation.
2. Remind people that, due to time constraints, you've shared all you can but there is much more to learn.
3. Reiterate the benefits of what was taught.
4. Describe the potential transformation if they take the next step.
5. Reveal your offer and invite everyone to participate.
6. Disclose your return policy.
7. Present a special, discounted price if they sign up today.
8. Offer a value-add bonus.
9. Add a fast-action bonus for a limited number of people.

Here's how that might sound:

"Wow, what a tremendous group. Thank you so much for your participation. In our time together today we took on three exercises that helped you release stress, hopefully provided a bit of back relief, and discussed the importance of practicing yoga. You also met Bob, Sally, and Mary and heard about how Yoga has transformed their lives.

"The challenge now is helping you achieve a permanent, pain-free state. While we covered a lot of ground, remember this is just the beginning of the journey. For anyone who is ready to finally put an end to your back pain, we put together something very special just for you. We'd like to invite you to join the next session of *Back Pain Be Gone!*, which begins May 1st. In just 12 weeks, our team of expert instructors will work directly with you to help you move beyond the pain. The program is fun, simple and, as you've seen today, leads to amazing results. While the benefits of this program are truly priceless, we offer this program for just $500.00. And I'm so confident in our system, and the abilities of our instructors, we offer a full 100% satisfaction guarantee.

"If, within four weeks, you attend class and follow our instructions, but don't feel it has had a positive impact on your body, we'll provide a full refund. You have nothing to lose. As a special thank you gift, everyone who signs up today will receive $100 off the price, and an additional week for free, to help get you started. Plus, we'll give you your own *Back Pain Be Gone!* yoga mat. We're now going to pass out the order forms. Please be sure to check the 'Yes, I'm ready to erase my back pain' box so you can take advantage of the bonus gifts. And, as a special bonus for the first seven people to enroll, we'll also include a *free* 90-minute meditation CD. Once you've filled out your form, please bring it to the back of the room where I will make myself available to answer any questions. When everyone has completed their form, I'll return to the stage with a few closing words."

After the order forms have been completed, move to the presentation's conclusion. "Now let's talk about what you can do tomorrow..."

This formula works flawlessly and many of the world's leading presenters follow it to the letter. Positioning the sale is paramount to your overall success. There's a clear difference between the failing and the thriving approach to closing. Serve their needs, solve their problems, and make the offer so irresistible they'll have little reason to say no. Model this formula and you'll realize a steady stream of clients, cash, referrals, and leads.

Stay Humble

With the expert outline in hand, your future awaits. People intuitively want to emulate the successful and learning from those with experience is a sure-fire way to accomplish one's desired objectives. From media appearances to bestselling books, sold-out workshops, and high-paying speaking opportunities, the possibilities for sharing one's expertise are endless. Yet fame has a tendency to breed a sense of superiority and it's far too commonplace for this mentality to lead towards audience alienation. To avoid this fate, keep these concepts in mind:

- **Stay grounded:** No matter how many zeroes are in your bank account, share from a position of servitude, not attitude. Everyone learns, progresses, and prospers at her own rate. Patience is an important quality of the expert. Remember that each person has a varying definition of success. One of my favorites is from author George Sheehan:

> *Success means having the courage, the determination, and the will to become the person you were meant to be.*

Nothing in this quote refers to zeroes in the bank, only the degree to which you honor your natural gifts. When attendees shift to simply being a number, one will likely enter the statistics of another business falling victim to the state of the economy. Reality, however, is that the expert fell victim to operating in the state of self-absorbing arrogance.

- **Large audiences start out as small audiences:** Whether you're invited to speak at a Rotary Club with five members or to appear on a television show with millions of viewers, consistently over-deliver. One never knows who's in the audience and the impact a well-positioned, value-laden message can have. Leaders understand that numbers are rarely the driving factor behind success. Commitment and caring are. Both a small pebble and large boulder dropped in the middle of a body of water will create rings that reach the shore. Regardless of the size of one's stage, provide an outstanding performance.

- **Share stories of the road traveled:** With the exception of those born with silver spoons and trust funds, most experts are self-made. Experts who maintain longevity in the marketplace encourage their audience to replicate their success and reveal specific details, shortcuts, tools, and strategies that can help them along their path. Remember where you came from and there'll be no limit to where you can go.

To catapult your business to the next level, harness the power of turning presentations into profit by creating beneficial content while establishing deep connections. Interestingly enough, by inspiring others to rise up and transform their lives, you'll inevitably transform yours.

 TAKEAWAYS

Presentation Prowess

- "A great pitch is not about procedure. It's about getting and keeping attention." Oren Klaff.
- Moving prospects to take action is the direct result of implementing the compelling combination of content, connection, and inspiration.
- The brain filters out what isn't urgent, important, relevant, or new.
- Avoid being "the accidental philanthropist" by adopting simple yet effective presentation and closing strategies.
- Follow the recipe for becoming an expert.
- Use Kristin's gathering questions to engage your audience.
- Remember Kristin's mindset shift for closing: You're not selling; you are serving those who need you most.
- Understand the power of remaining grounded, treating all audiences equally, and sharing stories of personal trial and tribulation.

CHAPTER 8

PROFIT FROM PODCASTS

S uccess in business requires addressing the "Four M's:"

- Market
- Message
- Medium
- Monetization

Before launching a new business, you need to make sure there's demand for your product or service. If market demand exists and the message and medium are nailed, odds are good you'll be able to monetize the endeavor. Jason Van Orden is a man whose current enterprise, *Internet Business Mastery,* addresses each of the Four M's perfectly.

The market? People who are looking to take control of their finances and their lives, are sick of the 9-5 grind, and/or want something different out of life.

The message? Anyone can achieve financial freedom using Internet marketing.

The medium? Podcasts.

Monetization? We'll get to that shortly.

Jason and his partner, Jeremy Frandsen, created their first podcast in 2005. Today, their show consistently ranks at the top of all Internet marketing-related podcasts on iTunes and has been downloaded over 2,000,000 times by listeners in more than 140 countries. Like most successful business owners, however, Jason readily admits that getting to this point wasn't easy.

The good news is that he will flatten the learning curve for you and by leveraging his proven approach any aspiring podcaster can achieve phenomenal results. He's figured out exactly how to address the Four M's and, while this chapter describes how to find success with podcasts, these same concepts can be applied to virtually any medium or business.

Recording Your First Podcast

When getting started, don't worry about fancy gadgets. You can purchase the necessary equipment for less than $100. Once your podcast gains traction and popularity, you can opt to upgrade. To create a high-quality sounding podcast, follow these seven simple steps:

1. Buy a USB microphone and plug it into your computer.

Jason recommends the Snowball from Blue Microphones, which is an affordable, high-quality USB microphone. To learn more and/or purchase the Snowball Microphone, visit EZ.com/snowball or use your mobile device to scan the QR code to the left.

2. **Download Audacity or other software to record and edit your audio files.**

Audacity is a free recording and editing program you can download at Audacity.sourceforge.net. Even with Jason's success, he *still* uses Audacity, proving it's absolutely possible to record high-quality podcasts without dropping an arm and a leg to do so. Once you've completed steps 1 and 2, you actually have everything you need to record your first podcast. If you're the star of the show, click Audacity's record button, talk into the mic, play some music, and you're good to go. If you want to take things to the next level, bring on guests and/or co-hosts. Unless they're in the room with you, though, proceed to Step 3.

3. **Use Skype and/or other software to connect with others and record conversations.**

   If you're going to have guests from around the country and/ or the world, you want to be able to connect with them inexpensively. A popular favorite is Skype (Skype.com). Next, you need software to record your conversations. For a PC, Jason recommends Pamela (Pamela.biz/en), SuperTinTin (Supertintin.com) or Vodburner (Vodburner.com); and for a Mac, Call Recorder (Ecamm.com/mac/callrecorder) or Audio Hijack (Rogueamoeba.com/audiohijackpro). After the conversation is recorded, you'll need to import the audio into Audacity and edit it, removing delays and other nonessential elements. Getting the hang of this may take a little while; but once you learn how, it's easy.

4. **Condense your audio file by converting it to MP3.**

   When you're finished editing in Audacity, you'll have a large .WAV file. You'll typically want to condense it to a more manageable size. The best way is to convert it to the MP3 format. For example, a 100MB WAV file will shrink to around 10MB as an MP3. Two recommended programs for doing this are WAV To MP3 Converter (WavToMP3Converter.com) and ConverterLite (ConverterLite.com).

5. **Create album artwork to represent your brand.**

   Don't ignore this crucial step. When people listen to your podcast the album artwork and podcast description will be displayed throughout the show, so it really makes an impact.

> *If you fail to add artwork, you miss an incredible opportunity to burn your brand's image into the minds of your listeners.*

6. **Upload your podcast to an audio hosting site.**
   Jason recommends using Liberated Syndication (<u>LibSyn.com</u>) as your host for two key reasons:

   - You can subscribe for as little as $5 per month, which provides up to 250MB of storage.
   - <u>LibSyn.com</u> offers upgrade packages to easily handle your bandwidth and upload growth.

7. **Get your podcast listed on iTunes, YouTube, and other sites.**
   While iTunes.com and YouTube.com are the most famous directories of podcasts, there are many other sites where you'll also want your podcast to be listed. Use Google to find directories that are a solid fit for your topic. With these seven steps in place, you're now in the podcast business. To summarize:

   1) Buy a USB microphone and plug it into your computer.
   2) Download Audacity or other software to record and edit the show.
   3) Use Skype or another program to connect with others and record the interview. Edit as necessary through Audacity or other software.
   4) Condense your audio file by converting it to MP3.
   5) Create album artwork to represent your brand.
   6) Upload your podcast to an audio hosting site.
   7) Get your podcast listed on iTunes, YouTube, and other sites.

You've now completed Podcast 101.

Podcast Submission

Once your podcast is ready and hosted on LibSyn.com, it's time to cultivate a following. When Jason was starting out with *Internet Business Mastery*, he made sure to upload his podcasts everywhere he could. This provided his show with substantial exposure. Eventually his efforts paid off and pushed his podcasts to #1 on popular distribution sites such as iTunes. You should follow the same strategy.

Because of YouTube's enormous traffic, you want your podcast to be available there. So how do you make an audio file which appeals to YouTube's visual-oriented audience? The solution is to use a program such as Camtasia (TechSmith.com/camtasia) to add photos to your audio. Camtasia allows you to create a visual slideshow that incorporates eye-catching images to enhance your message as your audience listens to the program. These images can include charts, graphs, guest photos, bullet points, book covers, and virtually anything that is germane to the conversation. Leveraging the full power of Camtasia takes practice. However, your efforts will be amply rewarded if you take the time to learn how to use this powerful software.

iTunes As A Search Engine

When most people need to find something on the web, they turn to Google, Yahoo, or Bing. When Jason is online, he's typically looking for a podcast, video, or song, and so the search engine he uses most is iTunes. While you might not think of it that way, iTunes is essentially a search engine for media—this is why you want iTunes to list your podcasts.

In order to achieve success with any search engine, you need to determine its primary goal. Google is designed to find the most relevant and authoritative websites, which it lists on its first page of results. YouTube gives priority to videos with the most views. Along similar lines, when you search iTunes it'll display the podcasts, videos, or songs it considers most relevant to your keywords, and the most authoritative based on the number of views and audience ratings each item receives.

> *To increase the likelihood of your podcast appearing in search results, create compelling content so it receives high ratings.*

Becoming Oprah

Oprah is one of the most successful media personalities of all time. By using her TV show as a platform, she built an incredibly lucrative empire. An integral part of this process was ownership of her products. Oprah owns her own magazine, television network, and other media that promote her brand and message. Why take things to this level? To be in charge of distribution. When Oprah relied on third parties to distribute and promote her material, she lacked a critical degree of control over how and to what extent her message was delivered. Owning the distribution channel is the only way to ensure availability of your offerings.

Similarly, when creating a podcast it can be tempting to rely entirely on existing podcast distribution and promotional resources. After all, who doesn't want to be the next "YouTube Star"? There's just one problem.

> *Today's YouTube star can disappear tomorrow if YouTube chooses to remove his or her show.*

The same thing can happen to a podcast that relies solely on sites such as iTunes. So while *Internet Business Mastery* is the #1 show on a number of podcast distribution sites, Jason retains control of his product and brand by using his own website, InternetBusinessMastery.com, as the central hub for his podcasts. Whenever he records a new show, it's featured prominently on his site. If iTunes or YouTube dropped his podcast, it would be a blow. But it wouldn't be fatal, as he owns a distribution channel that can still reach his audience.

Jason recommends creating a website to host your shows from the start. Then, no matter what happens along the way, you'll always have a central distribution hub you control.

Addressing The Last "M"

The last, and arguably most important, of the Four M's is Monetization. Making money from your podcast can be difficult. In fact, few podcasts generate revenue. That's because most podcast publishers rely on advertisers with a compensation structure based on every 1,000 subscribers or monthly downloads the show receives. This is called a CPM model (Cost Per Thousand; "M" comes from the Latin word "mille," which means thousand). Rates typically range from $5 to $50 per thousand listeners. That means if you have 5,000 listeners per month, you'd make $25-$250 from a single advertiser.

The problem is you'd need to develop a *huge* following to achieve financial independence with your podcast. Jason recommends another route. Once your podcast gains traction and you begin capturing emails, create products and services that solve their biggest problems.

> *The single most powerful way to find out what your listeners want solved is to ask them.*

A wonderful tool for doing so is Survey Monkey (SurveyMonkey.com). Survey Monkey is easy to use and it offers a Basic Plan that allows you to create surveys for free. While you're able to include virtually an unlimited number of questions, there is a direct correlation between how many questions are posed and completed surveys you'll receive. Therefore, keep it brief. For example, if you publish an Internet marketing podcast, here are a few questions to consider:

- What do you find most confusing about Internet marketing?
- What is your single greatest Internet marketing need?
- If we were genies and could deliver one Internet marketing-related product that could help propel your business forward, what would the product do?

Good surveys ask yes or no questions. Great surveys include open-ended questions. It's from the answers to the latter that you'll find valuable clues for developing the right products and services for your audience. Once you identify your audience's problems, deliver solutions that specifically address their needs. This strategy has led Jason to earn $1 in revenue per podcast subscriber. In other words, instead of making just $5-$50 per 1,000 listeners, Jason is grossing $1,000 per 1,000 listeners. Which model do you like better?

The Money Map

One of Jason's most innovative monetizing ideas is The Money Map. This is a powerful concept that, until now, he's shared only with his private coaching clients. The Money Map's core concepts are as follows:

- Gain attention in the market.
- Once you have attention, secure permission to interact (e.g., ask your audience to subscribe to an email newsletter).
- Once you have permission, add value to the relationship (e.g., provide free content).
- Once you've established a strong relationship, offer valuable products and services for purchase.

Let's look at The Money Map in closer detail. Attention is a scarce commodity. After being inundated with advertising, audiences have learned to turn attention away from it or—through the use of TiVo, DVRs, satellite radio, and premium cable TV—avoid it altogether. To break through this resistance, you need to provide information that your prospective audience truly wants. This can happen only by adding value to the equation. You must begin by offering free reports, videos, audios, and other products, as well as deep discounts, in order to reign in pitch-resistant customers.

And once you have their attention, you need to gain their permission. If you offer a free report, for example, permission is granted when they opt-in with their email address to receive it. After you have your audience's permission, you need to build a strong relationship with them by providing information they can use.

> *Offer additional free reports, free videos, and more—essentially, shower them in value.*

Once you've developed a strong relationship, you can *then* begin offering products and services for purchase. These are products you've developed to go beyond the value you've already provided, or are third-party products you highly recommend and will receive a commission on each sale. Since you've built up a strong know, like, and trust factor with your audience, your conversion rates will far exceed the norm. People already like you and your message. If they didn't, they would have removed themselves from your mailing list. Jason offers three top moneymaking products to his podcast audience:

- **The Academy:** A subscription-based model, payable monthly or upfront for lifetime access. The Academy includes group training, and access to broadcasts and interviews not available to the general public.

- **Coaching:** Jason and his partner offer one-on-one training to help clients create effective podcasts or take their business to the next level.
- **Affiliate Marketing:** The sale of third-party products that comes highly recommended from *Internet Business Mastery*. A commission is earned for each product sold.

Since Jason has built a strong relationship with his audience, he's able to charge high prices and convert at exceptional rates. Successful Internet marketers understand the importance of The Money Map. If you want to earn significant money online, following this model makes good business sense.

What's Next?

After you've followed the steps outlined in this chapter and have a

popular podcast, what should you do next? Once Internet Business Mastery increased in popularity, Jason invested in higher-quality equipment. He replaced the Snowball microphone with a Heil PR40. It's more expensive, but it provides a better audio experience for his listeners. To learn more and/or purchase the Heil PR40, visit <u>EZ.com/ microphone</u> or use your mobile device to scan the QR code to the left.

Additionally, he invested in a Behringer mixer that allows him to further refine the sound of his podcast. His mixer of choice is the Behringer Xenyx 802 Premium 8-Input, 2-Bus Mixer with Xenyx Mic Preamps and British EQs. To learn more and/or purchase the Behringer Xenyx 802, visit <u>EZ.com/vocalmixer</u> or scan the QR code to the left.

He also streamlined his systems, hiring others to edit and upload the podcasts. This empowered Jason to spend more time with his family and still deliver significant value to his audience. While Jason has taken his game to the next level, you can still create an exceptional quality broadcast without going broke.

Become The Next Podcast Success Story

By starting with a subject he has knowledge about and passion for, Jason has been able to create a profitable business with a significant following. By choosing the right topic, honing your performance skills, and working tirelessly to promote your brand, you can too. A key component of this process is seeking feedback from your listeners and taking comments to heart. This has led Jason to tailor programming directly for his audience, helping to ensure he both hangs onto existing listeners and keeps attracting new ones.

Even if you start with just a handful of listeners, they will reward you with their loyalty if you honor their suggestions. If you don't, they'll simply change the channel.

 TAKEAWAYS

Profit From Podcasts

- Leverage the 4 M's: Market, Medium, Message, and Monetization.
- Save your cash and get started with inexpensive equipment.
- Brand your podcast with artwork.
- Create compelling content that attracts audiences and garners high ratings.
- Emulate Oprah by owning all aspects of your business including the distribution channel.
- Use The Money Map to profit from your podcast.
- Upgrade your equipment after you've attained profitability.
- Seek feedback from your audience and honor their suggestions.

CHAPTER 9

VIDEO VISIONARY

It's easy to forget the Internet is still in its infancy. The automobile has been a mainstream staple for over 100 years. Radio has been commercially available in the US since the 1920's, and television since the 1940's. In contrast, while it seems like the Internet has been a permanent fixture in business and life for decades, mainstream acceptance did not hit its stride until the 1990's.

A key difference between other media and the 'Net is the now-rapid pace of technological change. The Internet world moves so quickly that fundamental tools can become obsolete within a few years. The latter also applies to Internet marketing strategies. What worked in the past is largely irrelevant now. Far too many red-text squeeze pages and unethical online marketers have made it difficult for new product creators to seek exposure without being seen as snake oil salesmen. A number of Internet marketers haven't kept pace, and futilely continue to employ techniques that no longer persuade jaded customers.

Mike Koenigs isn't one of those people. Mike is the creator of several of the world's most popular and game-changing products, including Instant Customer and Traffic Geyser. He consistently leverages bleeding-edge practices to improve people's lives and increase profitability. Brian Tracy has called him "one of the smartest marketers in the world." Let's now benefit from the knowledge Mike's been generous enough to share.

Blind Vision

Mike took to computers like Gretzky to the puck. In his early teens he learned all he could about programming and immersed himself in the online world. As technology matured and the demand for computer experts exploded, Mike was well positioned to pursue developing opportunities. In 1991, he co-created Digital Café, a company that focused on the creation of special-market advertising, including promotional games and websites.

After successfully operating, selling, and in 2008 reacquiring Digital Café, Mike began concentrating on video. At the time, video sharing sites such as YouTube were growing in popularity, but few companies were utilizing the technology to its full advantage. Although Mike wasn't yet a video expert, he recognized its value from the many leads generated by promotional videos he'd created for clients. Seeking to expand his knowledge, he began filming and uploading content-laden videos to YouTube and Google Video to better understand the intricacies of the medium.

While he didn't do it on purpose, Mike instinctively created search engine friendly titles for his videos. As a result, Google and other search engines pushed the videos to the top of the rankings. Leads poured in. Best of all, the traffic received was targeted and pre-qualified. Because the videos spoke to a specific subject and linked to a related site, the majority of visitors had a demonstrated interest in the products offered. This meant customer acquisition costs were minimal.

It was during this period of experimentation that Mike released one of his first products, Infomercial Toolkit. While he had confidence he was sufficiently prepared to introduce his product to the world, he wasn't even close to being prepared for the difference the launch would make in his life and the lives of others.

Changed Lives

Shortly after the release of Infomercial Toolkit, Mike had a chance encounter with Frank, a man who had purchased the product. Frank was almost in tears as he shook Mike's hand, explaining that Infomercial Toolkit had literally changed his life. Before purchasing and implementing Mike's teachings, Frank had difficulty connecting with his audience. While he was offering a wealth of knowledge, he wasn't properly communicating the benefits of his products.

In desperate need of help, Frank invested in Infomercial Toolkit. It was exactly what he needed. In Frank's words, "Mike provided me with hope." Frank learned how to effectively present his material and sales boomed. Frank was extremely grateful and asked if there was anything he could do to help Mike further grow his business. Though reluctant to accept his offer, Mike did have a need: to automate his video marketing efforts. Mike had demonstrated admirable video prowess and developed a system that garnered desired results, however, the process of uploading new videos was time-consuming, as it was necessary to individually submit each video to a multitude of sites. Mike mentioned his idea for automating the submission process. Frank knew a programmer who was perfect for the job.

Within several weeks, the prototype was up and running. This product became known as *Traffic Geyser.* Traffic Geyser has revolutionized the video submission process. After a video is created, with one click, Traffic Geyser:

- Uploads the video to 30 video submission sites.
- Converts the audio into a text transcript.
- Converts the audio into a standalone podcast and submits the file to numerous podcast sites.
- Distributes links to the videos and podcasts on social media.

What had once taken hours to complete was now done in a matter of minutes. Word spread like wildfire. Mike began receiving offers to purchase exclusive rights to the software. The first offer was for $15,000. The second was for $25,000. Mike recognized the enormous potential and he and Frank created a sales page and offered the product to the public. In the first week they made $147,000. Mike's success snowballed from there. Traffic Geyser has become one of the top grossing Internet products of all time. Subsequent releases have brought in staggering numbers:

- Firepower grossed $1.6 million.
- Main Street Marketing Machines grossed $9.1 million.
- Social Media Marketing Machines grossed $4.2 million.
- Main Street Marketing Fusion grossed $7.1 million.

These are among the largest-grossing products in online marketing history. Further, Mike holds the world record for "online direct-to-camera sales," generating over $3 million *in a single day* during a webcast. Mike attributes his success to creating high-value products that address tangible needs, solve big problems, and substantially improve people's lives. Video is the medium he chooses to leverage. Let's step behind the camera.

Personalize = Monetize

Video has the ability to let you share your personality, provide relevant content, and connect with your audience in highly visual and visceral ways. It is not necessary, however, to be a polished presenter. You just have to be natural on camera. This establishes a level of trust and loyalty between you and your customers...and can lead to the development of a multimillion-dollar business. A key to establishing deep-rooted relationships is communicating effectively while being viewed by your audience. Video empowers you to connect with them in a far more personal way than text.

Video is especially effective when coupled with well-told, visually appealing storytelling. We're wired to love good stories and will quickly bond with an entertaining storyteller. Stories also make it easier to guide your customers through the ways your product will directly address their needs. An effective formula is to convey product benefits through a mix of storytelling techniques, metaphors, anecdotes, case studies, and testimonials. When done correctly, there are few more powerful ways to get your message across.

That said, video can be a double-edged sword because the camera doesn't lie. People tend to know insincerity when they see it. You need to have a high-quality product that over-delivers on promises so you can fully believe your words when you sing its praises. No matter how you may try to hide it, authenticity screams through the lens. Renowned author Kurt Vonnegut once related how early in his career he was nervous about getting in front of an audience for the first time to promote a book. The presenter told him to relax. "They don't really care what you have to say," he explained. "They just want to look at you and see if you're honest."

The Right Equipment

Most people assume a professional-looking video requires expensive high-definition equipment. It actually doesn't. Thanks to technological advances, all you need is a camera and basic video editing software. The Kodak PlayTouch and even the latest generation iPhone can create high-definition 1080p quality video for a reasonable cost. To learn more about and/or purchase the Kodak PlayTouch, please visit EZ.com/playtouch or use your mobile device to scan the QR code to the right.

A key component for shooting video is an external microphone. This allows for audio and video to perfectly sync. Marketers too often skimp on this crucial piece of equipment. When a delay exists between the auditory and visual components of a presentation, regardless of what's said, the brain correlates bad audio with bad information. Fortunately, many external microphones are inexpensive, including ear buds, and the $40 Audio-Technica ATR-

35S Lavalier Microphone. For more information and/or to purchase the Audio-Technica ATR-35S, please visit EZ.com/lavalier or scan the QR code to the left.

As for software, there are two free products that will likely be all you need. For Windows, Microsoft Movie Maker couldn't be much easier to use (Windows.microsoft.com/en-US/windows/downloads/get-movie-maker). For the Mac, Apple iMovie does the trick (Apple.com/ilife/imovie). Both are typically installed on newer computers and allow you to easily edit your video creations.

10x10x4

Mike has created a streamlined model for achieving success with video. It's called the *10x10x4* formula. The first *10* represents the top 10 questions customers typically ask about your product or topic. To address them, you'll create 10 separate videos, each typically running two to three minutes. To illustrate, assume you're doing a video promoting your yoga studio. Questions your videos might cover include:

- What are the benefits of yoga?
- How can yoga help me lose weight?
- Am I too old to practice yoga?
- Will yoga help relieve my lower back pain?
- Is it difficult to do most of the poses?

Once you've selected the top 10 questions and have articulated clear, concise answers, set up the camera, attach the microphone, and press record. Again, each video should be no more than two to three minutes long. After the footage is recorded, transfer it to your computer, edit and polish each segment, and add text (a headline) to each video reflecting the question covered. You can then upload your videos to the various distribution sites (again, Traffic Geyser is great at automating this step). This entire process can be done in under a day and is a key first step in establishing your position as an industry expert.

The next *10* in the 10x10x4 formula answers questions your audience *should* be asking. Mike refers to these as "holy cow questions," because they allow customers to view the topic in ways they hadn't previously considered. These are significantly different from frequently asked questions. "Holy cow questions" clarify exactly how your product will benefit your audience. Examples for a yoga studio include:

- Can yoga help me live longer?
- Does yoga provide better results than other forms of exercise?
- How does yogic breathing enhance my quality of life?
- Does yoga enhance my immune system?
- Will yoga increase my strength and help me tone?

In these segments you want to let your personality and warmth shine through. In addition to further establishing yourself as an authority on your subject, they help you create a deeper, more personal connection with your audience.

The final *4* of Mike's 10x10x4 formula represents the following four videos:

- **A call-to-action at the end of each of the 20 videos.** A strong call-to-action moves viewers from simply admiring your message to entering your sales funnel. The action can be opting in to receive your free newsletter, signing up for a trial class, or purchasing an entry-level product. It's best to position your call to action at the end of your video.
- **A personalized website video.** To develop a closer bond with customers, greet them with a welcome video that reinforces your brand and message. Also include information that provides immediate value, and a clear call-to-action that encourages opting-in to receive additional videos. This is a proven strategy for increasing conversion rates.
- **A thank you video for opting in.** When visitors opt-in, say "thank you" for doing so. This is courteous, indicates thoughtfulness, and helps further develop trust.

- **The sales video.** Internet marketing experts typically follow the opt-in with three value-added presentations that include some of their best material but do not attempt to sell products. Selling is reserved for the last video. In this fourth and final video, offer the solution to a very real problem...at a price. Conversion rates will vary, but odds are good many will decide to make the purchase decision if you proactively:
  - Establish trust.
  - Provide helpful free content.
  - Introduce the audience to an existing problem.
  - Offer an easy-to-implement solution with a 100% satisfaction guarantee.

Mike has used his 10x10x4 formula successfully for years. Even though significantly more customers are familiar with the model now than when he invented it, the right combination of personality, positioning, and product continues to open the door to profits. To see examples of the 10x10x4 formula in action, visit the sites of bestselling authors Harvey Mackay and Tim Ferriss:

- HarveyMackay.com
- FourHourBodyBook.com

In addition, for a free training video that demonstrates how to create a 10x10x4 video sequence—as well as six other helpful training videos—visit MikeKoenigs.com.

A Final Rabbit In The Hat

Video is here to stay. In fact, it will become an increasingly important part of the online experience as time progresses. In just a few years, selling through video may become mandatory to remain competitive. Mike recommends you hit the record button now and gain valuable experience with this medium. Many of today's top online marketers began with zero on-camera training and have spent years honing their craft and developing phenomenal products. Their status among elite industry icons is the result of a calculated, long-term process and has organically developed over time.

Contrary to popular belief, there's no such thing as instant success. However, the sooner you get started, the closer you'll be to becoming the next "overnight sensation."

⏻ TAKEAWAYS

Video Visionary

- The Internet has shifted from a transactional experience to focusing on "reputation and relationships." Learn the new rules of the game.
- Create products that leverage your strengths. Being someone you're not is a formula for failure.
- Price products based on demand and perceived value. The market will dictate exactly how much something is worth. What you believe is irrelevant. What the customer will pay is all that matters.
- Creating a multimillion-dollar business is the direct byproduct of the degree of loyalty and trust established with prospects and customers. The key to establishing deep-rooted relationships is learning how to effectively communicate a clear message to a specific audience.
- Find your authentic voice and let your freak flag fly. You have something unique to offer. The world is waiting for you!
- Build your own HD studio for less than $500. Today, high-quality productions can be created on a shoestring budget.
- Leverage the 10x10x4 model. Monetizing your expertise by broadcasting your message to the world and establishing yourself as an expert has never been easier.
- Invest your time wisely. There are only two ways to use your time: Spend it or invest it.
- Realize substantial dividends by creating and sharing content, cultivating traffic, capturing leads, building rapport, and asking for the sale. This is a sure-fire formula for success.

CHAPTER 10

WORKSHOP WEALTH

We live in times of rapid change, political uproar, security alerts, and financial peril. In the midst of this chaos, people are in part coping through an instinctual craving to *gather*. After all, we're social creatures. We intuitively believe there is *safety in numbers*. Our need to connect has contributed to the phenomenal success of social media services such as Facebook, Twitter, LinkedIn, and Meet Up. It makes good business sense to capitalize on this trend by providing forums for customers to interact with like-minded people.

Callan Rush is one of the world's leading experts on traditional and non-traditional communication platforms. She's created hundreds of live and virtual settings for the purposes of education, inspiration, connection, and commerce. In this chapter, Callan shares her proven strategies for generating profits through fostering connectivity. No matter what business you're in, Callan will teach you how to create wealth through workshops.

Know Your Strengths

As a child, Callan was known for her gift of gab. Much to the dismay of her older brothers, she'd present dissertations on everything from the attributes of her favorite doll to why she was entitled to the last slice of pizza. While her brothers tried to dissuade her from talking, her dad encouraged it. He explained to her that you can make a substantial living from speaking; and so the seed of her life's work was planted. Together with her dad, Callan began studying the work of the world's most successful speakers, including Napoleon Hill, Anthony Robbins, Brian Tracy, and Jack Canfield.

Callan went on to earn degrees in both Psychology and Education, and became a well-paid teacher. While she had steady work, she found teaching within the public and private school systems wasn't sufficiently fulfilling. Searching for answers, Callan attended a live personal development seminar. From the moment it began, something clicked inside. She knew this was the next step on her path.

To the chagrin of her family, Callan immediately quit her job and became a volunteer for the seminar company. Her eagerness and talent were evident, and she was soon hired. Before long, she was traveling all over the U.S. and Canada learning how to produce and facilitate large-scale personal development events.

From The Back Of The Room To The Front

The company's owner took notice of Callan's efforts, and promoted her to be his personal go-to person and event assistant. Callan eventually worked her way up to being an emcee, giving her the privilege of introducing, and working on stage alongside, many of her childhood heroes such as Jack Canfield, Brian Tracy, and Mark Victor Hansen. Callan used her backstage access to ask these world-class speakers questions such as, "How do you create a multimillion-dollar business?" Over time she gathered detailed information on achieving success from a wide range of industry leaders. With this knowledge, Callan set out to start her own workshop and seminar business.

Unfortunately, despite her years of experience, her workshop business struggled. While Callan's content and facilitation were rock solid, she'd neglected a vital part of the equation: attracting participants. After a particularly dismal event turnout, Callan had a stark realization: Even if she was the most mesmerizing teacher on the planet with life-altering material, it meant nothing if seats remained empty.

Callan threw herself into learning everything she could about sales and marketing. As her knowledge grew, attendance steadily improved. Within six months, her income reached the high six figures. Since then, Callan has earned millions leading workshops...and has realized her dream of helping people while talking for a living. Callan now focuses on helping workshop, retreat, and seminar leaders earn an extraordinary living doing what they love while making a significant, positive contribution to the planet. This is your opportunity to learn how to incorporate live and/or virtual gathering events into your business.

The State Of The Hall

Seminars, conferences, and workshops have long provided a way to satisfy the natural desire to congregate. As our economy hit the skids, however, there's been a decline in attendance at live events. For example, the American Library Association's annual conference suffered a 23% decline in member attendance from 26,201 in 2010 to 20,186 in 2011. Atlanta's convention center has experienced a 32% decrease in visitors, from 697,000 in 2008 to just 473,000 in 2010. Strategies traditionally used to pack large conference halls aren't working so well anymore. Even some of the biggest names in public speaking are finding it difficult to fill seats in venues they previously sold out.

At first glance, this appears to be a contradiction. I've been saying that people want to get together more than ever, and yet turnout at live events is declining. The problem is our weakened economy has made customers more cost-conscious. Languishing revenues, packed personal schedules, a feeling it's become a luxury to spend time away from the office, plus increasing travel costs all limit audiences for even the most popular functions.

Callan outlines the perfect solution: an online seminar, also called a *virtual workshop*. Like its traditional counterpart, a virtual workshop allows experts to provide information to, and interact with, a large audience. However, it takes place over the phone or the Internet and can be conducted without the expenses related to a live, in-person event.

A virtual workshop therefore allows you to create a similar experience to that of traditional seminars...but without requiring attendees to leave the comfort of their chairs.

There are two main types of virtual workshops: teleseminars and webinars. Let's look at each in closer detail.

Teleseminars

A teleseminar allows people interested in your message to dial a phone number at a specified time to access your presentation. There are free and low-cost services you can use that provide a *bridge line* capable of hosting hundreds or thousands of people. Platform examples include FreeConferenceCall.com, Rondee.com, and FreeConference.com. The many benefits of teleseminars include:

- Free or low cost to host.
- Simple to set up.
- Can accommodate both live and recorded presentations.
- Free or moderate cost to attend (e.g., phone charges if it's a long distance call).
- No travel, lodging, or meal expenses.
- Easy to digitally record and upload to your site so anyone can listen to the presentation at a later date.

When done correctly, a teleseminar lets you leverage your customer's innate desire to gather, while sparing both you and them the time and expense of an in-person conference. And, they are fairly simple to create and facilitate, while having wide reach and appeal. Equally beneficial, a recorded teleseminar becomes an *instant product* that many facilitators will offer to prospects either as a free gift in exchange for their contact information or will bundle several presentations and sell the lot as a package. This is particularly effective if the presentations are complimentary, focus on a specific topic, and/or are steps in a proprietary strategy.

When packaged and sold, a recorded teleseminar is known as an *evergreen presentation* whereby it can become a source of continual passive revenue. Month after month, you can send the recording to customers who purchase it as a standalone product or have subscribed to a membership program in which you've promised to supply continual helpful information.

Webinars

Also known as *Web conferencing, Web-based seminar,* or *live streaming conferences*, webinars add a visual component to virtual conferencing. Different from *webcasts,* which are one-way communication presentations from you to your audience, webinars allow for visual and audio interaction between you, your guests, and your audience. Some webinars are built around Keynote or PowerPoint presentations in which you guide your audience through the material. An equally popular approach is for you, and any guests, to speak directly to the camera so the webinar has the look and feel of a TV show. On top of the benefits of teleseminars, webinars also provide:

- The ability to provide detailed training.
- Enhanced comprehension and retention of your information thanks to the visual clarification and reinforcement of your spoken words.
- Interactive capabilities that include a visual Q&A (for audience members with webcams), live chat, voting, and brainstorming.
- Complete web-based communication, which means no *bridge line* needed on your end, and no phone line (and potential long distance phone charges) required from the audience.
- Hidden, anonymous participation (versus a teleseminar with the potential to capture the phone numbers of those who dial in).
- Social media plug-ins that allow for audience members to provide text feedback both during and after your presentation, as well as allow you to conduct viral marketing.

As with teleseminars, webinars are simple to set up and implement; have wide reach and appeal, and can be recorded as evergreen presentations that become a source of continuous passive revenue. Platform examples include: GoToMeeting.com/Webinar, Webex.com/webinars/, and Join.me. As with teleseminars, recorded webinars are extremely effective, can be offered for free or sold, and will act as an unpaid sales force working 24/7 to attract potential clients and convert them into paying customers.

The MMM...Good! Formula

If you've decided to offer virtual workshops, you can use Callan's *Three M* formula to help ensure success. The Three M's are *magnetize, mesmerize,* and *monetize:*

- **Magnetize:** Your first step is to figure out how to attract ideal potential customers to your presentations. It's not enough to pull in a large crowd. You must attract the people most likely to need, and be willing to pay for, your products and services. Once you've mastered how to magnetize, customers will line the block to work with you. However, if you don't get this part right, the other steps in the formula will be irrelevant as you'll be sharing your message with an audience not sufficiently motivated to take the next step on the path.

- **Mesmerize:** You must consistently design and deliver dynamic events. You can mesmerize your audience by presenting information that's breathtakingly well written and well organized so your message is clear, accessible, and enjoyable. In addition, you should strive to be an entertaining and inspiring speaker. Another way to mesmerize is to create space within the presentation for participants to bond with each other. These connections will make everyone feel good, and the positive feelings evoked by your event will translate to higher sales. Of course, it's very important to provide genuine value. But, you must also design your presentation so it naturally leads audience members to the conclusion they greatly need your product or service...and they need it right now.

- **Monetize:** To be successful, your presentations must result in sales. Most audience members actually *want* to buy from you. They simply need to be taken through the proper steps of the relationship development process. If you perfect the art of magnetizing the right people to hear your message and subsequently mesmerize them with value-packed, strategic, and immediately useful information, monetization will be a natural by-product.

Callan warns against falling into the trap of seeking to mesmerize and monetize before putting a great deal of effort into how you can magnetize your audience. Cultivating clients is similar to finding love. To develop a meaningful long-term relationship, you must invest time and energy, and follow societal norms. Moving directly to the close violates the implicit agreement between buyer and seller that requires value to be delivered prior to requesting compensation.

Never mistake a customer's "wink"—in the form of an opt-in or sign-up—as an open invitation to move to home plate. It's merely an indication the customer has some interest but needs to learn more. Too often, hosts neglect to provide massive value (that subtly sets up the purchase) in favor of a fast food, nutritionally bankrupt pitch-fest that breaks trust, ruins credibility, and destroys the presenter's reputation. Instead, think of your teleseminar or webinar as a first date. Be courteous, patient, and do your best to make a great first impression so your audience will come back for more.

> *Follow the rites of courtship with your customers by letting them bond with you, explore the relationship and, finally, commit.*

Profiting From Education-Based Marketing

Profitability depends on delivering pertinent content and desired solutions for a specific audience. This in part requires identifying what Callan refers to as your customers' *egoic label.* An egoic label represents a word or phrase someone uses to describe herself. Strong egoic labels include mother, father, and teenager. Other egoic labels are business owner, entrepreneur, cancer survivor, sports fan, and book lover.

The way you speak with, say, a sports fan should be very different from how you communicate with a book lover. Yet a common mistake made by marketers is to send the same promotional copy to all potential customers. To convert prospects to clients, engage in what Callan calls *intimate marketing.* This means speaking directly to one person at a time. Identifying your audience requires you to be clear about the following:

- Who you most want to serve.
- What egoic labels they use to define themselves.
- Where they're located.
- What their budget is.
- Where they gather.
- What their interests are.

Once you've honed in on your specific audience, discover what top-of-mind issues keep them awake at 2:00 a.m. Most problems fall into one of these five categories:

- **Health:** Wanting to feel better, look better, lose weight, cure ailments, eat smarter, etc.
- **Wealth:** Wishing to create it, double it, better manage it, share it, etc.
- **Relationships:** Desiring to get one, improve an existing one, break out of one, etc.
- **Sex:** How to get it, how to do it better, where to do it, etc.
- **Identity:** I'm not being a good enough x (parent, business owner, person, etc.).

Once you know your specific audience, the egoic label of its members, and their top-of-mind problems, you're ready to begin creating your marketing message. First, craft a compelling headline to magnetize your audience to your event. This must speak directly to both the egoic label and top-of-mind problem of each customer. If you do this correctly, the response will be "Hey! This event is perfect for me. I was just thinking about that problem last night. I have to attend this." Intimacy achieved.

For example, one of Callan's clients wanted to develop workshops that helped "women in relationships create a deeper connection with their romantic partners." Callan and her client started by brainstorming a list of strongly held egoic labels with which "women in relationships" might identify, such as *woman, girlfriend, companion, married, spouse, wife*. They chose to focus on the egoic label *married woman*. Their specific audience was identified.

Next, after conducting research, they discovered many married women were up at 2:00 a.m. hoping to create a deeper, more fulfilling connection with their husbands. They then wrote this headline for a free 75-minute introductory teleseminar:

> *3 Massive Mistakes*
> *Married Women Make*
> *That Keep Them Feeling*
> *Disconnected From Their Husbands*

They organized the teleseminar's content to provide immediate value while, at the same time, perfectly positioning the purchase of a three-day in-person event titled The Really Good Relationship Weekend Intensive. Ensuring your workshops solve real problems while positioning your products or services for sale takes significant effort. It's a form of teaching that doubles as a business-building tactic, and is sometimes referred to as *education-based marketing.* It provides value, which inherently builds trust and develops rapport, while creating excitement for an audience member to learn more.

Once you learn how to effectively and consistently execute the formula for education-based marketing, you'll be empowered to deliver your message to large audiences, have a ton of fun, and earn the income you deserve.

⏻ TAKEAWAYS

Workshop Wealth

- The challenges of our rapidly changing world lead people to crave gathering together for support, safety, connection, and community.
- Workshops are a great way to capitalize on this social trend.
- A simple and inexpensive way to conduct workshops is to offer virtual teleseminars and/or webinars.
- To achieve success, use the Three M's: magnetize, mesmerize, and monetize.
- Hone in on your specific audience by indentifying your target customer's egoic label.
- Articulate a major problem that keeps your target customer awake at 2:00 a.m., and then design your products or services, and the marketing of your workshops, to directly address that problem.
- Always provide substantial value in an introductory workshop to build trust and establish the foundation for a long-term relationship. At the same time, subtly position what you have to sell to eventually convert your audience members into paying customers.

CHAPTER 11

THE SECRET OF MOBILE

Every so often, a marketing campaign is launched that blows the doors off conventional wisdom. Everywhere you turn, people are discussing it. From *Oprah* to your next-door neighbor, you simply can't avoid the topic. In 2006, the product *du jour* was *The Secret*. It took the world by storm. With its controversial subject matter (The Law of Attraction—essentially, *thoughts become actions*) and sniper-like focused marketing efforts, *The Secret* sold more than $100 million in products and continues to maintain its reign of popularity.

The Secret's incredible success might be attributed to many, but its record-breaking online marketing magic came from Dan Hollings and his implementation of the Master Plot Marketing strategy. No one surpasses Dan's understanding of how to profit from web and mobile-based marketing.

Fasten your seatbelt. This will get very interesting.

The Internet In Diapers

Dan's first career choice was to be a musician. As a classically trained concert guitarist, he received his Bachelor's degree in Music and taught at the University of Illinois. Unfortunately, or perhaps fortunately for us, teaching didn't pay well and he was forced to leave the profession. Al Gore had not yet invented the Internet, so Dan became involved in network marketing, rising to the top ranks of a well-known company. This first venture into sales helped Dan earn a much healthier income.

When the Internet began to take hold, Dan was there in the trenches. Using an AOL floppy disc to get online, he began honing his Internet skills. Among them were programming, web design, and basic Internet marketing principals. Because of his wide skill set, he was able to offer consulting services to network marketing companies, teaching them how to best leverage the power of this new medium. Doing so provided a vast test bed for his newfound marketing creativity while also increasing his Internet knowledge and visibility.

By 2004, Dan had established himself as one of the best Internet marketing wizards, so when the producers of *The Secret* needed a proven master to help with their launch, they gave him a call.

The Master Plot Strategy: The Secret Behind *The Secret*

When *The Secret* was released, people were stunned by how quickly it captured attention. Everyone seemed to either be reading the book or talking about it. Then the movie was released and was featured on *Oprah, Larry King*, radio stations all over the globe, and the covers of numerous popular magazines. But before all this happened, what truly kicked off the phenomenon was the Internet marketing campaign. Even before the mass media publicity hit, *The Secret* was making millions online. In fact, without the enormous success of *The Secret's* website, the TV and radio frenzy might never have happened.

What few realize is that *The Secret* lacked a massive launch budget. Dan was the only Internet marketer hired. He more than rose to the occasion. From virtually the start of Dan's marketing campaign, *The Secret* hit #1 on the "Movers and Shakers" list of Alexa.com (a website that ranks Internet traffic). This was an achievement that many had thought impossible. ABC News hailed *The Secret's* marketing campaign as one of the most successful of all time.

What were the key factors leveraged by this master marketer that resulted in *The Secret's* inordinate exposure and unparalleled rates of conversion? The answer may surprise you. Dan wove a story arc into *The Secret's* marketing campaign.

Think about the last time friends recommended a movie for you to see. They likely spoke of the film in general but left out important details, especially the ending: "We can't tell you the rest. You just have to see it." If a story is told in a compelling but incomplete manner and piques your interest, you'll naturally want to know what happens. Dan leveraged this innate curiosity for *The Secret*. Every landing page and promotional video revealed just enough to capture a visitor's interest. The teasers provided a riddle that left viewers eager to solve the puzzle.

While no one really knew what *The Secret* was about, it didn't matter. They were ready for its release. When the book and movie were finally made available for sale, customers were already in line. This strategy is as relevant today as in 2006. Though technology has evolved and the vehicles used to disseminate messages have changed, creating a Master Plot Marketing Strategy will continue to generate great results.

To create your own Master Plot Marketing Strategy, check out *20 Master Plots and How to Build Them* by Ronald Tobias. This is a powerful read that, when viewed from the standpoint of Internet marketing, can create phenomenal results. To learn more and/or purchase *20 Master Plots,* please visit <u>EZ.com/20masterplots</u> or use your mobile device to scan the QR code to the left.

The Next Big Thing

If you're one of the millions who didn't make millions during the dot com gold rush, no need to cry over spilt milk. Grab your glass and get ready to stand at the spigot of a much bigger opportunity: mobile. Mobile phones are *everywhere*. As of this writing, roughly one-third of your traffic is likely to be from customers on mobile devices (Smart Phones, Tablets, iPads, Kindles, etc). Research firm IDC estimates that by 2015 the number of US mobile Internet users will surpass their wired counterparts. Amazon, eBay, PayPal, and Google already report annual mobile revenues in excess of $1 billion.

According to research firm InsightExpress, mobile buyers are three times more likely to buy than computer users. And research firm Chetan Sharma has found mobile tends to be twice as viral as other media. What's not to like about these jaw-dropping statistics? Quite simply, people love their mobile devices and they have become an integral and intimate part of our daily lives. They're our companions, assistants, trainers, and planners; and our sources for music, news, books, research, shopping, and social connection. And if you're a business owner, they can become your never-ending personal cash register.

It is this love and addiction to our mobile devices that offers a virtually untapped goldmine to aspiring entrepreneurs. Yes, mobile marketing is in its embryonic stages, but this means a staggering number of mobile millionaires and billionaires will be created within the next 10 years. You could be one of them.

So how can you capitalize on the mobile boom? Dan reveals eight specific opportunities that represent exponential possibilities within the mobile landscape.

Mobile-Friendly Websites

Your website must be mobile-friendly. When people visit your site on their phones, they're working with a small screen. Complex pages built for a full-size monitor can look terrible on a smart phone. To serve mobile users, it is preferred to build a mobile-specific site as their interests and needs are substantially different from those using desktops.

A number of free and low cost tools are available to create mobile-friendly sites and mobile blogs. To help you find them, Dan has created My Mobile Toolbar (MyMobileToolbar.com), a free toolbar for mobile marketers that links to over 400 mobile tips, tools, and resources. As for hosting your mobile site, the most widely accepted strategy is to use either <u>M.Domain.com</u> or <u>Domain.mobi</u>. Both will allow you to create a mobile-friendly site that effectively serves your mobile market.

Text Messaging

Smart phones are the go-to mobile devices. Starting with the iPhone, multi-feature phones that access the Internet have become increasingly affordable and prevalent. As of this writing, 40% of active US cell phones provide access to the Internet. Nearly 100% of active cell phones can send and receive text messages.

Text message marketing is the low-hanging fruit in mobile, providing the highest open rates of all marketing channels. You can achieve dramatic results with well-timed text messages that offer mobile coupons, discounts, and special offers to your customers. As with phone calls, you want to avoid being intrusive and annoying. Never text anyone who hasn't fully opted in to receive your text messages, and be considerate about timing. Messages that fail to provide direct benefits will be viewed as spam and irritate your customers. Remember, you're being granted the privilege of entering your customer's personal life. A campaign that offers what your customers want at the precise time they want it is likely to enjoy positive conversion rates.

QR Codes

Dan loves QR (Quick Response) codes, which he says "hyperlink the physical world." A customer can scan a QR code with an Internet-enabled mobile device and instantly be connected to your mobile page, YouTube video, Amazon product page, Facebook fan page, or any other web-based destination.

Wikipedia defines a QR code as "a matrix barcode (two-dimensional code) readable by QR scanners, mobile phones with a camera, and smart phones. The code consists of black modules arranged in a square pattern on a white background. The information encoded can be text, URL, or other data."

In other words, QR codes are grid-shaped barcodes that, when scanned with a mobile device, take customers to a webpage, insert contact details into their phone, or perform other actions. To receive a *free gift*, scan the QR code to the right.

Did you scan it? Odds are good that, if you have a smart phone, you did.[1] That's because QR codes hold a certain mystery, and everyone loves a surprise—especially when getting to the payoff is almost effortless. The combination of novelty and fun carried by QR codes carries the potential for viral popularity.

Location-Based Social Media

The phrase *social media* conjures thoughts of Facebook and Twitter. While these two giants garner most of the attention, there are other social websites gaining significant traction that should be a meaningful component of your mobile marketing mix. One example is FourSquare (FourSquare.com). According to the company, "FourSquare helps you explore the world around you. Meet up with friends, discover new places, and save money using your phone. Whether you're setting off on a trip around the world, coordinating a night out with friends, or trying to pick the best dish at your local restaurant, FourSquare is the perfect companion."

FourSquare allows you to "check in" to businesses or locations within your area. For example, when you're at a favorite restaurant, you can use FourSquare to let them know you've returned. This allows the business to identify you as a frequent customer and potentially offer rewards for your loyalty. Sites such as Facebook.com/places and Gowalla.com provide similar services. You can find dozens of additional location-based social media services at MyMobileToolbar.com.

Pay-Per-Click Mobile

Pay-per-click (PPC) advertising is one of the most common forms of Internet marketing. With PPC, you are billed only when a user clicks on

---

1   The QR Code connects to EZ.com/big8 which provides Dan's "Big 8" Rules for effectively using QR Codes.

your advertisement. This powerful tool allows control over acquisition costs and ensures that every dollar spent results in tangible action. PPC is a sound way to advertise. However, competition for clicks in certain areas has grown fierce; and the more businesses that bid to have their ads displayed, the higher the price tag for being noticed. In some categories, a single click can cost upwards of $100.

So far, the mobile world hasn't attracted nearly as many advertisers. The reduced competition translates to spending less per click while also enjoying a higher click-thru rate. Services such as Google's AdMob (AdMob.com) allow a well-targeted ad to garner tangible results for just pennies per click. Just keep in mind that, to be effective, your mobile PPC campaign should offer specific value to mobile users.

Proximity Marketing

Although still in its infancy, proximity marketing allows smart phone users to connect with businesses via WiFi or Bluetooth. When implemented correctly, proximity marketing is 100% permission-based. For example, you can send an offer directly to a customer's phone when she enters your store. You might feature a sale item, provide detailed information about a specific product, share a video, or offer a 2-for-1 mobile coupon.

As another example, you could offer a free gift or other incentive for a customer to visit your booth at a trade show. Proximity marketing is a highly effective tool. To learn more, visit Ad-Pods at EZ.com/adpods.

Near Field Communication

Even though mobile is exploding globally, most countries remain in a three-year lag behind Japan. So if you want to see the future in mobile, Japan is the place to look. There you'll find cutting-edge mCommerce technology in extensive use, such as near field communication (NFC).

NFC allows customers to buy products with a mobile device. Instead of carrying credit cards or cash, a customer simply waves her NFC chip-embedded phone across a reception device at the point of purchase. Providing NFC capabilities is a smart move that lets you serve early adopters and get a head start on a technology expected to be a necessity in the future. Some notable mCommerce sites include:

- Google Wallet: Google.com/wallet
- PayPal Mobile: EZ.com/paypalmobile
- Amazon Mobile: EZ.com/amazonflex
- Big Commerce: BigCommerce.com
- WikiPay: EZ.com/wikipay, a pay-by-text service.

Each of these provides easy-to-use purchase options for your mobile customers.

Apps

Mobile apps have skyrocketed in popularity. They include games such as Angry Birds and Scrabble; language translators; Siri voice-activated personal assistants; and GPS services that guide our every move. According to research firm Flurry Analytics, the typical mobile user spends an average of 81 minutes per day interacting with various mobile applications. As a result, these apps have become a multibillion-dollar business.

That's the good news. Realistically, though, most apps fail. A bestselling app requires a detailed understanding of the market, a phenomenal idea, and a commitment to spending the resources needed to outshine the competition. If SMS text messaging is the low-hanging fruit in mobile marketing, apps are the choicest fruit near the top that require a fair amount of climbing—and a dire risk of falling. So developing a mobile app might be best saved for later—after you have your other mobile strategies firmly in place.

Apps can add great value for customers and help you make money while building brand loyalty. But you must enter the app development process with attainable goals, proper funding, a killer idea, and stellar execution.

Mobile: A Recap

To summarize:

- Develop a mobile-friendly website and/or blog. Keep it simple and make sure it's optimized for the small screen. Hoping that technology will squeeze your PC site down to "fit" does not provide an acceptable marketing solution. The most critical aspect of any mobile page is making sure your content or message is focused on something that would be of interest to a mobile visitor.

- Take advantage of Mobile's low-hanging fruit—text messaging. Open rates for text approach 98% and well-timed, well-worded texts can have engagement rates of 30%-40%. Start by collecting mobile phone numbers of your current customers and existing lists.

- Get creative with mobile QR codes. They're growing in popularity because they're easy to use, spark viral interest, and allow your business to connect to customers both on and offline.

- Use location-based social media. It connects people and recommendations to your company, encourages viral sharing, and is both fun and rewarding for customers.

- Mobile pay-per-click advertising is largely untapped. Take full advantage while you can still target your desired audience for pennies. Focus your campaign on a mobile-specific audience and move them through a mobile-oriented campaign funnel.

- Use proximity marketing to target customers at the point of sale. Keep your mobile initiatives permission-based and combine with signage for maximum effectiveness.

- Mcommerce and Near Field Communication are upon us. Position yourself to take full advantage of these new technologies.

- While the creation of a mobile app should be on your radar, first focus on the lower-cost and more surefire technologies mentioned. When you're ready to create a mobile app, be realistic about your objectives and incorporate a robust marketing strategy around it.

The Time Is Now

If you had a time machine, you could go back to a time when Apple, Google, Facebook, and Amazon were just starting out and invest seed money to help launch the companies. Unfortunately, that option is not available. But you *can* invest in mobile right now. Mobile is the future and the time to profit from it is today.

Dan says, "Mobile is no longer optional." The secret to future success will be found by those who leverage the power of this game-changing medium and mobile presents an unprecedented opportunity not seen since the dot com boom. By implementing the strategies discussed, you'll be ahead of most of your competitors. Remember, you're either a leader or a follower. The view is always better from the front of the pack.

 TAKEAWAYS

The Secret of Mobile

- Entice your audience to act by implementing a Master Plot Strategy within your marketing campaigns.
- Think like your target audience. Would you buy the product you're promoting based on the way you've positioned it?
- Mobile marketing is not Internet marketing on a tiny screen. The biggest differences lie in the psychology of the mobile user and the environment or situation they're in when they interact with your campaign.
- Optimize your mobile website for the small screen by keeping it simple. Keep content limited to what's relevant for your mobile audience.
- With rare exceptions, expensive programmers aren't needed to build your Mobile site. Use free and low-cost mobile site builders, mobile software, and mobile blog plug-ins.
- Begin collecting mobile phone numbers for text messaging immediately. Effective ways to persuade customers to opt-in to your mobile list is to provide mobile-only offers, VIP treatment, and/or mobile coupons.
- Make sure there's a mobile call-to-action on every mobile page you build.
- Write for mobile as if you're writing for Twitter: Keep messages short and simple.
- Use language appropriate for the medium. For example, with mobile campaigns "click here" is inappropriate; use "tap here" instead.
- Learn about, and leverage, the areas of mobile opportunity described in this chapter.
- Set-up either a <u>M.domain.com</u> or <u>Domain.mobi</u> web address for your mobile site.
- Mobile is no longer optional.

CHAPTER 12

APP ATTACK

Have you ever received a birthday card from someone you barely know and thought to yourself, "How cool they remembered?" Or, maybe you ran into someone you've only met once or twice and they ask about your kids (by name) and know more about your spouse than you do? On one hand, it's a bit creepy. On the other, it's fairly impressive.

Business lives and dies on the strength of relationships cultivated. Modern technology, while it's certainly made many aspects of life easier, has largely killed the intimacy associated with developing tangible rapport with vendors, clients, and even employees. Far too many companies have abandoned developing sincere one-on-one relationships with customers and instead focus on reaching the masses in as cost-effective a manner as possible.

Think back to Main Street and the "mom and pop" stores. If you were a frequent customer, the storeowners not only knew you by name, they likely knew the names of everyone in your family. And, that's how you felt...like you were part of their family. As a result, you didn't even think of shopping anywhere else. Fortunately, the mentality for developing closer business relationships is coming full-circle. New technologies have been developed which empower you to connect with thousands of customers in a personal manner.

Leading this charge is one of the world's most renowned experts on relationship management—Mike Muhney. Mike is the co-inventor of ACT!, a customer relationship management (CRM) software application which allows for client and prospect details to be shared in a single database accessible by multiple users. ACT! has largely been credited with creating the CRM industry.

Originally developed for DOS in 1987, ACT! is one of the top-selling relationship management tools, has been continually updated virtually every year since its release, and has been used by more than 10M people worldwide. Mike and his partner sold the company to Symantec in 1993 for $47 million. Six years later, ACT! was sold to SalesLogix for $60 million. CRM applications are popular for two main reasons:

- Maintaining a companywide database allows for all team members to access the same information.
- CRM software provides for the establishment of conversion metrics and the creation of customer value criteria.

Both are crucially important. However, the latter is largely dependent on establishing meaningful relationships that can eventually convert to sales. Consider the following scenario. You meet with a client and, rather than diving straight into business, you first talk about their life and interests. As you're chatting, she mentions her son is having minor surgery at the end of the week. After the meeting, this detail is entered into ACT! Then, before the next meeting, you check her notes. Your memory is jogged about her son's surgery and you subsequently ask how he's doing.

There's little doubt this makes a strong impact. Few people are likely to remember the surgery, let alone someone she has yet to conduct business with. As a result, you're likely to demonstrate you're not just someone who's hell-bent on taking her money—you're someone who's interested in developing an actual relationship. Though it sounds incredibly simple, few people take the time to do so. Of course, you can take this as far as you'd like. For instance, if she's a Bulls fan, you could buy her tickets to a game. If she loves chocolate, you can send her Godiva.

> *Small thoughts can lead to big deals.*

People sincerely appreciate when others recognize their needs, wants, and passions. This is, perhaps, the single most effective way to build your business. People inevitably tell their friends about your attention to detail and word spreads like wildfire. Today, Mike continues to be a leading advocate for customer relationship management and is the CEO and co-founder of VIPorbit—a company dedicated to bringing the power of CRM to mobile devices. Let's take a detailed look at how Mike utilizes apps to enhance business value and turn relationships into assets.

The App(etizer)

Ever since the iPhone was released, mobile applications (or "apps") have grown steadily in popularity. Today, an app exists for nearly anything, and with the market penetration of the Android operating system, the number of app developers and users have exploded. Barely a day goes by without hearing about the newest app millionaire. Truth is, however, very few apps make real—if any—money. There are two key reasons for this:

1. **Competition:** Tens of thousands of apps have been created and more are released daily. Working through the muddle of options and being noticed is difficult.
2. **Price:** The majority of apps are available for free, and many are them are quite useful. This has made it increasingly difficult to get customers to pay for an app. And even if you sell an app, your marketplace will receive a commission on

each sale. That means you need to sell a ton of product to earn real money.

You should absolutely think twice before spending substantial cash creating an app, because recouping your investment is far from a sure thing. If you're ready to enter the fray, however, Mike offers tips for maximizing your chances of success.

A Smart App(roach) To Starting

First, you must be clear about what app you'd like to create. Ideally, the app should compliment your business or reflect your unique abilities and/or interests. For instance, if you're a fitness guru, offer daily fitness tips. If you're an accountant, offer tips for saving money daily. The beauty of creating an app is there are myriad structures to consider. Some opt to create interactive tools whereby data is entered and a specific program is presented. Others send daily reminders or thoughts for the day. It is crucially important to understand your audience, what they can most benefit from, and deliver desired content via preferred learning modes. Three proven ways to start include:

- Determining your client's needs.
- Researching existing apps serving this market.
- Drafting your plan.

The first point is self-explanatory. The second may seem basic, but it's surprising how many skim past this step with a mere cursory glance, only to find out after significant time and resources have been expended that a more sophisticated tool exists. Do not be afraid to identify competitive products that may thwart your plans. Successful entrepreneurs embrace similar products and focus on what they can do better and more effectively.

The third point is essential. You want to strategize and formulate your vision before the clock begins ticking. Thinking on someone else's dime is not only expensive, but also unnecessary. Instead, brainstorm with partners, friends, and other trusted sources and create and refine an outline of how the product will look and how it will work. Unless you have money to burn, start the fire with the kindling of your efforts and let the professionals toss in the heavy logs.

Designing Your Apps Features

Let's look at Brazilian Jiu-Jitsu as an example. As a skilled teacher, you are clear on the needs of your students. In researching the marketplace for competitive apps, you're unable to find a suitable product and believe an opportunity exists to create one. After discussing the idea with a wide spectrum of practitioners and formalizing your vision, you identify the following app elements that will best serve both those unfamiliar with the sport and BJJ experts:

- **Describe the art of Brazilian Jiu-Jitsu.** This will enable you to provide a general overview of the discipline for those who may not be familiar with it.
- **Show it being used (either in competition or as a means for self-defense).** This provides a practical application so potential students can begin to understand its effectiveness.
- **Offer a "move of the day" for the various belt levels.** In BJJ, there are five belts—White, Blue, Purple, Brown, and Black. Offering moves for each empowers you to teach material that is directly applicable to the individual student at their respective stage of learning. Video is the perfect tool to use.
- **Provide information on your facility.** The purpose of creating an app is to market your business and increase sales. Otherwise, there's little reason to engage in the time, effort, and expenditures associated with development and marketing.
- **Put forth special offers.** This will, hopefully, result in moving people to action. Special offers are very powerful for encouraging people to shift from perusing to participating.

Creating an app must be viewed as an investment that can *potentially* provide meaningful dividends. Many aspiring authors dream of getting rich once their book is published. Similarly, many people believe developing an app will lead directly to a massive fortune. The key is to act responsibly and recognize that the only one in the equation to have guaranteed income is the developer. With these ideas in mind, let's shift towards programming options.

Accepting App(lications): Finding A Programmer

With your idea formalized, the next step is identifying a suitable programmer to bring the concept to fruition. There are multiple options.

FREE

Numerous free development options exist. However, it's important to note that in app-land, you really do get what you pay for. That said, if giving things a test run before fully committing is your preference, consider the following:

- Sencha: Sencha.com/Touch
- AppMakr: AppMakr.com
- Free iPhone App Maker: FreeIphoneAppMaker.com
- Free Android App Maker: FreeAndroidAppMaker.com

Each enables you to create a functional app which can be a great tool for creating a working prototype and begin securing feedback. The downside to free is that, once your name and brand is associated with the app you've put forth, an impression has been made and there's no turning back. If the app's functionality, appearance, or value is minimal, the consumer will tie this directly to you. Make 100% sure the app is fully representative of the impression you want to make before hitting the "release" button.

LOW-COST

A fully functional, cost-effective app can be built for less than $5,000. Many capable developers have the ability to create a professional looking product that represents your brand and image well. Three sites are solid resources to consider when searching for a developer:

- ELance: Elance.com
- ODesk: oDesk.com
- Freelancer: Freelancer.com

Each enables you to provide various criteria such as developer location, experience, and total budget. Talent, of course, varies so be sure to check references and ratings. The caliber of developers available can be outstanding as many have salaried positions and moonlight to make extra cash. Ask for examples of their work and, contrary to popular belief, do not be afraid to select the lowest bid.

HIGH-END

Developing a full-blown, highly robust app can be prohibitively expensive. It is not unusual for companies to spend upwards of $1 million to create an app with virtually every bell and whistle. Such apps typically involve detailed, interactive components and move far beyond the options offered by template-oriented products. For most, developing a high-end app is not an option. When it is, there are multiple companies who are more than capable of delivering per your specifications.

Preparing For The App(ocalypse)

There's simply no disputing the enormous potential mobile has to offer. According to The International Telecommunication Union, more than 5.3 billion people had mobile phone subscriptions at the end of 2010. This represents 77% of the world's population. By December 2011, more than 1.5 billion smart phones were in use. Further, over 300,000 apps were developed between 2008 and 2010, translating to an astonishing 10.9 billion downloads. Leading categories include games, news, maps, social networking, and music.

The study concludes, though, that not everything is coming up roses. The average download price of a mobile app continues to fall and one in four, once downloaded, is never used again. Standout sensations such as *Angry Birds*, *Where's My Droid?* and *Tiny Flashlight + LED* demonstrate that creating a viral movement can subsequently lead to profits. Mike is certainly banking on this trend continuing. He has invested several years and significant capital into VIPorbit with the intention of surpassing the success realized with ACT!

Intentions are one thing; realizing cash flow is quite another. Fortunately, there are proven strategies for monetizing one's efforts. Get your deposit slips ready.

(App)roved Tactics

Not every app is created to generate income. Many companies seek to spread goodwill and garner exposure by giving their apps away for free. This is not unusual as thousands of firms implement this approach. If generating awareness is the core objective, the app typically serves the singular purpose of being a *digital brochure*. If the plan is to monetize your efforts, there are three proven tactics to consider.

1. **Sell It!**

   Fees typically range from .99 to $2.99 with more robust apps costing significantly more, such as VIPorbit's Business version which sells for $9.99 on the iPhone and $19.99 for the iPad. While seemingly expensive, the robust functionality of VIPorbit is equivalent to desktop software that can cost significantly more. Additionally, it is available at your fingertips 24/7, which no desktop software can claim. For example, Sage ACT! was recently available for $466.99…on sale!

   A recent study from MobiThinking.com highlights that the number of mobile-only users continues to grow. By the end of 2011, more than 25 percent of mobile web users reported owning no other device to access the Internet.

   As more people move away from using traditional desktops and laptops, their computing needs will remain constant, though the device for interactivity will be markedly different. Given that VIPorbit provides similar functionality as Sage ACT!, yet costs 98% less, the smart money is pursuing mobile. Now is the time to capitalize on this shift.

2. **Sell Ads Within Your App**

   In similar fashion to AdSense, Google's AdMob.com has made it extraordinarily simple to place ads on your app via their proprietary platform. AdMob "allows earnings to be generated by placing targeted ads based on the site's content and users." Additional options include Greystripe.com and Smaato.com.

   Revenue is directly tied to traffic. Therefore, as more ads are shown, income will increase accordingly. And, while a significant number of views and clicks are required before more than just pocket change will be generated, each provides a reasonable opportunity to offset a portion of development costs.

3. **Offer A "Light" Version And Encourage Upgrading**

   This strategy can be very effective. VIPorbit offers a free "light" version, as do thousands of other apps. The free version typically provides customers with a solid user experience, but refrains from allowing access to many key components. In consumer product marketing, this is often referred to as *sampling*, whereby a taste is offered to whet the consumer's appetite and, hopefully, leads to the product being purchased.

   A 2011 study from Piper Jaffray in review of Apple Company data found that "the average iOS device owner downloaded 83 apps in 2011 of which 18% were purchased." Given that in December 2011 alone, the 18% represents 925 million downloads at an average cost of $1.05, that's more than $971 million in gross receipts. These figures do not account for sales generated via Android operating systems. Bottom line, apps can be lucrative but must be viewed as a component of the overall marketing/branding mix. For every one *Angry Birds*, there are likely thousands of angry developers who have yet to sell a single download.

App(lause)

Ultimately, developing an app can not only increase your company's exposure, it can be a very effective tool for reaching a diverse audience quickly and have a profound impact on customers already familiar with your brand. Apps are proven to engage and offer a wide-range of digital media features for promoting your products and services. Mike strongly believes in the technology and, while fun and games have their place, apps go far beyond shooters and puzzles. When leveraged correctly, apps can help your company:

- Optimize Sales and Marketing.
- Enhance Customer Service.
- Communicate More Effectively.

As Mike has demonstrated, virtually any idea, process, and system that streamlines productivity can be adapted for mobile application. By providing high-value products that address a specific market's needs, a strong opportunity exists to differentiate your firm and realize significant rewards that, in the end, will more than justify the initial expenditure.

 TAKEAWAYS

App Attack

- Modern technology has largely killed the intimacy associated with developing tangible rapport with vendors, clients and even, employees.
- Few apps make real money due to competition and price.
- Ideally, your app should compliment your business or reflect your unique abilities and/or interests.
- It is crucially important to understand your audience, what they can most benefit from, and deliver desired content via preferred learning modes.
- Over 300,000 apps were developed between 2008 and 2010, translating to an astonishing 10.9B downloads.
- By the end of 2011, more than 25 percent of mobile web users reported owning no other device to access the Internet.
- Apps can be lucrative but must be viewed as a component of the overall marketing/branding mix.

CHAPTER 13

QR CODES

One of the great things about the Internet is that it's helped level the playing field. Anyone can secure a domain, build a decent-looking site full of content and items for sale, have it hosted on a reliable server, and attempt to go head-to-head with industry leaders. Due to the ease of start-up, millions of websites have been created and the competition for traffic is steep. The landscape has become so crowded that some have grown concerned the opportunity to make money online is over.

Riel Roussopoulos is not one of these people. A Montreal native and marketing rock star, Riel got involved in the tech world at a very young age. In 7th grade, he frequented a local department store that sold Commodore 64s. They allowed him free access to the machines, and he became an expert at playing its games. The owner wasn't just being kind, though. As customers came in and witnessed Riel's mastery, they became interested in buying a computer. Riel was essentially providing product demos and communicating valuable presale information about the capabilities of the system.

Therefore, when computers were sold, the department store clerks would inform customers that, for a small fee, Riel could come to their home, set up the computer, install software, and provide an overview on how to use it. This marked the beginning of a long and mutually beneficial relationship between Riel and technology.

The Power Of Lists And Tracking Software

Virtually every business lives and dies on its ability to communicate with customers. Today it is common practice to capture names, email addresses, and as many other details as the customer is willing to share. The more demographic layers, the more valuable the data can be. Consider the following. You can buy a list of people who live in the United States—93,786,526 names and addresses—from InfoUSA. com for $3,282,528. That's $35 per thousand names.

But let's say you want additional demographic layers—for example, women between the ages of 45 and 49 who live in California and earn between $100,000 and $249,999 per year. That reduces the list of contacts to 259,778 and costs $13,768. This equates to $53.16 per thousand names, or 52% more than the baseline cost. Adding two additional criteria, Religion (Catholic) and Marital Status (Married), reduces the list of contacts to 60,361 at a cost of $3,622. This reflects a CPM cost of $60.07—a 71.6% premium over the baseline cost. The lesson is clear:

> *Detailed customer data equals dollars.*

Though it's now common knowledge that building and mining a customer database can be very fruitful, it wasn't always this way. Riel was one of the early pioneers to recognize the potential. After working at the local computer shop ran its course, Riel went to college and majored in film. On the side, he'd DJ and promoted private events. Instinctively, he recognized the importance of keeping track of the people who attended. To capture their contact information, he encouraged them to join his mailing list so they would be the first to have access to future parties, special offers, and VIP opportunities.

In short order, the list contained over 200,000 names. Given his massive reach, he had little difficulty filling a wide variety of venues. Concurrently, he developed an innovative ticketing system that accurately monitored response rates and other details. This enabled him to identify the specific promotional campaign to which a guest responded. While commonplace today, it was a highly sophisticated tool for its time that allowed a promoter to be credited with sales generated from his efforts.

Riel soon realized he possessed a groundbreaking system and seized the opportunity to shift focus from promoting other people's events to creating his own. So Riel held a party. He secured a suitable location, invited established promoters to participate, and together they were able to assemble a larger crowd than any single promoter could do on his own. Prior to Riel's system, promoters distrusted one another and seldom collaborated as it was virtually impossible to accurately track the results of each company's efforts. His unique ticketing system eliminated this issue. As a result, business soared and he thrived in the industry for another 10 years before selling the company. This early foray into the world of list building and tracking foreshadowed Riel's next business.

The Opportunity Of QR Codes

Reviewing his options, he shifted attention towards Internet marketing. Given his marketing experience, technical savvy, and ability to build lists and monitor data, he strongly believed he could help business owners take full advantage of the medium. Most have enough on their plate simply trying to run a profitable operation. Understanding how the Internet works—building an effective site, SEO, SEM, PPC, landing pages, capturing leads, etc.—is often one of their last thoughts.

Riel recognized a tremendous opportunity: Create an end-to-end platform that takes care of virtually every aspect of online business. By utilizing tested techniques, he set up websites, landing pages, tracking systems, and marketing initiatives for brick-and-mortar business owners who were not yet online. His business quickly flourished. Most recently, Riel has been emphasizing sales via mobile marketing—and specifically

QR codes. As smart-phone devices proliferate, business owners have a unique chance to engage with existing, and potential, customers in ways not previously seen. However, there's a right and wrong way to use the technology.

The Wrong Way To Use QR Codes

Riel's strategy for QR codes is simple: If a customer takes the time to scan your code, give her what she wants. Too many companies fail on this simple initiative. As an example, while waiting for the bus one day, Riel noticed a luggage advertisement on the side of the bus stop canopy. It had a QR code. As is frequently his practice, he scanned the code using his smart-phone and Google Goggles (a free downloadable program accessible in almost every smart phone's Marketplace). The QR code directed him towards the company's website.

Although it may seem like the campaign worked flawlessly, it was anything but. The ad failed for two key reasons:

- The ad lacked a strong *call-to-action*. Riel only scanned the QR code because he's interested in mobile marketing. For everyone else, the advertisement provided zero incentive to interact with it.
- The QR code directed customers to the company's basic site. Not only wasn't the site optimized for mobile phones, thereby making it difficult to navigate, there were no specific offers to entice mobile phone users to request information or purchase product.

An effective QR campaign contains both a strong call-to-action and encourages scanners to provide contact details and/or make a positive purchase decision…immediately. If a company provides enough incentive, *impulse buying* is a very real possibility. One of the common complaints from smart phone users is that, while they enjoy the convenience of interacting via mobile, it is a cumbersome process to type in the requested data. Riel incorporates a simple widget to address this concern.

In December 2008, Facebook introduced Facebook Connect, which replaces traditional form submission systems. In the past, customers would be required to enter their name, email, and possibly other data if they wanted to request information or join a mailing list. And, depending on the offer, they may also need to provide the ever-annoying CAPTCHA code. Facebook Connect eliminates this task by enabling visitors to allow access to personal information via their Facebook account. Therefore, instead of needing to fill out a lengthy, time-consuming form, they are able to complete the process with just one click.

Given the number of Facebook users, this has greatly simplified the smartphone data-entry process as most mobile phone users also have a Facebook account. Though available for a number of years, strangely, few offer this timesaving feature. Riel consistently looks to streamline the customer experience and make it as easy as possible for someone to conduct business with one of his clients. Online or via mobile, keeping it simple is the cornerstone for improving conversion rates.

Bottom line: The easier you can make it for people to interact and purchase, the greater the return you'll realize.

The Right Way To Use QR Codes

To illustrate the power of a properly executed QR code initiative, let's look at one of Riel's marketing campaigns. His client was a relatively new personal-training facility. The gym has a closed-door policy. Meaning, if someone wasn't a monthly due-paying customer, they were not able to enroll in any of the available classes. While business was decent, they needed to ramp-up membership. To attract new members, the company chose to promote free "spin classes" and provide a limited-time opportunity to view the space.

Their budget, however, was miniscule. Recognizing their constraints, Reil drafted a proposal that would cost the gym a mere fraction of traditional advertising and, hopefully, drive meaningful traffic into the facility. His campaign was built around an outdoor strategy and sought to leverage the power of stickers. Eye-catching decals would be placed around town, with a special emphasis on the vicinity of competing gyms, and only contain the phrase Free Spin Class and a QR code.

The gym's membership was comprised primarily of people in their 20's and 30's—those most often associated with being early adopters of new technology. Given that QR codes were not widely utilized or accepted, ownership liked the idea, loved the cost, and decided to give it a spin (pun intended). Because of the strategic placement of the stickers, hundreds of ideal clients scanned the code and were brought to a landing page where they could opt-in for the special offer. Many did and, subsequently, viewed the facility, tried the class and, within a small window of time, 60 people became new members.

The campaign provided a tremendous return as the gym's only expenses were printing the stickers, having them distributed, and paying a commission to Riel for each new member secured. Further, because of the significant buzz created around the use of the relatively new QR code technology, a local newspaper featured a story on the facility. This resulted in additional coverage and inevitably, an increase in the number of visitors to the facility and new member sign-ups. So what can we learn from this story? Mobile marketing is *powerful* and *affordable*. Ready or not, it is changing the way business is conducted.

An Effective QR Campaign

Riel's techniques are proven to work. By implementing his strategies, any business can realize similar results. There are five core strategies for an effective QR code campaign:

1. **Set attainable objectives.** QR codes must be viewed as one component of the overall marketing mix. While they can absolutely generate sales and leads, they will not be saviors of any business. It is important to be realistic about the potential outcome and view QR codes as a method with which to target a developing subset of the population. Current response rates average less than 1%.

2. **Be clear on what happens when the code is scanned.** Customers view QR codes with a stringent cost to benefit analysis radar. Random codes are ineffective unless tied to a clear reward. The

luggage ad failed because it offered zero incentive for scanning the code. People expect a solid return on their investment of time. Had the ad said, "Scan this code to receive $50 off your next luggage purchase," customers would know exactly what to expect and could respond accordingly. When you provide customers with a clear directive, your conversion rates will soar.

3. **Separate sales initiatives from data collection.** Immediate conversion doesn't always have to be your goal. You can use QR codes to simply collect data. One effective way to do this is to give a customer a chance at winning a valuable prize (e.g., an iPad) in exchange for her scanning the code and providing her contact information. Remember, data has inherent value and, once the customer enters your sales funnel, you're able to communicate with her and, eventually, build a relationship that converts her into a paying customer.

4. **Combine mobile payments with on-premise bonuses.** This is an extraordinarily effective strategy made famous by Groupon and Living Social. For example, a restaurant might offer a $40 voucher for only $20 with an ad saying, "$20 in Free Food! Scan the QR Code now!" After scanning, the customer is taken to a mobile-friendly page that describes the restaurant, provides details of the deal, and offers the voucher for sale. The hope is that, when the customer redeems the discount with friends, she spends more than the $40. But even if the bill ends up at precisely $40, the customer's data has been captured, the $20 likely covered hard costs, and the restaurant has a potential new long-term customer. Everyone wins.

5. **Deliver on what's promised.** This may seem like a no-brainer, but too often an organization's sales, marketing, and IT departments fail to connect. This can result in marketing spending many hours putting together a campaign that should convert, IT failing to receive the memo, and sales sitting on their hands. Worse, the customer is left with a negative first impression that is difficult to repair. Few things propel a company towards disaster faster than customer disappointment.

If you follow these techniques, your QR code campaign will typically result in substantial leads and sales.

Creating Codes

Creating QR codes is simple and there are a number of free tools available to get started. Riel offers an innovative product that can be found at Scan2.co. Other products include Microsoft Tag (Tag.Microsoft.com/home.aspx), Delivr.com, and Scan Life (ScanLife.com). Even if you're a complete beginner, you can create a QR code using one of these programs in seconds. And, while QR codes are in the early stages of adaptation in the United States, their use is likely to spread rapidly over the next few years. Some businesses will try them, make serious blunders that prevent converting traffic to sales, and give up. Other companies will get everything right and increasingly use the codes for profit.

Like any other tool, a learning curve is required. The hope is you'll eventually land in the latter category and QR codes will become an increasingly powerful weapon in your overall marketing arsenal. To the scanners go the *prophets...*

⏻ TAKEAWAYS

QR Codes

- Your business depends on its ability to continually communicate with potential and existing customers. Data and reach equates to dollars.
- QR codes and mobile sites are a cost-effective way to engage and capture high-value customers.
- If a customer takes the time to scan your QR code, give her what she wants.
- Effective QR code campaigns contain a strong call-to-action.
- Use the five rules for an effective QR code campaign to consistently generate leads and sales.
- Take advantage of free QR code-generating software.

1
0
1
1
0
0
0
0
0
1
0
1
0
1
0
1
1
1
0
1
0
1
0
1
0
0
1
1
0
0
0

PART III

LEVERAGING
THE 'NET

CHAPTER 14

DOT COM PRINCIPLES

Money. Love it or hate it, you can't live without it. And you can't run a business if you don't have it. Taking an idea from inception to execution requires significant capital—be it from personal funds, friends and family, angel investors, traditional lenders, or institutions.

This is a key reason why successful entrepreneurs are relatively rare and so many small businesses fail. Securing adequate funding requires knowledge, finesse, and tenacity, and it always takes more—usually much more—cash than the eager businessperson can imagine to achieve profitability. The road to success is littered with obstacles. Consider what you face:

- Raising funds from angel investors or institutions? They'll typically throw capital only at those with a high probability of providing meaningful returns. No track record? Not a big idea? Not a large enough market opportunity? You're in for a tough sell.
- Need a loan? Unless you already have collateral, the banks won't lend you a dime. Of course, if you had a meaningful

net worth and sufficient liquidity, you wouldn't need the bank. It's a classic Catch-22.

- Feel like approaching friends and family to participate? Nothing will end close bonds faster than failing to return their cash. Asking those you love for a penny, let alone thousands of dollars, requires serious intestinal fortitude.

Though difficult, raising funds is not impossible. The key is preparation. Having a game-changing idea combined with an energetic, knowledgeable team and solid business plan that excites, overcomes concerns, provides answers, and clarifies profitability is a proven start-up formula. Investors put capital behind those they believe in. Your ideas are a huge factor, but demonstrating personal dedication to realizing long-term dividends is even more important.

Christopher (Kit) Codik has perspective from both sides of the table as he's an entrepreneur and an investor. The majority of Kit's business ventures have been backed by significant capital. This includes <u>Liquor.com</u> which Kit co-founded and has run as CEO since 2009. To ensure Liquor.com's success, Kit has leveraged his personal and professional network of investors and his sharp business acumen to develop a new media brand and large-scale digital platform for the cocktail and spirits industry. Let's grab a drink and learn more.

An Apéritif

After graduating from Princeton, Kit moved to San Francisco to be close to the epicenter of the start-up world, Silicon Valley. Here, he witnessed the incredible growth of numerous companies, and had the opportunity to develop a network of young, sharp entrepreneurs. Choosing to start his career at an established, yet rapidly growing, corporation Kit joined The Gap and was part of its first structured management and merchandising training program at its San Francisco headquarters. He gained an invaluable education in retail and product development, and was able to tap into The Gap's extensive network of talent and resources.

After nearly five years, Kit left to help launch Infant Advantage with one of The Gap's senior executives. This marked the start of his entrepreneurial career. Attempting to help build the company with little capital proved challenging. Infant Advantage achieved moderate success, but it never fully flourished due, in large measure, to its lack of adequate financing. Kit learned it's wise to secure sufficient funding before attempting to bring a great idea to life.

Kit then helped launch <u>Della.com</u> (originally Della & James), which was the first online gift registry platform, initially focused on weddings. Della.com was well-funded by top-tier venture firms (Kleiner Perkins Caufield & Byers and Trinity Ventures), and also received investments from many of their partner retailers, including Amazon.com, Crate & Barrel, and Tiffany. Della.com grew quickly, and was acquired by The Wedding Channel within two years of launch. While at Della, Kit was recruited to join a new venture capital group created to focus on corporate ventures. The firm, eVolution Global Partners, was set up by Texas Pacific Group (now TPG Capital), Kleiner Perkins, and Bain & Co. Kit joined as a principal on the U.S. Venture team and was initially focused on sourcing and developing new investment opportunities.

While at eVolution, Kit helped to fund, set up, and build a new financial services firm, Finacity. The company was created in partnership with Bank of America, EULER Hermes, Amroc Investments (now Avenue Capital) and ABN Amro Bank. Originally structured as an online receivables finance firm, it evolved into a unique, sophisticated accounts receivables securitization platform. Within months of launch, Finacity's newly hired CEO asked Kit to stay on as executive vice president and focus on business and corporate development. Kit did, and subsequently helped build the business into a global, profitable endeavor.

In 2006, Kit's entrepreneurial bug kicked in hard. Recognizing the Internet still had massive potential despite the NASDAQ's previous implosion, he and a friend, Nicolas Darveau-Garneau, created The Green Lake Group, a venture advisory firm focused on helping entrepreneurs and start-ups build and grow their business. As fate would have it, I had recently reclaimed the <u>Liquor.com</u> domain and, along with Warren Yamakoshi, secured space in the TechCrunch 40 Demo Pit to find operational and funding partners. As Kit and

Nic traversed the event in search of possible clients and emerging companies, we discussed our plans.

Several months later, we executed an agreement to collaboratively build a substantive business around the high-value domain. Leading the charge, Kit and Nic reworked the model, established compelling metrics, and raised angel funds. In late 2009, Liquor.com went live. Within two short years, Liquor.com established itself as the leading digital media platform for spirits and cocktail culture. The company currently has more than 280,000 Facebook fans, nearly one million unique monthly visitors, and over 130,000 email subscribers, and has built a network of media partners extending the brand's content and advertising reach to over four million consumers per month. Liquor.com has also successfully partnered with most of the major spirits conglomerates to help market at least one or more of their brands.

While the final chapter is far from written, Liquor.com's story represents an entrepreneur's dream: build a game-changing company in expedited fashion. Belly up to the bar as Kit shares his entrepreneurial blueprint.

The Sidecar

Although Liquor.com is a fantastic domain name, the URL itself did not guarantee the creation of a profitable business. Like all start-ups, Liquor.com had to meet major challenges. These included:

- Establishing credibility
- Developing relationships
- Providing high-value content
- Fending off competition
- Attracting a following

Rather than addressing these sequentially, Kit decided to tackle them concurrently. His first step was to meet as many influencers and insiders in the cocktail and spirits industries as possible. These included top writers, historians, bartenders, brand managers, wholesalers, and mixologists.

After developing an understanding of the cocktail community and the people who played an influential role in the industry, he invited a select group to join the Liquor.com advisory board. They received equity in the business and were asked to both provide content and advise the company as it built its brand and presence.

Kit also recruited business advisors who each brought different skills and areas of expertise to augment Kit's own, including design, advertising, sales, product development, and strategy. Bringing in experts provides compelling advantages:

- **Helps to quickly establish credibility and relationships:** By enlisting a team of renowned experts, Liquor.com was able to establish credibility relatively quickly post-launch. When brand managers, venues, and the press took a look at Liquor.com's team and contributors, they saw an impressive line-up of writers, content providers, advisory board members, and experts. This helped to shorten the vetting process.
- **High-value content:** Kit recruited people who live, eat, and breathe cocktails and spirits. The depth of knowledge these insiders provided was reflected in their content and helped to quickly differentiate Liquor.com from competitors.
- **Fast track the moat:** A significant challenge most start-ups face is fending off competition and maintaining position in a crowded field. By enlisting the industry's best and combining their talent with an industry-defining domain, an initial barrier-to-entry was created. Liquor.com used its early credibility, quick start, and increasing scale to make it difficult for other media platforms (existing and new) with an alcohol beverage-related focus to usurp Liquor.com's developing position as the leading authority for consumers and top tier bartenders.

Providing social proof can play an important role in gaining early traction for a business. Even if you don't have the budget to immediately hire a team of experts, you can consider sharing equity with those who'll add extraordinary value. The incremental dilution is minimal and greatly offset by selecting advisors and experts who will support your business. Enrolling them as partners and sustaining their enthusiasm is an important key to ensuring they'll remain long-term ambassadors for your company versus just being names on a masthead.

Customers, potential partners, and advertisers are all wary of being the first through the door. That's why it's wise to validate your brand's worthiness, be it in the form of media attention, celebrity testimonials, a high-powered advisory board, or an enormous number of Facebook fans.

Happy Hour

Within every niche, there are industry leaders. For the world of soft drinks, it's Coca-Cola; for online commerce, it's Amazon.com. One strategy for gaining larger-scale exposure is to develop meaningful partnerships with the leaders in your field. Doing so enhances your company's credibility, and can result in increased revenue opportunities. Gaining the attention of industry-leading companies can be very difficult. They're solicited daily with offers.

To interest media stars such as *The Huffington Post, 7x7,* and *SF Gate,* Liquor.com offered to provide spirits-related articles at zero cost. Given the company's stable of world-class writers and high-value content, the sites happily accepted. Liquor.com benefits from these relationships in four powerful ways:

- The articles are Liquor.com branded, establishing Liquor.com as an authority on these respected media sites.
- Each of the articles links to Liquor.com, which enhances the site's search engine rating and points to Liquor.com's Facebook and Twitter pages.
- A large number of readers are exposed to Liquor.com from a site they already trust.
- New potential customers may result from readers clicking the Liquor.com links and visiting the site.

At the same time, Liquor.com's media partners benefit as:

- They receive, and feature, exclusive content their readers appreciate.
- They save the time and expense of creating such content themselves.

Running a large website is difficult. Consistently adding interesting articles is expensive, time consuming, and requires extensive management. If you can provide fresh content at no cost, many sites will jump at the chance to exchange real estate for engaging material. This model holds true for *every* industry. For example, if you're a chef or own a restaurant, it would make sense to pitch providing a column for <u>Food.com</u>; or, if you're a martial arts instructor, consider submitting articles to <u>MartialInfo.com</u>.

If you already run a blog, you may be able to tweak existing content to speak directly to the third party's audience. Professional writers often look for ways to reuse their material. You should too. (The only exception is when a site is paying you for "first publication" or "exclusive" rights, which rules out already-published material.) In the end, credibility is a two-way street. An "As Featured On" badge allows you to take advantage of the larger site's name recognition and receive validation via their implied stamp of approval.

From your customers' perspective, this credibility can make all the difference. Instead of buying a product or signing up for a newsletter from a random website that could have been created yesterday, they'll be placing their trust in a company that has been featured on a site they recognize and respect. At the same time, your contributions help sustain the larger site's position as a leader in its field by supporting their initiative to offer massive content that adds value for their audience.

I'd call this a true win(e)-win(e).

Make Mine Red-Eye Too

When reviewing a new business opportunity, Kit asks six crucial questions. These apply to any industry and almost any type of business. The questions, and the answers for Liquor.com, were as follows:

- **Is the market large enough?** Answer: Yes. According to the Distilled Spirits Council of the United States, the U.S. beverage alcohol industry is, "a major contributor to the U.S. economy, responsible for nearly $388 billion in total U.S. economic activity in 2008." The spirits industry alone generates $60 billion at retail and spends $3+ billion a year in advertising, marketing and promotional activities. Fact is, when times are bad, people drink; and when times are good, people drink. While not recession-proof, it's pretty darn close. For your own business, always begin by asking whether there are enough customers to sustain it. If the answer is no, head back to the drawing board.

- **Is there an existing customer base?** Answer: Yes. Beverage alcohol is a widely accepted, albeit somewhat controversial, product that has been manufactured, distributed, and sold for centuries. Little education is required to inform the public as to what the product is, whom it's for, and how one uses it. This allows marketers to shift directly to positioning. Whatever business you're planning, try tapping into an existing customer base with demonstrated interest in your products or services. Attempting to create a market where one doesn't already exist is possible, but it's much more difficult and expensive.

- **Is there an opportunity to dominate the market?** Answer: Yes. Even though billions were spent annually on alcohol beverage marketing, little was being directed towards online advertising in 2008. As spirits brands began to realize that digital often provides a more cost-effective means for marketing their products over traditional media, Liquor.com was well positioned to take advantage of this shift.

  Establishing the leadership position in your chosen niche is far from easy. But if you select an unadulterated market that meets the first two criteria and lacks a dominant player, you have a strong opportunity to reinvent the industry.

- **Can existing technology be used to rapidly grow the business?** Answer: Yes. Thanks to the widespread acceptance of the Internet, social media, email newsletters, mobile, and video, many digital solutions are flourishing and provide the necessary platforms to help Liquor.com succeed. Of course, whenever technology is involved, it's important to be flexible and make adjustments based on evolving trends. For example, Kit recognized email newsletters in excess of 500 words were largely falling on deaf ears and consumer preferences were gravitating towards short, easy-to-digest articles, mobile content, and video. Action was immediately taken to revamp its offerings.

Liquor.com has released several high-quality videos and continues to produce more. To view one of Liquor.com's videos, scan the QR code to the right or visit EZ.com/behindthedrink. All of the site's videos are uploaded to its YouTube channel at YouTube.com/liquor.

Kit and his team also made heavy use of Facebook (Facebook.com/Liquor.com). The consensus was to engage its target audience where they gathered, prior to building tools and incorporating them into the Liquor.com site before significant traffic existed. The team, therefore, developed a formula for daily Facebook postings that blended their existing articles with outside content—the latter ranging from quotes and polls to comments designed to evoke an emotional response from visitors. (A number of posts have received more than 700 comments.)

- **Can the company be profitable and will investors participate?** Answer: Yes. From day one, Kit saw great potential in maximizing the value of the domain. The initial business plan has been tweaked several times, but creating a profitable business that would appeal to investors has been a constant. In just 24 months, the company borders on profitability while raising only $2 million from outside investors. Additional

rounds of funding may be completed to help the company
achieve its vision.

- **Is there a meaningful exit opportunity?** Answer: Yes. There
  are a number of viable scenarios, ranging from going public to
  being acquired that will provide participants with a significant
  return on their investment. Further, even if things don't go
  according to plan, the value of the domain alone is a tangible
  safeguard against the company becoming worthless.

Before moving forward with developing Liquor.com, Kit insisted
on being able to answer each of these six questions with a definitive
"Yes." It is advised you do the same when pursuing your own business
opportunities.

One For The Road

There's no one strategy for creating a thriving online business. It
requires a creative mix of approaches, including working synergistically
with others and having everyone dedicated to achieving a clear goal.
What's most important is to continually stay in motion. In business you
can never know exactly what will happen and when, so flexibility and
adaptability are key. Salespeople have learned to focus on the ABCs:
Always Be Closing. As an entrepreneur, you should also focus on the
ABCs, but assign them a different meaning: Always Be Challenged.

Without challenges, growth is impossible. An unfettered path leads
to an unrewarding destination. Adversity represents opportunity. And
it's at the precipice of challenge that you'll find success. Stay thirsty,
my friends.

⏻ TAKEAWAYS

Dot Com Principles

- For your start-up to have a good chance of success, aim for a game-changing idea combined with a dedicated, knowledgeable team and a solid business plan that excites, provides answers, overcomes concerns, and makes clear how you'll achieve profitability.
- A highly compelling domain name doesn't guarantee your company will be profitable. But it also doesn't hurt.
- Leveraging others' notoriety and abilities can play an important role in gaining early traction for your business.
- Gain large-scale exposure by forming meaningful relationships with the biggest companies in the game. Expand exposure through the reach of others.
- Credibility is a two-way street that helps enhance a mutually beneficial relationship.
- Before pursuing potential business opportunities, ask yourself Kit's six crucial questions.
- To succeed, work synergistically with others dedicated to achieving a clear goal, and always be ready to tackle challenges with flexibility and adaptability.

CHAPTER 15

SEO STRATEGY

There are many factors involved with creating a successful website. Most can be easily and quickly learned so long as one critical ingredient is present: traffic. No matter how ugly or poorly designed a website is, if traffic exists, product will be sold. On the other hand, one might have the world's best site with copy so compelling it could sell gym memberships to your bed-ridden grandparents, but without visitors, not a dime's worth of product will sell.

There are dozens of sources of traffic, both paid and free. However, the source universally recognized as the "pot of gold" stems from Search Engine Optimization (SEO). Wikipedia defines Search Engine Optimization as, "the process of improving the visibility of a website or webpage in search engines via the 'natural' or un-paid ('organic' or 'algorithmic') search results. In general, the earlier (or higher ranked on the search results page), and more frequently a site appears in the search results list, the more visitors it will receive from the search engine's users."

This is an accurate, albeit sterile, definition of SEO. But it fails to address how search actually works and can be used to increase profitability. By understanding how SEO differs from alternative traffic-generating tools, you can leverage its power for building your online business. SEO has three great advantages: it's free (with qualifications), your webpage will appear in search results related to your specific topic, and it continues the conversation taking place in the consumer's mind. Let's look closer at its core benefits.

SEO Is Free...Sort Of

There is a cost to implementing SEO, but it comes in the form of time, energy, and other resources invested in creating content and securing links to achieve a top ranking. Once you've established this position, however, maintaining ideal placement requires little additional effort. Unlike pay-per-click (PPC) and traditional forms of advertising which require continual out of pocket expenditures, SEO continuously drives targeted traffic to your sites, thereby providing long-term rewards for your initial efforts.

Your Message Places Itself

With offline media, such as television, radio, and print, an ad is created and you're able to select where and when the ad should run, such as "drive time" or during a particular program. Online advertising works similarly in that you can select which sites the ad will be featured on, identify audience criteria, and schedule the timing for it to be visible. SEO works differently. Once you create your webpage—which, for marketing purposes, is a sophisticated form of an ad—the search engines determine where and when it will appear.

Typically, your page will appear at the precise moment a prospective customer proactively seeks information about your topic. If your subject matter is popular and a top ranking is achieved, it is possible for your page to appear countless times over an extended period. This differentiates search from all other forms of advertising.

Search Is Non-Interruptive

Imagine that while watching your favorite TV show, an ad appears for car insurance. If you're happy with your agent and coverage at the time, the ad is irrelevant. Now imagine that a year later you're in an accident and your insurance company does a poor job handling your claim. You immediately decide to explore alternatives.

As you type "best car insurance rates" into Google, you're consciously thinking about finding a new provider. As a result, the choices shown simply continue the *conversation* you've already begun. This is a crucial feature of search. A search engine is ostensibly an oracle that answers your question and allows you to select from the results provided. Instead of being subjected to unsolicited advertising, search delivers the related information you want at the precise moment you need it.

The Target Or The Bull's Eye?

Search often demonstrates pinpoint accuracy, such as how to convert currency from one form to another, identifying where a street address is on a map, or obtaining background information about a prospective client. This is known as a "targeted" query. A "non-targeted" query is broader in scope and delivers a wider range of possible matches. For example, if you search for "yoga," your failure to supply sufficient criteria will lead to the engine providing millions of pages to choose from. If, however, you type "yoga classes in Chicago," you'll receive fewer results that better reflect the exact information you seek. Your goal is to rank at the top of the results for the search criteria that best define your business.

When search engines first came onto the scene, there was no shortage of speculation as to how to make this happen. Today, we know far more about this process—and that's in no small part due to the work of one man, Leslie Rohde.

SEO Breakthrough

Leslie began his online career in 1998 by selling products from a website. He enjoyed being a merchant, but was also curious about how the Internet worked behind the scenes. He toyed with different ways of generating traffic and pioneered a number of strategies. As the early search engines gained traction, he shifted his attention to the power of search. Then Google exploded in popularity. Given its massive influence on the ability for a company to establish category dominance, Leslie chose to pursue the knowledge needed to master achieving a prominent Google result ranking.

He was not alone. He, and hundreds of others, sought to break Google's code and decipher how its complex algorithms worked. Much to his dismay, there was little reliable information available and most continued to focus on the outdated technique of "keyword density" that had worked previously. After months of research, Leslie came across a public document written by the founders of Google before they left Stanford to go into business. In it, they explained in highly technical detail the two major factors used in ranking pages. While the document was available in the public domain, few outside of Google understood its complexities. Leslie was a software engineer, however, and quickly grasped the key concepts. Google's search structure had fallen into his hands...and it was gold.

With this powerful information, Leslie set out to create a program that allowed site owners, IT professionals, and consultants to identify any site's linking structure and provide the necessary tools for vastly improving its ranking. In 2002, he released OptiLink. Described as a "program to assist in the development of *top ranking* at the major search engines," it was widely heralded as ushering in a new era of SEO technology. Within a few days of release, Leslie went from being virtually unknown to the center of the SEO universe. His software explained in detail the power of "link text," and provided tools any webmaster could implement to achieve better rankings through the adjustment of links.

> *There was another "secret" in Google's document that would end up being equally crucial: the mathematics behind page ranking.*

Ranking pages depends on two primary factors: relevance and authority. These form the foundation for search and Google's algorithms actively compute values for each. *PageRank*, a link analysis algorithm named after Larry Page, is a key factor used to establish authority. While the algorithm was openly disclosed, it was not clearly understood until Leslie published his ebook *Dynamic Linking* in 2003. *Dynamic Linking* described what is now known in SEO as *PageRank sculpting*, and is the foundation for how to control and optimize Google's measure of authority.

Since then, Leslie has developed numerous other products and methods, and in partnership with Dan Thies (another early pioneer in search), formed The SEO BrainTrust (SEOBrainTrust.com), a teaching and mentoring company devoted to helping online entrepreneurs grow their businesses. Today, link text and PageRank remain the two most important factors in achieving top rankings. Let's cut through the clutter and examine why these two elements are so important.

Relevancy And Link Text

A page that's highly relevant for a given search has three elements:

- Search keywords that appear in the page title.
- Content that's pertinent to the query.
- Inbound links pointing to the page.

The first two bullets are self-explanatory. For example, a page that features spicy horseradish mayonnaise should have "Spicy Horseradish Mayonnaise" as part of its title and feature related content. Inbound links are clickable text featured on another site that link to your page. For instance, this link, if clicked on an e-reader, will take you to InternetProphets.com. The link text associates the phrase *this link* with *Internet Prophets*. If this link was used often enough, eventually the book would rank under this search term.

Leslie points to the example of searching for "click here" on Google. More than 9 billion results will be returned—and the number one search result is almost always Get.adobe.com/reader. Adobe's site doesn't appear first because *click here* is scattered across it. It's at the top of the list because tens of thousands of other sites link to the free Adobe Acrobat PDF Reader using *click here* as the anchor text.

In other words, even though Adobe doesn't mention *click here* on its site, Google considers it the most relevant site for the phrase. With enough links pointing to a page, it can be top-ranked for any search query. This aspect of Google's ranking structure has frequently been exploited. For example, in 2003 hundreds of sites linked the phrase *miserable failure* to a White House biography page of President George W. Bush.

As a result, whenever someone typed "miserable failure" in Google, President Bush's photo and information would appear. Google has since changed its algorithms to prevent this type of prank, called *Google bombing;* but the underlying principles of its search for relevancy remains consistent. Some people also occasionally try to fool Google's algorithms for profit using tricks referred to as *black hat* tactics. These may work short-term, but Google actively looks for such ways to subvert the system. When Google identifies violators, it may ban these marketers from being included in any Google searches—which can be devastating for a business owner. It is best to avoid such attempts and stick to approved techniques.

While link text is an important component of the SEO equation, it's far from the being the sole variable. The other major factor is determining authority.

Authority

Because there can be millions, or even billions, of pages that are relevant for the most popular topics, search engines rank "more important" pages before "less important" ones. A "more important" page is considered to have greater *authority*, which is measured by a number called *PageRank*. In practical terms, what this means is a highly relevant page for a query can fail to appear at the top of the search results because its PageRank is lower than others. PageRank math is complex, but in essence the more links that point to your page, the more authority your page is considered to have and the higher its PageRank.

Many of the links pointing to a page will stem from other websites. However, links from a site's own pages count as well. That's in part why larger sites tend to do far better in search results than smaller sites. Some refer to the latter as "the Wikipedia effect." Wikipedia is one of the most authoritative sites on the web because it has 1) an enormous number of pages, and 2) thousands of links from other sites. With this in mind, let's examine one of the most powerful SEO "secrets."

Top Ranking Isn't Enough

Attaining the highest ranking shouldn't be your primary goal. A top-ranked page that receives few clicks or fails to convert traffic into leads and sales is a site that requires major modification. Your first goal should be to create products and services that customers want to buy. Only after this core objective is accomplished should you focus on ranking high for the search terms relevant to your target market. Ranking that converts to leads or paying customers is the only sustainable strategy.

For example, let's say you own a Bikram yoga studio in Chicago. Entering the search term "yoga" into Google returns around 400 million pages, of which YogaJournal.com is typically number one. Suppose you spend thousands of dollars for your site to achieve page one status for this search term. Reality is, you may have a difficult time recouping your investment, as a Bikram yoga studio in Chicago is unlikely to be what most actually seek.

While there may be a select few who are indeed, looking for a Bikram yoga studio in Chicago, 99.999% are not. They could be searching for yoga apparel, yoga poses, a yoga studio in Tokyo, or one of millions of other possibilities and simply need to be more specific with their query. As a result, your page will receive minimal traffic regardless of its prominent position. Now suppose you narrowed your focus and searched for the term "Bikram Yoga in Chicago." This returns around one million pages, of which 105f.com is number one.

While the odds have dramatically shifted in your favor for achieving page one status (one million pages versus 400 million), major competition for traffic remains, as does the possibility that a great deal of those entering the query may still be seeking something other than what you offer. So, what to do? Identify what makes your business unique. Looking closer at your studio, you recognize that you offer classes for beginners, classes for advanced practitioners, daytime classes for moms and tots, senior classes, and a kids-only class on Saturday. Related search queries for these might include:

- Bikram yoga classes for beginners in Chicago
- Advanced Bikram yoga training in Chicago
- Daytime Bikram yoga classes for moms and tots in Chicago
- Senior citizen Bikram yoga classes in Chicago
- Saturday kids only Bikram yoga classes in Chicago

These highly targeted search terms are known as *long-tail queries*. Because they laser in on your clientele, if you attain top ranking for these phrases conversion rates will be exponentially greater. Another advantage of narrowing focus is you're likely to find it easier to achieve page one placement. In Leslie's words, "That's why the *O* in SEO stands for *optimization*." To achieve a solid return on your investment, anticipate your customer's thoughts and plan accordingly. Then, at the exact moment they're ready for your products or services, the groundwork will be in place and they'll have little difficulty finding you.

Maximizing SEO

With SEO, content absolutely rules. Creating content requires time, of course, but nothing achieves higher rankings faster. There's a direct correlation between the number of pages your site has and the amount of traffic it receives. For a Bikram yoga facility in Chicago, Leslie recommends creating pages that speak to:

- Bikram yoga poses
- Your facility
- Client stories
- Industry news
- New personal discoveries
- Answers to frequently asked questions

- Featured teachers
- The city of Chicago
- Anything and everything related to what prospective students may want to know about Bikram yoga

Driving traffic through SEO requires you to be in the publishing business. While this may not be what you had in mind when you opened shop, there's no way around it. Every time you publish a new webpage, you increase your site's authority and the chances of a web user finding your business. And if your content is engaging, that visitor may become a long-term paying customer.

Google Love

You now possess the modern-day recipe for search:

- Target search queries directly relating to your specific business.
- Create pages that provide detailed answers to popular queries.
- Include the search query for which you'd like to rank high in every page's title.
- Create attractive, engaging pages with pertinent content.
- Use links between pages to help visitors find what they need.
- Create link text that includes targeted keywords and phrases.
- More webpages on your site will result in greater authority.
- Secure inbound links from related sites to increase authority.

SEO is a very powerful tool but must be used within Google's guidelines. Google bombing and black hat tactics won't fly. In the words of Joe Cortez, one of the world's most famous boxing referees, Google is "fair, but firm."

By following Leslie's advice, you can create an effective, layered site that addresses the needs of both your customers and the search engines. While there are no guarantees for landing on page one for your desired search terms, using Leslie's proven strategies will greatly improve the chances of Google taking notice of your site. And, when they do, so will potential customers.

⏻ TAKEAWAYS

SEO Strategy

- Cultivating traffic is mandatory for online success—SEO-generated traffic is ideal.
- Well designed SEO strategies lead to higher rankings.
- Good page titles, accurate link text, and establishing PageRank are key factors for achieving top ranking.
- Search is a "conversation." Therefore, think about your prospect's queries and create pages that answer their questions.
- Short-tail queries may have a higher volume, however, they convert poorly and require high authority to attain prominent ranking.
- Long-tail queries are significantly more targeted, easier to rank well for, generate less traffic, but convert exceptionally well.

CHAPTER 16

CRACKING THE FACEBOOK CODE

I n every generation, there are game-changing advancements that redefine business. From the automobile and television, to the VCR and Internet, the evolution of technology drives our consumptive habits. Today, there are arguably fewer more engrossing, time-consuming habits than that of the world's current phenomenon, Facebook.

While more than 900 million people worldwide have active accounts, few businesses take full advantage of this enormous marketplace. For most, this is not due to a lack of desire—it stems from a lack of knowledge. Realizing massive success begins with understanding one's limitations. It is not only difficult for one person to do everything in an organization, attempting this near impossible feat ultimately equates to the undeniable kiss of death.

When industry stalwarts such as Anthony Robbins, Eben Pagan, Frank Kern, Trey Smith, and James Schramko sought to leverage Facebook's tremendous reach and recognized their limited ability for effectively making this happen, they turned to Jennifer Sheahan. A serial innovator, she is one of the most visible and sought-after social media experts in the world. Jennifer has cracked the Facebook code and created powerful strategies that are neither complex nor expensive. To affect a veritable Facebook frenzy and drive this powerful, captive audience towards your products and services, follow Jennifer's advice.

Apples And Oranges

First and foremost, create both a personal and business page. Do not make the mistake of having one Facebook presence that combines personal and business items. Taking this approach will result only in confusion. Business customers may be temporarily amused with funny pictures of your nephew, but in the long run they'll view you and your company as being out of touch with their needs and wants. And while those close to you may find your new white paper intriguing, they're not likely to be your ideal customer and may be annoyed by your business-related postings.

A personal page should be exactly that—personal—and reserved for friends and family. In other words, avoid letting everyone into your home. Doing so is not only potentially dangerous, but could also have harmful repercussions. A business page should be reserved for business—nothing more, nothing less. It should serve to enhance your brand, generate sales, and disseminate corporate information. There are three key advantages of creating a Facebook business page:

- **Inexpensive communication:** Creating a Facebook business page is free and empowers companies to speak directly to those who have expressed interest in their products and services. Most importantly, it provides a powerful, interactive forum for customers to provide, and exchange, direct feedback.
- **Unlimited reach:** Personal accounts are limited to 5,000 friends. A business page has no limitation on the number of Likes, or *fans*, it can have. There are over 150 Facebook pages with 10 million or more fans—including the most popular page, Texas Hold'em Poker, which has over 55 million.
- **Engaging content:** From video and email capture to direct contact with customers and the introduction of new products, there are many tools and options available to create customer loyalty, engagement, and interest.

Successful marketers view Facebook as a must-buy medium, and budget accordingly. The key is to implement effective ad strategies which provide the highest ROI and drive meaningful traffic to your page.

Ad Strategies

There are two main Facebook ad strategies. The first is structured for businesses that seek to expand their online presence but do not sell products online. These include companies such as Coca-Cola and Starbucks. Yes, they may offer t-shirts, mugs, coupons and special offers that can be redeemed locally, but you can't put a cup to the monitor and grab yourself a Venti Vanilla Latte or a Diet Coke. Therefore these businesses are considered *indirect sellers*.

The second strategy is structured for those who sell products and services directly to end-users online. These include companies such as TechSmith, Zynga, and University of Phoenix and are known as *direct sellers*. Regardless of company type, adhere to the new world mentality. Prior to the rise of social media, customers were too often viewed as numbers. Anything a corporation could do to shake the last few pennies from their pockets was the ultimate objective.

As direct communication, and the ability to easily share thoughts on one's experience became commonplace, the race to quarterly profits with no regard for customer satisfaction has largely dissipated. Today, developing personal, one-on-one dialogue with your tribe is absolutely essential. On Facebook, this stems from creating a compelling business page that encourages customers to hit the "Like" button. Once their approval has been granted, the floodgates open and consistent, quality interaction leads to building solid trust and value-based relationships.

Indirect Sales Strategy

Brand recognition in business is like oxygen for the body. Without it, you're toast. From slogans and logos, to advertising and PR, the world's largest companies spend billions of dollars ingraining their message, and cultivating interest in their products and services, into the minds of customers. Fortunately, social media has largely leveled the playing field for those who lack multimillion-dollar budgets. More than 44 million people have viewed Maria Aragon's rendition of Lady Gaga's, *Born This Way* on YouTube (Youtube.com/watch?v=xG0wi1m-89o); Tim O'Reilly, founder of O'Reilly Media, has more than 1.5 million Twitter followers (Twitter.com/#!/timoreilly); and, Evan Bailyn's Facebook page has over 110,000 fans (Facebook.com/EvanBailyn). If you haven't yet heard of them, you likely will soon. A huge following begets huge exposure. Through the provision of valuable or entertaining content, each has developed a significant, and loyal, following.

Successful Facebook indirect marketers understand that building and maintaining a successful company hinges on its ability to engage. Coca-Cola, for example, runs contests, encourages interaction, and offers customers the opportunity to send a "virtual pick-me-up" to friends and family. They currently have 36 million fans. Pepsi, on the other hand, introduces multiple products but fosters little interaction among customers. They currently have slightly more than 6 million fans. Considering Coca-Cola sells around *twice* as much product as Pepsi, that it garners *six* times as many fans is remarkable.

Coca-Cola clearly understands that, above all else, its Facebook presence is about the creation of an entertainment-driven experience, not the provision of a direct call-to-action. Loyalty is created when strong intangibles are delivered. In other words, what's not said ultimately creates permanence and establishes position in the customer's subconscious. When customers head to the marketplace, purchase decisions are directly tied to their brand connection. Indirect sellers view Facebook as an opportunity to strengthen such customer relationships.

This requires creating professional-looking, well-branded fan pages that properly address their key demographic and entice visitors to click the "Like" button. From 2-for-1 coupons and no-cost product downloads to gift cards and free apparel, there are many ways to provide immediate rewards for taking action. Even though a sale won't occur immediately, the creative investment will typically be rewarded many times over. Let's now shift focus from engagement to closing the deal.

Direct Sales Strategy

Although branding and community building are important regardless of business structure, a modified Facebook strategy is required for those who sell products online. Proper product positioning is essential. Effective direct sellers focus on benefits and encourage *sampling*. The harsh reality is no one cares about fancy logos or gimmicks. In the social media world, people have little patience and want to get right to the meat of the product.

Answering the customer's question of, "Why do I care?" as quickly as possible is key. Today's marketers leverage the power of video and show the product in action. This is often complimented with video testimonials. Once hooked, discounts and incentives to purchase should be provided immediately. The online customer loathes waiting for the "ask." Once they're ready, show them where to enter their credit card information.

For example, consider Dell's Facebook page. When you enter "Dell" into the Facebook search box, it takes you directly to the page shown for Dell's XPS 14z computer. The call-to-action couldn't be clearer: *Buy now*. Once clicked, the purchase process begins. This is exactly what both customers and the company want.

Drama doesn't cut it. Neither does fancy. Customers today are much too wise and have moved far beyond old methodologies. If they feel too much money was spent on building a site, they automatically equate this to increased costs. Attempts to over-impress lead to the worst sound in the world—wallets snapping shut.

Hewlett-Packard takes a slightly different approach than Dell. HP encourages you to click a "Like" button first (building community) and entices you to do so by offering "access to exclusive HP ink deals." It appears that HP is on the right path.

However, once you click "Like," you're taken to a second page requiring *another* click. A third page follows...that requires another "Like." At this point, not only have you grown tired of the process, you may opt to "Unlike" the page.

To take full advantage of Facebook, direct sellers must adhere to the rules as created by customers. More clicks means fewer conversions...and opportunities lost. While mid-six figure marketing execs may believe they're behind the wheel, 900 million users hold the keys to the ignition.

Facebook's Ad Network

Generating Facebook traffic largely stems from proper utilization of their ad network. There is no single more powerful tool for generating "Likes" and securing visitors. Billions of dollars are spent annually on the network. Similar to Google, Facebook enables businesses to target a specific demographic with their ads. The ad buyer can choose from either a PPC or CPM model.

With PPC, there's a charge each time the ad is clicked. With CPM, there's a charge for every thousand impressions the ad receives. Since millions of people who meet defined criteria access Facebook daily, you can blow your budget in short order.

Creating an ad begins with clicking the "Create An Ad" option to the right of the word Sponsored. This leads to a second page where ad construction begins. The first section is where you design your ad. With most advertising, copy is paramount to your campaign's overall success. On Facebook, copy is still important, but even more critical is the image. Facebook users have many choices and short attention spans, so you need to grab their attention.

One of the benefits of Facebook is that you can create and test an unlimited number of ads. A typical approach is to keep the same copy but vary the image and determine which version of the ad receives the best response. Jennifer suggests selecting five images relevant to your product and five amusing but not on-the-nose images. Create 10 ads, each using the same copy but a different image. You're now positioned to find out how effective each image is in garnering response.

Your next step is to select your target audience. If no criteria are selected the potential audience for your ad will be every Facebook member in the country. This will need to be refined. Facebook allows you to select location, gender, income, interests, and other criteria. To test effectiveness and hone in on your ideal client, Jennifer recommends A-B testing with a budget of less than $10 per day per ad. This allows for the creation of multiple ads to check effectiveness. In the end, the only metric that really counts is conversion. Facebook makes it possible to identify your perfect customer. Use its technology to your full advantage.

The best Facebook marketers leverage the Connections on Facebook option to the hilt. There are four distinct segments of the Facebook community:

- **Anyone:** As discussed, targeting *anyone* is a direct path to bankruptcy. You might as well make a donation to your favorite charity; at least the money will be well spent. One of my favorite charities is <u>SteveOlsherNeedsANewFerrari.com</u>. Feel free to save the time, energy, cost, and frustration of creating ads that won't work. Send me a check now and support this worthwhile cause.

- **People who have not yet "Liked" one of your pages:** Facebook lets you build multiple fan pages. For example, if you're a book writer, you can have a fan page devoted to you as an author, and also a fan page for each of your books. It's not unusual for companies to maintain several dozen distinct fan pages. Targeting those who are not current fans is a smart strategy, especially when used in conjunction with other criteria, such as 'Interests'. Ideally, you'll want to learn as much about existing fans as possible. Post interesting topics, ask for feedback, and poll them. Invest in gaining additional information about what sites they visit, magazines they read, and people they respect. Having this information will empower you to target subscribers who have similar interests. Conversion rates for those with similar profiles of existing fans will consistently outperform other marketing efforts.

- **Those who already 'Like' one of your pages:** Why spend money targeting those who have already indicated they "Like" what you have to offer? Many Facebook users "Like" hundreds of pages but seldom take the time to read posts or visit the "Liked" pages. They may even forget they clicked "Like" in the first place. Targeting existing subscribers keeps your message near the top of their attention. When new products are released, those who already "Like" what you're doing should be the first to know. Think about it this way: Would you continually mail new catalogs to customers in your database? Of course you would. Victoria's Secret does this every month (at least that's what I've heard...). Facebook works the same way. Start by preaching to the choir. They're already prepped and eager to hear your newest message.

- **Friends of those who "Like" your page.** Of the available options, this may be the most powerful. When you target friends of those who "Like" your page, they'll see your ad along with the thumbs up icon, the word "Like," and the name of the friend who "Likes" the page. Though not a direct endorsement, ads targeted to friends of those who "Like" a page appear to come well recommended. Because of this, these ads convert at a higher rate than the other options mentioned.

Your next step is to select your budget. Based on your selected criteria, Facebook will generate a suggested cost per click. Do *not* accept this amount! Guerilla marketers enter less than half of Facebook's recommended bid. Remember, Facebook is a business. Though it may seem like simply a fun place to hang out online, its main objective is to generate income...and they're damn good at it. Don't get suckered into paying retail. While your ad may be shown with less frequency, it will still receive exposure.

Finally, set the times when your ad runs. For example, if you're targeting stay-at-home moms, run the ad weekdays after they've dropped their children off at school; while if you're targeting doctors, have the ad run before they go to work and after they've had dinner. Facebook ad success is a product of detailed knowledge and consistently monitoring ads. Also keep in mind Facebook offers a 'Pause' button to stop and restart ads. Don't hesitate to use it whenever your ad isn't needed or requires adjustment.

Using Facebook For Free Market Research

Many marketers capitalize on Facebook's valuable technology without placing ads at all. They do so by:

- Beginning the process of creating an ad.
- Moving directly to the 'Targeting' option and entering the location of their target audience.
- Selecting pertinent additional criteria, such as age range, gender, and interests.
- Noting the number of subscribers who match the criteria.

Without spending a dime, they're able to determine if enough demand exists for their products and services. If the numbers are strong, it would likely make sense to move forward. If not, significant pain has easily been avoided.

A Final Facebook Thought

There's little doubt that Facebook offers immediate and powerful opportunities. That said, so did CompuServe and MySpace. The Internet is a vast, often volatile, landscape reminiscent of the Wild West, and can be just as unpredictable. Business longevity is the direct result of being proactive, maintaining awareness of the market's evolution, getting while the getting's good, and being adequately prepared for what's next.

Facebook should absolutely be a component of your overall promotional strategy, but you shouldn't depend on any one resource for your marketing. As with investing, always diversify, because there's no telling what the future will bring.

⏻ TAKEAWAYS

Cracking The Facebook Code

- Create both a personal and business page. Don't make the mistake of having one Facebook presence that combines personal and business items.
- There are three key advantages to creating a Facebook business page. Inexpensive communication, unlimited reach, and engaging content.
- Be clear on business structure. Are you a direct or indirect seller?
- Social media has helped level the playing field for those without multimillion-dollar budgets.
- Successful Facebook indirect marketers understand that building and maintaining a successful presence hinges on the ability to engage.
- Effective direct sellers focus on benefits and encourage sampling. Answer the customer's question of, "Why do I care?" as quickly as possible.
- Leverage Facebook's ad network. There is no single more powerful tool for generating "Likes" and securing visitors.
- Nail your niche, be proactive, maintain awareness of the market's evolution, and be adequately prepared for what's next.

CHAPTER 17

BLOGGING FOR DOLLARS

How cool would it be to wake up in the morning (at 10:00), make yourself a bowl of grits, and check your PayPal account to see you've made $1,000 while you slept? Next, you huddle at your computer to practice your foreign language course and, midday, grab lunch with a friend. After lunch, you head home to peruse your stock market lesson for the day, make a few trades, and head out for martial arts. By 5:00, another $450 has poured into your PayPal account. Charged up and energized, you head out for Salsa dance lessons with your significant other followed by a delicious Ethiopian dinner.

Even while you're on vacation, the money continues to arrive. Whether you're awake or asleep, at home or on the beach, passive income keeps rolling in...every single day. Never in history have so many been able to make this happen. Automated online payment processing and product distribution now makes it possible to reach millions and effortlessly sell content and services to them. The process of selling products in perpetuity without significant additional work is referred to as generating *passive income*.

> *Wikipedia defines passive income as "income received on a regular basis with little effort required to maintain it."*

If you have a typical 9 to 5 job, you go to work, spend a minimum of eight hours completing assigned tasks, and receive a paycheck on a defined schedule. The amount of money you earn is based on the hours you put in; and if you aren't receiving a huge salary, it'll be hard to accumulate savings, resulting in the common problem of living "paycheck to paycheck."

Conversely, if you craft passive income products, you perform a great deal of work upfront to create the product and then market it. Once completed however, the product can continue selling with little additional effort on your part, aside from providing customer service and occasional updates. Making money while doing virtually nothing sounds great...and it is. But it's far from easy to get to that point. To create a commercially viable product, you need to invest substantial time, energy, and resources. During the development process you aren't earning a dime from your efforts—and you might be too busy to do anything else that produces revenue.

Since product creation can take months, or even years, your savings will likely dwindle. Meanwhile, you can't know for sure whether your product will actually be successful and that all your hard work will pay off. However, if you're willing to take such risks, and have the wherewithal to create profitable products, it's well worth planting the seeds to make it happen and harvest your own online "money tree."

Pat Flynn is a huge advocate of this process. He has spent years developing his online success and his website, <u>SmartPassiveIncome.com</u>, currently ranks in the top 5,500 of all sites worldwide. Let's explore how Pat arrived at the desired destination of enjoying substantial passive income every day.

From Architect To P.I. Expert

Pat began his career with a B.A. in Architecture and a job at a well-known firm. He then decided to study for the LEED (Leadership in Energy and Environmental Design) exam, as being accredited would help him climb the corporate ladder. To help himself and his peers study, Pat created a blog where he posted test preparation materials. Within a few months he had created hundreds of pages. Though he passed the test with flying colors, several months later, he was laid off. He needed to generate income…fast.

Searching for options, he began to wonder if it would be possible to monetize his LEED blog. He first installed tracking software to discover if the site was attracting any traffic. To his astonishment, he found it was receiving thousands of visitors every day. To capitalize on the traffic, he immediately added Google AdSense ads to his blog. Within a week, he was earning $7.50 a day in passive income. And, while the $225 a month wasn't going to replace his salary, it validated his notion that the web held income opportunities.

Pat then searched for advertisers who might benefit from targeting the unique demographic attracted by his material. He quickly secured four. At $150 apiece, plus the AdSense revenue, he was suddenly making over $800 a month from passive income. With a bit of breathing room, Pat invested time into developing a commercial product. He scoured the site's content for the most pertinent LEED information and put together an easy-to-read ebook. Pat created an eye-catching cover and then posted the book for sale on his homepage. In its first month, the ebook generated $7,906.55 in sales. In its second month, it made $9,782.89. And in its third month, it pulled in $12,193.59.

Thrilled by his success, Pat chose to create more products. Noting that students are always on the go, he created an audio guide to make studying easier. Almost immediately, his sales doubled. He was now generating $25,000-$35,000 per month in passive income.

> *Pat had increased his monthly cash flow from $0 to $35,000 per month—all from a hobby-based site created to help him and his friends study.*

Was Pat lucky? To the extent that he stumbled upon a passive income opportunity, yes. But what made Pat successful wasn't dumb luck. It was his ability to quickly recognize the potential of his discovery and being willing to invest the time and energy necessary to produce quality products that directly addressed the needs of his audience. The passive income provided Pat a very comfortable lifestyle. Soon after his online venture was in full swing, he became a father and the continuing revenue allowed him to spend almost limitless time with his newborn son.

Pat became inspired to teach others how to duplicate his success. This led him to create SmartPassiveIncome.com, which is now one of the web's top resources for learning how to build a profitable online business focused on passive income. The site has more than 45,000 RSS subscribers, over 21,000 Facebook fans, and alternates with Wikipedia for the #1 position on Google for the phrase *passive income*. Further, Pat has over 55,000 Twitter followers. Let's take a detailed look at his strategies.

Blogs Versus Standalone Websites

Both Pat's LEED and Smart Passive Income sites were built as *blogs* (short for web log). One of the key differences between a blog and a standalone website is that a blog encourages user feedback and interaction, whereas a website is generally static in nature. Using free hosts such as WordPress.com or Tumblr.com, you can start a new blog in minutes, even if you lack technical savvy. According to Nielsen

Company's BlogPulse, in 2011, the web had more than 156 million blogs.

While WordPress.com is the most popular home for blogs, Pat prefers installing WordPress software from WordPress.org as the template, as he feels it provides more options and greater site-building flexibility, and hosts the site using BlueHost.com (HostGator.com and 1and1.com are additional options). Pat likes WordPress for its robust content management system that launches in one click and allows for easy site maintenance and drag-and-drop modifications. Current versions also incorporate audio, video, and audience participation widgets.

You can watch Pat's how-to video for installing WordPress and creating a blog in less than four minutes by scanning the QR code to

the left, or visiting EZ.com/4minutes. Because starting a blog is free (or nearly free if you opt to register your domain—which typically costs less than $20 a year and is a recommended course of action), there's virtually no risk in setting one up. However, you should take great care in choosing the right domain name, identifying your core message, and packing the blog with value before you officially launch it.

Selecting The Tree

Identifying your *WHAT*—that is, the one thing you were born to do—is a key component of building a formidable business. Pat's

WHAT, and his inspiration for launching SPI, is to teach others how to generate enough passive income to sustain their desired lifestyle. There are a number of resources available to help you become clear on what you're most passionate about, including my award-winning book, *Journey To You: A Step-by-Step Guide to Becoming Who You Were Born to Be*. To purchase

Journey To You, please visit <u>SteveOlsher.com</u> or scan the QR code at the bottom of the previous page.

There are many ways to describe your *WHAT*. One of my all-time favorites can be found in the 1991 movie *City Slickers*. In the film Mitch Robbins (played by Billy Crystal) takes a break from his hectic Manhattan grind to vacation at a dude ranch in the country in an effort to "find himself" and work his way out of a midlife funk. During his journey he meets Curly Washburn (played by Jack Palance), who represents everything Mitch is not: carefree, tough as nails, and—most importantly—centered.

I've seen hundreds of movies in my life, but only a handful really hit home. What stuck most in my mind from *City Slickers* was a scene that seemed oddly profound at the time, but I didn't take in its full meaning until years later. It involves Curly and Mitch, each riding horseback, conversing about life. Curly is a tough, no-nonsense old cowboy who wears a black cowboy hat, red bandanna, black riding gloves, and always has a lit cigarette hanging precariously from the corner of his mouth.

His voice sounds like it was passed down from Moses, and he talks with the confidence of a man who's seen it all. In comparison, Mitch is a small, unassuming city guy who's wearing a New York Mets baseball cap, and a shirt and khakis that might have come from L.L. Bean. The best way to describe the difference between them is this eloquent comment Curly makes to Mitch earlier in the movie: "I crap bigger than you."

In the scene that had the greatest impact on me, Curly says, "You city folk, you worry about a lot of shit."

Mitch replies, "Shit?! My wife basically told me she doesn't want me around."

Curly chuckles. "Is she a redhead?"

Mitch: "I'm just saying…"

Curly interrupts. "How old are you…38?"

Mitch: "39."

Curly: "Yeah. Y'all come here at about the same age; with the same problems. Spend about 50 weeks a year getting knots in your rope and then you think two weeks out here will untie them for you. None of you get it. Do you know what the secret of life is?"

Anxiously, Mitch says, "No, what?"

Curly smiles and holds up one finger: "This."

Looking perplexed, Mitch asks, "Your finger?"

Still holding up one finger, Curly says, "One thing…just one thing. You stick to that and everything else don't mean shit."

Mitch holds up his own finger and looks at it. "That's great. But what's the one thing?"

Curly says, "That's what you've got to figure out…" And then he rides away.

Curly calls it "one thing." I call it your *WHAT*. It doesn't matter what you call it. You just need to figure out what it is. Once you can answer the question of "What is your *WHAT*?" it's time to build your blog.

Blog Components

Thanks to the wide array of widgets, plug-ins, formats, and display options, no two blogs are identical. That said, the most popular blogs consistently offer the following:

- Extensive, fresh, topic-specific content
- Videos
- Pictures
- Interesting interviews and guest contributors
- Visitor interaction

Technorati.com offers a list of the Top 100 blogs and continually updates its rankings. The number one rated blog is frequently *The Huffington Post*. Started by Arianna Huffington in 2005, this Internet newspaper features a wide range of topics, aggregates content, and publishes articles compiled by its in-house journalists. *The Huffington Post* consistently attracts more than 50 million visitors per month and receives more than one million monthly comments on its articles. Purchased by America Online in 2011 for $315 million, the company is a stunning example of the massive profit potential available to sites that can attract a large following.

What *The Huffington Post* and other top blogs do exceptionally well are:

- Understand the needs of its audience and deliver applicable content.
- Capture the voice and personality of its owners.

TechCrunch (TechCrunch.com) delivers news of the tech world and largely reflects the voice of its founder Michael Arrington; *TMZ* (TMZ. com) delivers entertainment news and clearly reflects the personality of its creator Harvey Levin; and PerezHilton.com delivers celebrity gossip and has attained worldwide notoriety thanks to the outrageous personality of its founder Mario Armando Lavandeira, Jr. (a.k.a. Perez Hilton). Forget about blending in. When you run a blog, you want to stand out from the crowd. To become one-of-a-kind as opposed to one-of-many, get comfortable with taking a stand and having people line up on either side of you. Dr. Theodor Seuss Geisel (a.k.a. Dr. Seuss) said it best:

> *"Be who you are and say what you feel, because those who mind don't matter and those who matter don't mind."*

Once your blog is operational, meaningful content has been added, and you've begun cultivating traffic, Pat offers three powerful rules for creating momentum and generating income: find partners, sell products and/or services, and spread your wings.

Find Partners

One of the most effective strategies for building major traffic is to contact top bloggers in your niche. First, tell them you're an up-and-coming blogger who respects their work and enjoys their content. Then, add you're writing an article and would love to get quotes from industry experts like them. The vast majority will take time out of their schedule to answer your questions.

Once the article is published, send each contributor a follow-up thank you note with a link to the article. Most will post the link on their site and/or offer a link to your homepage, thereby introducing their audience to your work. This provides you with free exposure and credibility as these top bloggers are effectively endorsing your content. Few things establish brand recognition faster than endorsements from renowned peers. With significant effort and patience it is certainly possible that your blog may become so popular that other bloggers will get in touch to obtain quotes from *you*.

Offer Products And Services For Sale

Pat created high-value products that best served his LEED audience. To profit from your blog traffic, you can create products and/or services that best serve your tribe. Examples of content-based products include books, interviews (in video, audio, and/or transcript form), white papers, and research studies. Alternatively, you can become an affiliate by offering products and services created by others for sale and receive a percentage of each transaction.

A growing trend is to create a membership program. Some memberships require a one-time fee and provide access for life. Others, known as continuity programs, provide ongoing content and require subscribers to pay a monthly, quarterly, or annual fee. The membership model works great for certain industries—e.g., finance, in which many customers will gladly pay for ongoing news and analysis. It wouldn't work for Pat's LEED site, however, because once students pass the test they have no incentive to continue visiting the blog.

If you have the talent to continually create great products and high-value content, creating your own membership program is your best option since you keep 100% of the sales revenue. If you don't feel ready or able to pursue this strategy, becoming an affiliate is a proven way to earn substantial passive income as evidenced by a growing number of "super affiliates" who consistenly gross six or seven figures per year.

Spread Your Wings

One of the great things about a blog is its flexibility. For example, it's simple to update text and photos so information remains current without the need for relying on an expensive programmer to update the site. It's also easy to modify on the fly to adapt to the changing needs of your audience. You can even run A/B Split tests, in which you post two versions of the blog to determine which strategies are most effective for achieving higher conversion rates. Remember, online, no one builds monuments. Be willing to periodically play around with layout, content, and structure in order to keep attracting the largest number of potential customers for your message.

You should also consider including advertising to generate additional passive income and/or to capture your audience's contact information. Options include:

- Google AdSense (and other ad networks)
- Banner ads
- Ads for training or certification programs related to your field
- Paid guest posts
- Ads for teleseminars and webinars that compliment your offerings
- Advertorials which feature beneficial products and services
- Ads for personal and group coaching
- Ads for on- and off-site consulting
- Ads for newsletters (often free in exchange for a visitor's contact information)

Watering The Tree

While your products can perpetually generate passive income, maintaining and increasing the traffic to your blog typically requires ongoing effort. Especially when you're starting out, you should ideally post high-value content daily, or at a minimum weekly. Once you're established, new content should be added no less than every two weeks.

As with a tree that must be continually watered to flourish, building a popular site requires steady attention. While blogging creates a platform for selling products and generating passive income, there's nothing passive about maintaining the blog itself. Customer loyalty is difficult to attain and easy to lose. Always over-deliver on audience expectations.

If you model Pat's strategy, you can earn exceptional revenue from passive income. The joy of making money while you sleep is that when you're awake you'll live the type of life most others can only dream about.

 TAKEAWAYS

Blogging For Dollars

- Passive income allows you to earn money on a regular basis without significant effort to maintain cash flow. Arriving at this juncture, however, requires a meaningful investment of time, energy, and resources.
- Value-packed content focused on the needs of a sufficiently large niche is likely to result in substantial traffic.
- One advantage of blogs over standalone websites is that blogs encourage user feedback and interaction.
- To build a formidable business, you must identify your **WHAT**—that is, the one thing you were born to do.
- Don't hesitate to let your personality shine through online. You want to stand out from the crowd.
- Monetize your blog's traffic by selling your own products and/or services, or by becoming an affiliate and selling the products of others for a commission.

CHAPTER 18

PRODUCT LAUNCH LIFTOFF

You've likely heard stories of entrepreneurs who make millions and, after a handful of bad decisions, lose everything. Then after a few years they reappear on the radar, making even more money with a new company. How is it that when self-made millionaires (or billionaires) lose their fortune, they tend to recover quickly? What makes it possible for them to duplicate their previous success?

The answer is simple: The steps for creating a profitable endeavor don't change. Similar to riding a bicycle, once the skill is mastered, it becomes an integral part of you and can be called upon whenever needed. For corporate leaders, crafting a lucrative venture is not significantly different than Lance Armstrong switching his bike from Schwinn to Trek. The vehicle may change, but the mechanics remain the same. Part of what enables replication of past victories is that money follows money. Even when huge flameouts occur, those who've mastered the game have little trouble dreaming up potentially profitable ideas, finding willing partners, and tapping new sources of capital.

Investors are more than willing to buy in, because those with a track record have already developed a proven system for realizing extraordinary results. Christopher Van Buren understands the power of leveraging effective systems. Over the years he's transitioned from literary agent to entrepreneur to Internet marketer, each time implementing the same tactics for creating outstanding success. Today, Chris owns and operates LaunchMoxie, a company dedicated to helping Internet marketers construct seamless, problem-free product launches that attract attention and maximize revenue. Get ready for liftoff.

Understanding Product Launches

A product launch is defined as a "focused campaign that revolves around an online event or series of events that are designed to draw in customers." When executed correctly, a product launch can generate a massive number of leads, increase name-brand recognition, and create substantial income. For example, Brendon Burchard launched Experts Academy in 2011 and grossed over $4.6 million. Jack Canfield and Bill Gladstone were able to achieve bestseller status for their book *The Golden Motorcycle Gang* by building interest and orchestrating a coordinated purchase process.

A launch can entice customers to purchase books, DVDs, and virtually any other product or service. In fact, information that may have previously been released as traditional nonfiction books is now being packaged as online courses, video training series, audio programs, and other products of the digital age—products that fetch significantly higher prices than their paperback counterparts. Though an effective launch requires a lot of time and energy, the monetary costs can be relatively low. There are six phases for a successful product launch: product design, scripting, technology, soft launch, securing partners, and official launch.

Product Design

Regardless of whether your product is physical or a service, it must be designed to meet the following criteria:

- Appeal to the target audience.
- Answer, and solve, burning questions and problems.

- Include free and low-cost entry points to attract potential customers.
- Look professional and function as described.
- Define why it improves upon, and truly outshines, existing products.
- Over-deliver on its promises.

If you're creating an information product, you must also determine the best way to deliver it—for example, printed text, ebook, PowerPoint presentation, audio, video, interactive website, or live seminar. Your choice should be based on the preferences of your target audience. In some cases you'll want to use multiple delivery methods because different people are "wired" to absorb information in different ways—e.g., some like to read, others prefer watching DVDs, and many enjoy interacting face to face.

Another consideration is pricing. A product's price must meet both customer and affiliate expectations, and be properly positioned against competition. A price that's too low may not generate enough revenue, but a price that's too high may prevent the product from selling. A common range for online sales tends to be from $197 to $2,497.

Scripting

Scripting is far from easy and creating superlative copy is an acquired skill. Have someone on your team who understands the importance of building a compelling story that attracts attention, engages, and moves people to action. Scripting is needed for:

- Creating the overall theme
- The pre-launch narrative
- Site and email headlines
- Email subject lines
- Affiliate recruitment
- Text affiliates can use for their audiences
- Sales copy
- Video copy

- Email copy
- Site copy

Each word must be pored over, reviewed, edited, and rewritten until the look and feel is directly on point. While each phase of the launch process is crucial, nothing can extinguish the fire quicker than scripting that fails to properly capture the essence of the product. Here are a few tips for writing good copy:

- Answer the customer's question, "Why should I care about the product?"
- Focus on the product's benefits and the problem being solved.
- Touch the customer on an emotional level. This can be accomplished with humor, storytelling, and/or something provocative.

Technology

Leslie Rohde said, "The tech side of the equation has never made a launch successful, but it's damn near killed a whole bunch of 'em." Nothing is ever as hard as it looks or as easy as it seems. In the case of product launches, it's much more difficult to flawlessly execute one than meets the eye. There are myriad components that hold the launch's potential success or failure in a continuously swaying, highly delicate balance. These include:

- Choosing a provider, properly configuring servers, and hosting the content. For *Internet Prophets* we used StormOnDemand, which is LiquidWeb.com's cloud-hosting service. For video, Amazon S3 is a reliable choice.
- Obtaining and installing a secure server certificate if a hosted cart system won't be used.
- Identifying and installing a content delivery mechanism. For *Internet Prophets* we used Digital Access Pass. Other options include Kajabi and WishList Member.

- Identifying and installing a shopping cart plug-in that's compatible with the payment gateway and selected billing options.
- Identifying and installing affiliate management software. For *Internet Prophets* we used Synergyx for both a shopping cart and affiliate management software.
- Setting up at least two merchant accounts to accept and process payments compatible with billing requirements. For example, if multiple payment plan options are offered, the gateway must support recurring billing. You want to have more than one merchant account so if something goes wrong with one, your system can instantly switch to the other without losing sales.
- Selecting an email service provider to capture leads and contact information. For *Internet Prophets* we used AWeber. InfusionSoft is another option.
- Integrating the email service provider with both the shopping cart and affiliate software, as well as integrating the shopping cart with the content delivery system.
- Testing functionality of all components.

Of course, this is merely an overview, not a step-by-step guide. It should, however, provide you with a sense of just how much is involved in the product launch process. While almost no launch takes place without a few hitches, these can be kept to a minimum by enlisting others who have meaningful launch experience and can add value to your team.

Soft Launch

Before the official launch, many recommend a *soft launch* during which associates are contacted and provided with early access to the materials. The hope is they'll like what they see and subsequently introduce your product or service to their contacts. In exchange, many Internet marketers will pay the soft launch partners a much higher commission than what will be paid during the release—often 75% to 100% of proceeds. This is done for three main reasons:

- It allows for testing of the system. Far too many people simply expect things to work as they should. As Murphy has taught us, this seldom happens. Do everything possible to avoid failing to deliver at crunch time.
- Feedback, and hopefully testimonials, can be secured. Testimonials are hugely helpful in recruiting additional partners and garnering customers. When customers reach for their credit card, the last thing that should happen is hesitation. Hearing from others how they'll benefit from the product instills a sense of confidence they're making the right purchase decision in buying it.
- Metrics can be established. These provide specific detail regarding opt-in figures, conversion rates, average spend per customer, and percentage of returns. Potential partners outside of your circle will typically ask for this information to decide whether or not to participate in your launch. High conversion rates mean high commissions.

By engaging in a soft launch, you'll be able to extrapolate performance and apply real data against the expected number of recipients for the official launch. This allows you to establish a strong sense of staffing requirements, materials needed, bandwidth to allocate, and approximate amount of funds to hold back for returns.

Securing Partners

Now comes the fun part. After you have tested the launch, solicited feedback, and established metrics, it's time to assemble the troops. Successful launches require collaboration, as most companies do not have enough subscribers to reach a meaningful number of potential customers. Therefore, partners are sought to help spread the word. In partner land, there are typically four players:

- A players have a list of more than 50,000 subscribers.
- B players have a list of 25,000-49,999 subscribers.
- C players have a list of 10,000-24,999 subscribers.
- D players have a list of fewer than 10,000 subscribers.

In an ideal world, everyone and their mother would support the launch. Unfortunately, reality says this is unlikely. Therefore, a more attainable strategy should be pursued. Most product launches take place without a string of A players participating. This is not because the majority of products aren't worth supporting—quite the contrary. Most products are very good, but it is difficult to access many of the game-changers. Their calendars fill up very quickly supporting their own launches and those of people with whom they have long-standing relationships.

Realistically, one A player, several B and C players, and a solid number of D players will suffice. Many will argue that millions of touch points must be established in order to turn decent numbers, but this isn't the case. Success is certainly related to the number of people who receive your message. However, they must be the *right* people.

If, for instance, your product provides solutions for small business owners, reaching two million high school football players who are looking to increase their speed and strength makes zero sense. On the other hand, if you partner with a handful of office product suppliers who have access to 25,000 presidents and CEOs of companies with annual sales of under $25 million, conversion rates should be impressive. Avoid getting hung up strictly on numbers and reach out for those who share your vision, knowledge, and operate within a similar sphere of influence. These are the key people with whom to partner. Others can be invited to the party, but whether or not they dance is up to them.

Official Launch

The heavy lifting is complete, the product is solid, the script is compelling, the system functions correctly, metrics are in place, testimonials are in hand, and your partners await the signal...wait for it...*bam!* Open the cart. The worst-case scenario is that no one buys your product. The best case is that millions of dollars flow in, your merchant processor can't keep up, and the next thing you know you're on the beach in Hawaii sipping piña coladas.

While both scenarios are possible, your first launch will probably fall somewhere in the middle of these extremes. With experience under your belt and affiliates on board, subsequent launches will be easier to execute. The important thing to remember is you now possess the knowledge required to improve upon acquired skills.

A Typical Product Launch

Jeff Walker's *Product Launch Formula* has been used by many to generate significant sales. Others have adjusted the sequence by putting more emphasis on one aspect or another, but the original model still holds up well. The basic product launch formula consists of releasing four content-rich videos, each averaging around 20 minutes. The videos are structured as follows:

The first video, *What It Is*, is released on Day 1 of the launch. It accomplishes these five core objectives:

- Provides a general overview of the product.
- Agitates the known (or unknown) problem the potential customer faces.
- Provides examples of what life is like without the product.
- Offers valuable information that can be applied immediately.
- Introduces the viewer to the product's creator.

This is commonly known as setting the stage. The first video establishes trust and familiarity with the presenter (typically the product's creator), and entices the viewer to want to learn more.

The second video, *How It Works*, is released around Day 4. It meets these goals:

- Shows the product in action.
- Demonstrates how easy it is to use.

- Explains how it can help make the viewer's life easier.
- Goes into further depth about the product's benefits.

After seeing this, the viewer should have a solid sense of the solutions the product provides and how simple it is to use.

The third video, *Proof*, is released around Day 7. It meets these objectives:

- Introduces viewers to people just like them who have used the product. This is commonly known as *social proof.*
- Discusses how each customer's life has vastly improved as a result of using the product.
- Puts the microphone in the hands of customers so they can explain why they highly recommend the product.
- *Optional*—Provides endorsements from celebrities who have used the product and/or interact with the product's creator.

Hearing how people have successfully used the product is a powerful persuader, and it provides support for a customer's decision to purchase the product. Similarly, endorsements from public figures help legitimize the product and boost the product creator's credibility.

The fourth video, *Get It Now*, is released around Day 10. It meets these objectives:

- Introduces the concept of scarcity.
- Provides "here's how to order" instructions.

Scarcity can be very powerful, as the idea that the cart will close at a specified time, or a huge bonus will be pulled off the table, often moves people to action. Many of the biggest product launches in history were built around a limited-time offer. Then again, others were evergreen products, i.e., always available. Either course of action works. The important thing is getting people to click the 'Add to Cart' button.

Mike Koenigs is a true product launch master. In December 2011, Mike released Cross-Channel Mojo. For this launch, Mike offered a fifth video, titled *The Whole Package*. This video accomplished three things:

- It agitated the problem by providing a summary of the product, demonstrating the product's attributes, and introducing viewers to others who've used it.
- It reminded viewers of the limited opportunity to buy.
- It repeated the "here's how to order" instructions.

While not commonplace, this additional video provided one last chance to take advantage of the program before registration closed, giving Mike the opportunity to land a few last-minute sales. The product launch process has been replicated thousands of times. People continue to rely on it for one simple reason—it works. Over the course of an approximate 10-day period, word spreads, leads are generated, anticipation builds, knowledge is shared, and product is sold. While other means for introducing and releasing new products exist, few match the effectiveness of this strategy.

The Blueprint

You now have the exact blueprint needed to become an Internet marketing superstar. Whatever size company you choose to build with the plans in hand, the choice is yours. And, therein lies the beauty of a system. Once created, it can easily be replicated to create extraordinary results. Time to get to work.

⏻ TAKEAWAYS

Product Launch Liftoff

- Systems help replicate success. Once the formula has been established, leverage it time and time again to create desired results.
- A product launch is a proven way to generate a massive number of leads, increase name-brand recognition, and create substantial income.
- There are six phases to an effective product launch. Each is important to success.
- A typical product launch uses four 20-minute videos to build a compelling story arc, attract attention, engage, and move people to action.
- Your partners are the heart and soul of your launch. Make sure you build strong relationships and always consider your partners' interests at every stage of the process.
- Becoming a successful Internet marketer is difficult, but definitely achievable. Follow the footsteps of the pioneers who've made millions online.

CHAPTER 19

CREATING COMMUNITY

Learning is an ongoing activity. Unfortunately, far too many people consider their education completed when they graduate college. The wonder-filled openness experienced as children disappears, and life becomes solely about what's most comfortable and familiar. It's as if they toss away their "record" button and operate solely via their "rewind" and "play" buttons, experiencing life through a filter of preconceived notions that leave little room for profound new discoveries.

Imagine Leonardo da Vinci trying to paint the Mona Lisa over his previous classic The Last Supper; or Michael Jackson singing *Thriller* over the track for *Billie Jean*. The result of each of these attempts would be disastrous, as the intent of the artist would be lost amid the chaos of conflicting ideas. How the world would have suffered if our great creators had been unable to spawn new works of art due to their inability to move beyond what they had already produced. To realize a new vision, you must begin with a blank slate while leveraging existing knowledge.

Your life is being held captive if you deny yourself the ability to create new thoughts and ways of being. When such a repetitive condition exists, growth stops and is replaced by a constant state of complacency. The world's most successful people subscribe to the notion that education never ends. And, thanks to the Internet, huge amounts of free information on virtually every subject is accessible without needing to return to the classroom.

One of the Internet's most popular educational resources is SelfGrowth.com. Co-founded by David Riklan, SelfGrowth is described as "the Internet supersite for self improvement and personal growth." Its popularity consistently leads to its ranking within the top 10,000 of all sites. David is a huge proponent of continuing education and has devoted a significant portion of his professional life to helping others craft a powerful existence. Getting to this point, however, required traversing the road less traveled.

From Scratch

After graduating from college and landing a position with Hewlett-Packard, the company sent David to a variety of training seminars where he learned from renowned public speakers and personal development experts, such as Dale Carnegie. Fascinated by their teachings, he contemplated creating a website where like-minded individuals could gather to share and review available information on self-improvement strategies. He discussed the idea with his girlfriend, Michelle (now his wife), and both agreed they faced a meaningful opportunity. Working together to put the pieces in motion, they identified SelfHelp.com and SelfGrowth.com as viable domain name options. Upon contacting the owner of SelfHelp.com, they learned he wanted what sounded like a lot of money for the domain: $1,000. Since SelfGrowth.com was available for just $35, they chose the latter.

> *In hindsight, David wishes they had splurged for SelfHelp.com.*

Nonetheless, the site has done tremendously well. The Riklans' success demonstrates that with the right content and community, a name brand domain isn't mandatory. Today SelfGrowth.com and its three sister sites attract more than 1,200,000 monthly unique visitors and over 950,000 subscribers receive their weekly email newsletters and ezines. With visitors in over 100 countries, SelfGrowth has created a vibrant cadre of individuals and experts focused on furthering their knowledge and improving the world.

David shares his strategies for generating and monetizing significant traffic, cultivating loyalty, and establishing position as the go-to authority in a very competitive niche. Professor Riklan will now preside.

The Magnificent Seven

Category-dominating sites are difficult to create and there's little doubt why. Creating a formidable entity not only takes time, energy, and resources, but it also takes an in-depth understanding of oneself. There are seven crucial factors for success that must be mastered in order to establish front-runner position. Most would-be industry leaders find it nearly impossible to master *one* of these areas, let alone all seven. The requisite success factors—in no particular order—are:

- **Specific Area of Focus**: Identify your core interests and desired target market. In other words, what do you have innate love for and whom do you want to serve? From forensic accountants and third grade teachers to underwater welders and golf coaches, exhaustively providing relevant information and continuously adding beneficial, focused content to one specific subset of the population often equates to long-term success. This is not to say that expansion to other products and services is forever removed from the equation; however, this should only happen after market dominance has been established (think Amazon).
- **Professional Website Design:** Clearly a no-brainer, but there are so many poorly designed sites it bears repeating. Model competitive and other category-leading sites that receive significant traffic. Customers flock there for a reason.

- **Visibility to Target Market:** Where do potential customers gather and how can they be reached? One can have the best products and services in the world, but if no one knows about them, their business is irrelevant. Identifying high-return opportunities to spread the word is crucial.

- **Expert, Valuable Content:** Nothing breeds credibility and stickiness (the amount of time a visitor stays on the site) as will pertinent, well crafted content from both contributors the clientele knows and up-and-coming game changers. To establish authority, combine cutting-edge, exciting ideas and information with proven industry products and services.

- **Interactive/Social Visitor Experience:** Leading sites encourage visitors to contribute content, comment on articles and products, and share thoughts via social networks with their tribe. From Facebook and Twitter to StumbleUpon and LinkedIn, today's customers insist upon leveraging social media to disseminate positive and negative feedback while cutting the learning curve down for fellow surfers.

- **Free High-Value Products:** Like it or not, free is mandatory. To drive traffic, one must offer something of inherent value that pushes beyond articles, helpful resources, and videos. Doing so not only enables site owners to capture leads as the customer typically opts in to receive the free product, it also fulfills the unwritten obligation they have to connect with their audience in a deeper manner than simply posting relevant content.

- **Products/Services for Sale:** Without products and services to sell, the rest of the equation is moot. Even not-for-profits ask for donations. Why? Because hosting, updating, and maintaining even the simplest of sites has related expenses. Creating for-sale products and services is a necessary part of doing business.

Like spokes in a wheel, each element of *The Magnificent Seven* carries equal weight. And, while it's certainly possible to survive for an extended period of time without each being firmly in place, eventually the road will get very bumpy. Let's smooth out the ride.

Honor The Hierarchy

Category dominance takes time...a LOT of time. Therefore, the recommended manner for establishing authority is to first gain credibility within one specific aspect of the industry and then, if desired, seek to expand. Far too many look to take on the big dogs and get buried. It's virtually impossible to become the next Food.com, Cars.com, Liquor.com, or Soap.com, given their head start and significant funding. However, it is very possible to become the go-to-choice for content and community related to say, 'Mastering Dorm Food.'

On the surface, it may appear as though this focus is too narrow. Not true. According to the National Center for Education Statistics, 19.7 million students attended American colleges and universities in 2011. If just 15% of these students live in dorms, the potential audience is nearly three million. And each fall a new batch of students arrives on campus, ushering in an untapped audience.

Translation: Huge monetization opportunities await and a massive, captive audience exists. Would MasteringDormFood.com appeal to every person on the planet? Certainly not; but it doesn't need to. A site or product that attempts to serve too broad a market serves no one particularly well. This is a common and critical error.

> *Although it may seem counterintuitive, the more narrow your focus, the wider a net you can cast.*

MasteringDormFood.com has tremendous potential. From credit cards and bicycles to pizzerias and clothiers, countless companies would love to reach this highly-targeted audience and will pay above-average CPMs to do so. Focus and creativity begets opt-ins, traffic, and sales. Think about it for a moment. Would college students opt-in for a 30-

page guide titled *Free Crock Pot Recipes*? Of course they would. And would Campbell's pay tens of thousands of dollars to feature their soups as the base ingredient? You bet.

Would these same students be interested in a monthly e-newsletter that offers easy dorm room exercises, articles such as "Best Cafeteria Foods to Eat to Lose 10 Pounds in 10 Weeks," and videos that introduce relevant content such as "Gourmet Cooking on the Cheap?" Absolutely. And, would Kroger, Bally's, and The Food Network have an interest in advertising in this newsletter? Without a doubt.

SelfGrowth.com began with this strategy: Dominate one niche—personal development—before expanding. After generating substantial traffic and income in this area, only then did the owners begin exploring expansion possibilities. They identified seven core topics of interest: Success Skills, Relationships, Health, Finances, Mental Health, Spirituality, and Lifestyle, and then began featuring synergistic content.

Digging deeper empowered them to better serve their audience and avoid losing traffic to competitors. For instance, under Health, various topics include: Aerobics, Stretching, Yoga, Dieting and Weight Loss, Martial Arts, Pilates, and Reiki.

Each sub-section offers a plethora of information, resources, and products and services for sale. Perhaps most interesting, each can operate as an autonomous business unit. This allows SelfGrowth to uphold their desired image while establishing a rev-share structure with independent contractors who are responsible for content creation and community development. After significant time and effort are expended, a robust, search engine friendly site that ranks at the top of its industry can absolutely be created. The key is to follow the formula: traffic first and then contemplate expansion.

As with attempting to cash a carbon copy of a certified check, this order is non-negotiable. Honor the hierarchy and future fortune is a distinct possibility.

Provide Expert Content

There's no faster way to establish credibility than to solicit content from experts in their respective fields. SelfGrowth has done a yeoman's job leveraging this concept. Their homepage highlights the massive number of articles, experts, websites, products, events, and videos available. With rare exception, others contributed ALL of this content.

This model clearly supports the creation of a tight-knit community and encourages participation that rewards contributors, visitors, and SelfGrowth alike. Contributors are viewed as experts in their respective industry; visitors can access massive amounts of free information; and SelfGrowth is viewed as the go-to conduit that makes it all possible. Getting to this point, while challenging, is not impossible...nor is cultivating content. In today's competitive marketplace, nearly every expert wants additional exposure and few will turn down the opportunity to secure leads or put their name in front of potential customers.

Like any startup, SelfGrowth's initial traffic was minimal. Nevertheless, because it provided free publicity for experts who contributed articles and high-value material, most felt there was nothing to lose and everything to gain by supporting their endeavor. Worst case, the experts would establish additional "authority" both via search engines and customers. Best case, visitors like what they have to say, buy one of their products, visit their site, and/or attend one of their live events.

> *When experts promote other experts, credibility flows both ways.*

SelfGrowth offers "As Featured On" badges that contributors can post on their site as well as reciprocal links. This helps to differentiate one expert from another, and mutually boosts traffic while SelfGrowth reaps the benefit of publicizing its family of contributors. Most experts have a bounty of articles, videos, and how-to-guides they're willing to share. One simply needs to ask for them. Continuously receiving updated content, however, is not easy.

As with other media, the customer wants fresh, state-of-the-art material. *The Simpsons* hasn't stayed popular for over 20 years by playing the same episode week after week. To remain relevant, contributors must be encouraged to post new information on a consistent basis.

Generating Traffic

Without community, there is no traffic. Without traffic, monetization is irrelevant. Without cash flow, so is your business. It's a dangerous chicken and egg game of needing cash to generate traffic and traffic to generate cash. Traffic is typically generated in one of three ways:

- **Your Website:** Each month, a defined number of visitors descend upon a site and stay there for a specific period of time. In the next section, we'll discuss how this traffic translates to income.
- **Email/E-Newsletters:** Like magazines and newspapers, subscribers equate to dollars. Many of the world's most well known people have databases that exceed several million subscribers and e-newsletters that reach just us many. As discussed previously, the fastest way to quickly increase subscribers is to offer free products and services. Everyone likes a bargain. Internet marketers love names and emails.
- **Social Media:** Facebook, Twitter, LinkedIn, and other social media provide a powerful platform for cultivating community, followers, and interaction. Needless to say, the larger one's numbers, the greater the potential for creating meaningful revenue.

SelfGrowth vigorously pursues all three means for generating traffic and has developed a replicable model for producing substantial income once eyeballs and fingertips are in place. What follows are the six key components for converting visitors to cash flow.

1. Banner Ads

Because SelfGrowth offers a targeted audience of known self-improvement enthusiasts, companies with personal development or related products are able to access a captive group of potential customers in a cost-effective manner. This is primarily accomplished through the placement of banner advertisements throughout the site.

The company allows marketers to target specific subsets of their clientele and charge according to traffic received. For instance, an exclusive advertising opportunity to reach people with a demonstrated interest in *goal setting* may cost X over a 30-day period, while an ad targeting those seeking information on *stress management* may cost $2X$ or more. Effective marketers seek to target one person who has a defined interest in their genre versus 100 that might. And, while the cost to reach them may be higher than traditional advertising, the conversion rates will be far superior.

To set pricing, review competitor's rate cards and test the waters. Both provide a solid indication of price elasticity. SelfGrowth prices its ads based on demand and aims to sell available inventory 60 days in advance. If successful, pricing for the next 60-day period increases. If sales are slow, specials are offered to fill remaining slots. This ability to retain flexibility while maintaining focus on organizational objectives has empowered the company to easily adapt to changing economic times and customer needs.

2. AdWords

Through their increasingly popular Google AdWords program, sites with consistent traffic profit from displaying ads from the Google ad network and receive payment for each click generated. Google's ad network appears on millions of sites, including SelfGrowth. Their algorithm seeks keywords on the page where Google's ads are featured and displays related advertisements most likely to be of interest to viewers. For example, <u>PersonalHomeLoanMortgages.com</u> features ads that speak to interest rates, lenders, home equity loan information, and obtaining one's credit score.

This is a *serious* business. Many companies do nothing more than create a simple WordPress site, add loads of relevant content, and feature

Google AdWords throughout. Millions of dollars are made every day and some sites generate upwards of $100,000 monthly solely from Google AdWords revenue. SelfGrowth effectively incorporates both banner ads and Google AdWords into its revenue mix.

3. Newsletters

SelfGrowth offers a wide range of weekly and bi-weekly newsletters. From Personal Development and Business to Natural Health and Self-Improvement for Entrepreneurs, the company does an effective job of consistently delivering information their clientele seeks. Within each newsletter, advertising is interspersed with useful content. Advertisers pay for exclusive placement and costs vary based on the respective newsletter's circulation. Given the number of publications sent on an annual basis, revenue adds up quickly.

4. Affiliate Marketing

Promoting products and services from other companies and receiving a percentage of each sale is a huge component of SelfGrowth's annual income. Given their massive database and traffic, they are in the enviable position of having established a proven know, like, and trust factor with their audience and can easily introduce new opportunities to their customers.

From books and ebooks to audio courses and personal coaching, a wide array of third-party offerings exists. Commissions paid vary from 5%-10% for high-value, high-cost for delivery products, such as physical books, to 50% or more for easily distributed products, such as an online course. Generating income begins with identifying niche products in your marketplace, vetting them to confirm value, and creating email blasts or promotional site copy to offer the products or services for sale. SelfGrowth consistently sells goods from Brian Tracy, Joe Vitale, Jack Canfield, and many others.

To profit with affiliate marketing, stay on top of trends and offer timely products that fulfill immediate needs. As your audience builds, so will the number of buyers and, subsequently, your bank account balance.

5. Products And Services

As SelfGrowth's popularity exploded, so did requests for products that teach businesses how to emulate their success and individuals how to improve their life. One of their best-selling products is an ebook written by David titled *Self Improvement: The Top 101 Experts Who Help Us Improve Our Lives.* The ebook features interviews with many of the world's most successful people including Tony Robbins, Marianne Williamson, Zig Ziglar, Les Brown, and others who reveal their "inside secrets for becoming successful." After a large, multi-media promotion, more than $100,000 of ebooks was sold in less than 24 hours.

Other products created by the SelfGrowth team include courses on list building, attaining high search-engine rankings, creating ebooks, and dozens of other topics. Given their massive platform and ability to produce value-add products, their in-house creations have grown to become a large source of income for the organization.

6. Coaching

Reading and attempting to implement what's learned is sufficient for some. For others, more guidance is needed. As SelfGrowth established category dominance and released high-value, educational products, a number of people began asking for one-on-one assistance to bring the lessons to fruition. While a structure had not yet been developed, David created one. Within short order, personal coaching became a lucrative component of the income mix. Though unforeseen at the beginning of the journey, the market often presents opportunity even the blind can see.

Like an Indian buffet, it is better to offer far too much than not enough. Attempting to guess what potential partners want is senseless. By providing myriad ways to work together, they'll make it very clear what they're actually willing to pay for.

Riklan's Triangle

After 15+ years, he has witnessed both massive online business success and incredible failure. Based on his experience, he encourages implementing three proven tenets for moving powerfully forward.

- ## Avoid The Shiny New Toy Syndrome

Most entrepreneurs begin with an idea and work hard for a limited period of time to turn their dreams into reality. However, as soon as a new idea comes along, they bury their original plan and lose focus on their initial objective. This cycle of leaving half-eaten plates of food continues ad nauseam. Unfortunately, this way of being never creates wealth and only serves to leave one hungry. To join the 1%, you must fully develop your ideas.

- ## Make Technology Your Friend

Technology can be complicated, but it's essential to learn and leverage available tools. Customers expect you to use the latest technology to serve them. Using outdated tools is as foolish as releasing new music on an 8-track.

- ## Model Successful People

The formula for success is consistent and people in every city, state, and country have broken the code. While some have lucked into it, others have worked for decades to reach the pinnacle. Regardless of their path, model their actions. The learning curve has been shortened and there's absolutely no shame in following their lead. Emulating those you admire requires reaching out, destroying perceived limitations, and creating a supportive environment of like-minded people who share your desired standards. This is the way leaders are created.

In the end, David named his company SelfGrowth because he understands that if you're not growing, you're dying. Plant the seed, water it daily, and allow it to evolve. Everything else will happen organically.

⏻ TAKEAWAYS

Creating A Niche Community

- Smash the 'Rewind' button. Life is significantly more interesting when you hit 'Record.'
- The "perfect domain" doesn't exist. A powerful brand can be built regardless of the domain name selected.
- Leverage *The Magnificent Seven*. To establish front-runner position, master the seven crucial success factors.
- Honor the hierarchy. Traffic first and then contemplate expansion.
- Ask experts to share their content. Most have a bounty of articles, videos, and how-to-guides they're willing to provide.
- Understand traffic-building strategies. Once traffic is in place, monetization is inevitable.
- Know the three powerful mindsets for creating success in life and business.

1
0
1
1
0
0
0
0
0
0
1
0
1
0
1
1
1
0
1
0
1
0
0
1
1
0
0
0

PART IV

STRENGTH IN NUMBERS

CHAPTER 20

NETWORKING NIRVANA

etworking is one of the most essential business building skills. Who you know can end up being much more helpful than what you know. If you establish a strong network, the answers and resources you need are only an email or phone call away. Need venture capital? Someone in your network might be of help. Looking for a Twitter rock star? Sound the horn. The bigger your Rolodex, the more doors you can open.

Dean DeLisle is a networking guru. He's embraced the Internet since BBS (Bulletin Board System) groups were the cool place to be. After 20 years online, his company Forward Progress has a following of over 50,000 professionals in more than 35 countries, including many who have attended his coaching and training programs. Dean understands how to leverage the power of the Internet while keeping two goals in mind:

- Inexpensively secure as many leads as possible.
- Convert leads into sales.

While these are both common sense goals, they elude most businesspeople. Some easily secure leads, yet fail to convert. Others are great at conversion, but lack enough traffic to make significant money. Dean successfully addresses both objectives through power networking. His medium of choice: LinkedIn.

According to LinkedIn, the company was founded in 2003, and "Connects the world's professionals in virtually every industry to make them more productive and successful. With more than 120 million members worldwide, including executives from every Fortune 500 company, LinkedIn is the world's largest professional network on the Internet." Although LinkedIn provides a phenomenal platform, few consistently leverage its extensive reach and are able to realize the full potential of this massive professional social network. Then there's Dean DeLisle. In this chapter, we'll review his core strategies that will benefit both the LinkedIn novice and those with significant experience. But, first, a brief look at Dean's journey.

From Merrill Lynch To Forward Progress

Dean began working for Merrill Lynch in 1981. Long before the Internet became popular, he was globally conversing on the company's Intranet, building comprehensive systems and procedures via mainframe computers. Inquisitive by nature, he attended classes at IBM and began conducting his own technology-based research. He was fascinated with technology's continual evolution and wanted to stay ahead of the curve. While at Merrill he began to contract with other companies to write programs which allowed people to better communicate via the existing Intranet platforms.

After a productive stint at Merrill, he formed his own company, focusing on mainframe computing and programming. This was during the time personal computers were first released to the public. Like any new technology, only those with deep pockets could afford to take full advantage of the forthcoming shift. First-generation computers cost in excess of $10,000. This translated to minimal penetration. Larger companies, however, jumped at the opportunity to streamline operations and required experienced computer consultants. Dean chose to focus on the accounting market as they required complex programs to support their business, and costs for the appropriate hardware and software often exceeded $30,000.

In those early days, programs such as QuickBooks and Peachtree didn't exist, so personalized software had to be created for each company. As an experienced programmer, Dean was able to deliver and within short order, he sat at the helm of a $5 million company. His clients included Sears, BlueCross/BlueShield, and other Fortune 500 stalwarts. By 1999, his company was valued at over $100 million. Unfortunately, the dot com implosion eroded valuations across the board and Dean was forced to restructure his business.

Ever open to opportunity, by late 2001, Dean created one of the first online universities in response to the decline in travel due to 9/11. Companies that regularly sent employees cross-country for training sought new alternatives to save money, time, and address travel-related fears. Technology, though, had not yet caught up to Dean's vision. Broadband limitations often caused a significant delay between the teacher's voice and the student's ear. This tended to make learning more distracting than convenient. Over time, however, the university was able to identify teachers who could handle this delay and it began to flourish. It was during this period that Dean began to recognize the power of networking.

Leveraging LinkedIn

If you want to take your business to the next level, you need to begin making powerful connections. These connections will ultimately provide massive business opportunities. LinkedIn is one such tool you can leverage to accomplish this objective. One of the largest social networks, LinkedIn has more than 200 million active users and is a virtual 'meet and greet' breeding ground. To optimize your LinkedIn experience, begin with these fundamental steps:

- **Create a consistent profile that actively works for you.** Most LinkedIn profiles fail to create business and networking opportunities. You want a strong profile that works to your benefit. A key to making this happen is consistency. Your LinkedIn details should mirror those of your other social media accounts and your marketing materials. For example, if your Facebook page says you're a real estate investor but your LinkedIn profile says you're looking for a job as an office manager, prospective employers and networking allies are likely to notice the discrepancy.

- **Create a strong headline.** People steer away from boastfulness and are attracted to those who can help them. Your headline should therefore emphasize your skills rather than your job title. For example, Dean is CEO of his company Forward Progress, but his headline simply says, "Author and Speaker." As a result, Dean is frequently contacted about speaking and writing opportunities.

- **Complete the entire LinkedIn profile.** You don't need to write a dissertation for each section, but do fill in all the blanks, ranging from work experience to personal details. This includes posting your photo. People want to work with someone they trust. Including a warm, inviting face enables visitors to connect your name to a real person. And while it may be cute to show how you looked when you were 10, it's not a helpful representation of who you are now. Unlike Facebook and other social media sites, LinkedIn is a business network. Save the shtick for the other platforms.

- **Create both a personal and business LinkedIn profile.** Your personal profile should tell the story of who you are, what your interests are, and why others should connect with you. Your business profile should focus on your professional skills and/or the capabilities of your company. Keep these profiles distinct, and connect them with links to each other. This allows visitors to read about your business without being distracted by personal information, and vice versa, while giving them the option of learning more about you.

As one of the world's leading LinkedIn authorities, Dean has spent years developing proven strategies for maximizing its platform. To follow are Dean's five best practices for high-powered LinkedIn networking.

The 20-Minute Rule

Many people avoid LinkedIn because they can't bear the thought of spending hours upon hours adding connections, sending emails, and updating profiles. Dean recommends investing just 20 minutes each workday to effectively cultivate meaningful relationships on LinkedIn. By limiting your participation to 20 minutes, you can set specific daily and weekly goals while avoiding social media overload.

After Meeting Someone, Connect Via LinkedIn

Most people fail to do this. Whether it's at a networking event, social gathering, or online forum, connections made should become connections kept. Ask for permission to connect via LinkedIn and then send an invitation. Most initial conversations simply scratch the surface as to what someone does or how you may be able to help one another.

By connecting, you'll gain immediate access to the person's work and personal experience, allowing you to further develop the relationship as you learn more about the person's capabilities and business. One of the best ads ever, stated, "The difference between a friend and a stranger is a conversation." Begin enough conversations and you'll end up with a lot of quality friends and referrals.

Ask For Introductions

It's often been said that you're just six connections away from anyone in the world. On LinkedIn, this number is substantially reduced. One of the most powerful aspects of LinkedIn is the ability to easily connect with others. People you'd like to speak with are often no more than one or two connections away. Ask your connections for an introduction by choosing the "Get introduced through a connection" option when viewing the desired contact's profile. Alternatively, upgrade your account to send the person a direct InMail. With enough perseverance, it is possible to connect to anyone.

Always Look For Potential Interactions

When you log into LinkedIn, scan your homepage. This provides instant updates on your network of connections. Post a substantive status update; or 'Comment' or 'Share' regarding what your connections are talking about. Your words will become visible to both your network and theirs. Add value to a conversation by posting interesting content from which you feel others would benefit. To be successful on LinkedIn, you must interact.

Providing helpful tips or other valuable information can lead to several thousand people seeing your message. Even if just one person contacts you from your post and you're able to convert that connection into a customer, you've come out ahead. What are the odds that one in several thousand people might need your expertise or product? It's probably less than 1%. However, because the exposure is *free*, other than a bit of time invested, your return is incalculable and costs you ***nothing***. Conversely, what are the odds of no one finding you if you don't get in the game? 100%. What does that cost you? ***Everything.*** Which scenario do you prefer?

Join And/Or Form Groups

Among LinkedIn's most powerful networking opportunities are its groups. The service has over one million groups, and the most popular groups have hundreds of thousands of members. Groups can be private or public, and are moderated by the group's owner. You must be a member of the group to post messages and interact.

Groups run the gamut from Sewing to Technology to University Alumni, with the largest groups focusing on employment-related topics. No matter what you're looking for, you'll find a group that caters to your area of interest. Consider joining as many groups as possible (you can join up to 50), as long as they're related to your business or personal interests. Doing so will allow you to connect with like-minded individuals and share ideas, make friends, cultivate new business, and build your brand.

Guaranteed LinkedIn Success

In summary, these are the ways to achieve success on LinkedIn:

- **Build and Consistently Monitor Your Profile:** Your profile isn't a "one-and-done" deal. It needs to be continually updated. When your business evolves, update your profile. Land a new job? Update your profile. Receive an award or close a huge deal? Update your profile. Keep your profile current to reflect your current skills and accomplishments.

- **Keep Adding New and Meaningful Connections:** Look for people who add value to your network and/or may become customers (e.g., who you may be able to help professionally). Always choose quality over quantity. Even if you just add one or two connections a week, this will keep your profile active and maintain position on the LinkedIn radar.

- **Be Interactive:** Regularly scan your homepage looking for interesting content. Comment on or Share what others are posting. And post your own content that adds value for others.

- **Ask for Introductions:** LinkedIn is designed to help you access the people you'd like to meet. Take advantage of its inherent structure to make powerful connections.

- **Twenty Minutes a Day:** That's all it takes. Proactively use LinkedIn for just 20 minutes each workday. Your investment of time is likely to pay off.

LinkedIn must be viewed in a different light than other social media. It is an incredible platform for building your business and connecting with potential customers, partners, allies, and/or investors. Crossing the "magic" 500 connections threshold and sharing useless trivia and irrelevant content is not the goal. Establishing mutually beneficial relationships is.

Ultimately, your net worth is directly correlated to your net—work. What's in your wallet?

 TAKEAWAYS

Networking Nirvana

- Success requires a far-reaching vision. Understand where the market is headed and prepare for what's next.
- Listen to the experts. This is not condoning becoming a follower. However, if the majority of people around you are stating the same thing, take it seriously.
- Surround yourself with intelligent people you trust and use their knowledge to elevate your business to the next level.
- Leverage the power of LinkedIn. Post a professional, friendly photo, and keep your profile updated.
- Scan your LinkedIn homepage and participate. This will help keep you on the radar.
- Post helpful tips and other information. Add value and your message will spread.
- Spend 20 minutes each workday on LinkedIn. No more, no less. LinkedIn should be one of a multitude of business tools in your arsenal.

CHAPTER 21

ALLIANCE SECRETS

In 1986, a second-year NBA player named Michael Jeffrey Jordan scored 63 points for the Chicago Bulls in Game 2 of their playoff series against the Boston Celtics. The remarkable performance still stands as a league playoff record. At the end of the 2nd overtime period, the scoreboard read 135-131...in favor of the Celtics. Two games later, the Bulls were eliminated from the playoffs. In 1987, the Bulls once again met the Celtics in the playoffs and realized the same fate. They were swept 3-0 in a best of five series.

By 1988, Jordan had established himself as the game's most dominant player. Yet, the Detroit Pistons knocked the team out of the playoffs in three consecutive years. In 1991, under the guidance of third-year coach Phil Jackson, Jordan, Scottie Pippen, Horace Grant, Bill Cartwright and John Paxson gelled as a formidable team and led the Bulls to their first of three straight NBA titles. Jordan cried as he held the Larry O'Brien Trophy. Moral of the story: No matter how talented someone might be, it is impossible for any single person to outperform a finely tuned, highly focused group of individuals committed to achieving a unified goal.

> *Even in his prime, Bruce Lee couldn't defeat 25 hungry teenagers if he was holding the world's last loaf of bread.*

As Jordan learned, while individual accomplishments are appreciated, such accolades pale in comparison to leveraging individual strengths and coalescing as a team for the betterment of the common good. Success in business requires a similar approach. Profitable, growth-oriented companies continually reinforce and display the organization's current objectives while fostering a supportive environment that rewards collaboration. Creating and maintaining beneficial internal and external connections is paramount to establishing corporate longevity.

Janet Bray Attwood understands the power that exudes from assembling like-minded people for the attainment of a singular purpose. Over the years, and as a Founding Member of the Transformational Leadership Council, she's developed powerful, close relationships with many of he world's most influential people including Jack Canfield (*Chicken Soup for the Soul*), John Gray (*Men Are From Mars, Women Are From Venus*), myriad spiritual leaders, and has shared the stage with Sir Richard Branson, His Holiness The Dalai Lama, and Steven Covey.

By leveraging these, and countless other relationships, she's developed a burgeoning career. An in-demand media guest, workshop facilitator, teacher, and co-author of *The New York Times* bestselling book *The Passion Test: The Effortless Path to Discovering Your Life Purpose*, Janet has been recognized by the President of the United States for her efforts, and established herself as an expert connector and relationship builder. Strong relationships equate to measurable, sustainable returns. Establishing powerful relationship muscles, however, requires knowing the exact exercises to perform. Thankfully, we're about to learn from one of the best.

Relationship Building Secrets

Rhonda Byrne. Does the name ring a bell? It should—she's the creator of the mega-selling book and DVD *The Secret*. Long before *The Secret* was released, Rhonda faced a huge dilemma. She had a game-changing idea for established experts to share their thoughts on The Law of Attraction and envisioned traveling the world to interview them. And, while she unequivocally believed the final product could positively affect millions of lives, there were three problems:

- She had little credibility in the personal development space.
- She was unclear as to whom the right experts were to interview on the subject.
- She had no idea how to access the experts once identified.

Someone she knew, however, could help with two key aspects of the equation: Janet Bray Attwood. Rhonda was a member of Janet's program, Alliance Secrets. The course focused on developing long-term relationships and building powerful alliances. Over many years, Janet had practiced the concepts taught and built a substantial list of influential contacts. Rhonda leveraged *The Secret* to contact Janet and her partner Chris. In Janet's words, "It was her enthusiasm and heart that convinced me. While I liked the idea, I loved Rhonda. I was fully committed to helping her bring everything to fruition."

In short order, a who's who of thought leaders was on-board including Lisa Nichols, John Assaraf, Marci Shimoff, Michael Bernard Beckwith, and many others. Janet and Chris introduced Rhonda to 70% of the experts featured in the film. Since its release, *The Secret* has done phenomenally well. The movie has sold more than two million copies and the book maintained position on *The New York Times* bestseller list for 146 consecutive weeks. It has been translated into 44 languages and over 21 million copies are currently in print. Perhaps more importantly, its teachings and message of inspiration has reached hundreds of millions across the globe.

Like Michael Jordan, Rhonda would have faced tremendous difficulty succeeding alone. By partnering with others who added exceptional value, the results were exponential in scope. She not only transformed her life, she also provided significant benefit to those who received her message and helped propel the other participants to the forefront of the self-improvement world. By leveraging her previous experience and that of her partners, everyone was lifted to heights they may not have been able to attain on their own in an expedited time frame. It is this combination of selflessness and camaraderie that inevitably results in the creation of a win-win-win scenario.

Joint Ventures Versus Alliances

As Janet shared, far too frequently, Internet marketers view business relationships as limited-scope joint ventures. Often, product A is promoted by company B and a joint venture is formed for immediate, mutual benefit. After the promotion, each moves in a divergent direction and, likely, do not work together again. This approach is shortsighted at best and results in tremendous effort being limited to a one-time gain.

As an analogy, consider residential real estate developers. There are typically two types: apartment investors and condominium developers. Tremendous work is allocated for the creation of both for rent, and for sale, units. The condominium developer seeks an immediate return. The apartment investor seeks long-term dividends. Both have nails hammered into walls. The condo developer is paid once for the nail when the unit is sold. An apartment investor is paid for the nail over and over as they receive monthly rent for decades. Joint ventures can be thought of as condominiums, and alliances as apartments. Joint ventures represent the antithesis of forging long-term alliances that create high-value interpersonal relationships.

While potentially lucrative, joint ventures are the equivalent of a one-night stand.

Alliances are inherently cyclical in nature and each party seeks to provide benefit to the other. Therefore, as one party succeeds, both are rewarded. Janet chooses to conduct business only with those she feels so much resonance with she considers them to be friends as well as business partners. This approach has propelled her company from its embryonic stages to *The Passion Test* having 900 facilitators in 28 countries. The opportunity exists to not only make a ton of money, but to also have fun along the way. By surrounding yourself with those who dare to soar and encourage you to do the same, the possibilities for reaching astronomical heights are vastly improved.

Know Yourself

Developing and maintaining strong alliances requires understanding the art and science behind the magic. The first step is to *know yourself*. Grant yourself time and permission to understand who you are. Devote focused, quiet time to identifying your *WHAT*—that is, the one thing you were born to do. It's a good idea to set aside a part of each day to focus on what makes you tick.

Some people find meditation or yoga to be effective in starting inner dialogues. Others may prefer a quiet walk in a park, or time spent in a place of worship. Still others engage in the daily use of a Vision Board to focus on their *WHAT*. Whatever is the right approach for you, begin scheduling time to do it. If you've never tried this before, you'll soon realize that taking time out to listen to your inner self is one of the most valuable and satisfying activities to undertake.

> *This may require letting go of denial and recognizing that your life scarcely reflects your core identity.*

You may have even convinced yourself you're a whole other person. Is the true you buried beneath the emotional rubble of the past? If so, it's time to dig deep and rescue the real you. Explore why you've chosen to deny yourself and everyone else your innate gifts and then do everything you can to become who you were born to be. For others, you may need to vigorously explore your past. Think about it. When you were a toddler, you explored the world with unabashed curiosity. If you saw something that was of interest, you would be immediately drawn to it and pursue it unreservedly, without any worry about looking silly or what others thought.

Then you started being told "no." This was usually for your own good; such as the time you thought the oven was a TV. Still, you learned to avoid hearing "no," and that resulted in your taking fewer chances and only pursuing activities you were confident would garner approval. At some critical point, this may have led you astray from your true self and natural calling. If you believe this happened, think back and identify the point in your life when you took the wrong fork in the road and then reclaim your proper path. Give yourself a second chance to discover and live your passion.

In order to form powerful alliances, you must know who you are. The reason is simple: an alliance is predicated upon providing value to others. If you're unclear about what you have to offer, providing meaningful value will be met with consistent incongruities. The successful know exactly who they are and how they can best serve the world.

Identify Perfect Partners

Before seeking to form alliances, understand who are the most likely beneficiaries of your knowledge and identify partners who can provide access to those who fit your desired profile. Sadly, many business owners are unable to clearly define their client base. Get clear. Consider the following. Someone drops the yellow pages on your desk and asks you to call your ideal customer. Without specifics, you may as well start on page one and start dialing for dollars. Needless to say, conversion rates will be virtually non-existent.

However, if you've identified your typical customer to be female, between the ages of 35 and 54, lives in Manhattan, is a divorce attorney, and earns between $100k and $250k annually, you'll know exactly who to call and can begin identifying partners who serve this market. Assuming your product is solid, conversion rates will be off the chart. Odds are good there may be only three or four *perfect partners* to reach this demo. Yet, this small number of partners could have a monumental impact on your ability to monetize your specific expertise.

Ideally, the more you choose to live like a sniper and takes aim for the center of the bull's eye, the more success you'll realize. A shotgun approach whereby you opt to concentrate solely on reaching the masses with little regard for synergy is an effort in futility. Touch points may be impressive, however, sales will not. The successful focus on forging alliances with *perfect partners* and bring tangible value to the relationship. When you're clear about who constitutes your *perfect partner*, you'll know where to find them and immediately recognize them when they show up and avoid wasting time pursuing partners who do not align with your criteria.

Nurture Alliances

Like marriage, creating long-term mutually beneficial alliances takes work—a lot of work. The time and effort required for this to happen represents the single biggest difference between a joint venture and an alliance. Many of the world's leading experts gather twice annually at the Transformational Leadership Council Summit. Venues for the event vary from California and Arizona to Bermuda and Puerto Rico. Huge deals are structured, with many being solidified poolside or over dinner. Fact is, most people greatly prefer to transact business with those they know and like. The successful often reject proposals where there is a lack of alignment on core business practices or moral differences. Life is too short to compromise.

A vital component for achieving success is to establish a Circle of Four that not only encourages you to reach your full potential, but also accurately reflects who you want to become. Your Circle of Four is made up of the four people you consider cornerstones. It includes both those you admire—such as a

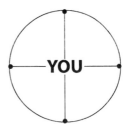

mentor whom you seldom see but have access to—and those dearest to you, such as your best friend or closest family member.

The sum of these four people directly reflects your life. For example, the median net worth of your Circle of Four is likely to be very close to yours. If two in your Circle are broke and two have just enough to scrape by, odds are good you're concerned about where your next meal is coming from. Conversely, if your Circle of Four includes three people who are living their *WHAT* and one who is on an amazing trajectory, it's likely you want to continually evolve and are consistently working to attain your objectives.

Be wary of those whose goals do not closely mirror or exceed yours. While it may be comfortable to surround yourself with familiar faces, they must emphatically support your mission or their weight is going to drag you down. Take a few moments to review your current Circle. Be honest about what you see. To flourish, you need accountability partners who both inspire and encourage you. Be conscious of the power your Circle holds. With the right people in your Circle, anything can happen. With the wrong people, little to nothing is more likely. Choose wisely.

Serve Before Being Served

The successful first seek to understand and then be understood. This is the polar opposite of how most choose to operate. A core strategy for serving first is to gather ample information to assess how immediate benefit can be provided to one's partner. Janet describes this process as identifying your partner's "critical need." Once their objectives are understood, value-added services can be implemented. Oftentimes, this happens without having to coming out of pocket. For instance, you can:

- Email your contacts about their work (newsletters, solo mailings, special offers).
- Interview your partner (phone, online, in-person) and share their wisdom.
- Invite them to be a guest at a live event.
- Use social media to spread their message.
- Introduce them to others (affiliates, media, like-minded people).

- Bundle their products with yours.
- Include links to their website from yours.
- Publish their article on your blog.
- Review their products and post your thoughts.

What's most interesting about providing service first is that, often, as you help others solve their most pressing issue you concurrently solve your own critical need. By helping first, you'll likely discover you don't have to ask others for assistance. If you provide significant value, their natural inclination is to reciprocate. Follow this formula and you'll be three feet from gold.

Maintain The Relationship

Janet creates a clear distinction between joint ventures and "enlightened alliances." While both are valuable, an enlightened alliance is fundamentally grounded in maintaining a long-term relationship with someone you genuinely care about *and* who can benefit your business. As new opportunities arise, you can return to the relationship again and again as the alliance is mutually beneficial. Of course there will be times when each party is actively engaged in pursuing specific business objectives, but throughout the journey, closeness remains.

Ideally, alliances become lifetime friendships, regardless of profits. This can only happen when both parties are fully committed to helping one another and selfishness disappears from the equation. Tremendous results awaits by understanding who you are, identifying *perfect partners*, nurturing the alliance by serving first, and consciously maintaining the relationship.

Aligning With The "Top Dogs"

Developing relationships is a skill. While not innate for everyone, it is a learnable talent. To succeed in business, connect with others. To grow one's business in expedited fashion, connect with industry leaders. As one might expect, established icons are difficult to access and receive thousands of "value-based offers" everyday. So, what to do? Smash the box. To attract name-brand players, you must play in the major leagues.

Consider this book. Prior to its release, few people knew who I was. While I've been in the online world since 1993 (we launched a store on CompuServe's Electronic Mall that year), and achieved moderate success as an author and entrepreneur, my name recognition was limited. I had always desired to align myself with the industry's biggest names, but lacked the right platform to capture their interest. After kicking around a number of ideas, the concept for creating this book, multi-media series, and a live event was crafted.

Shortly thereafter, I secured the related domain names, formulated the plan, and began networking. Within one week of formalizing my presentation, the first expert was signed on. Within eight weeks, 24 more agreed to be interviewed and most pledged to support the release of the book and the online series. One month later, Morgan James was secured as the publisher. Two months after that, 18 of this book's contributors agreed to speak at *Internet Prophets LIVE!*

The book, online series, and live event have been very well received. This is largely because everyone wins. You gain access to cut-to-the-chase, pull back the curtain information that can be immediately applied to your business, the experts gain access to new clients, and our firm has established position alongside many of the world's most recognized Internet marketing companies. Yes, a tremendous number of hours and an incredible amount of hard work have been invested into this endeavor. The rewards, however, are more than worth it.

The big dogs need room to run and a place to play. By addressing their needs, providing meaningful exposure, and offering tangible, no-cost solutions, many will be more than happy to join the pack.

The Secret Sauce

Hopefully, it's now crystal clear that, not only is it impossible to do everything on your own, it's highly detrimental to the long-term health of both you and your business if you attempt to operate in this manner. Most animals that travel alone in the wild soon perish. An individual animal's strength, though formidable, is no match when faced with the strength of a multitude of adversaries. Human beings are no different.

Your road to business success should not be traveled alone. Being willing to cut off a piece of the pie will:

- Require you to translate your internal understanding of objectives into spoken words. When you can clearly and succinctly communicate your intentions, you'll be much closer to it becoming reality.
- Empower you to realize far greater success. By opening yourself up to outside perspectives, the net sum of efforts far surpasses the value of its parts.

Life, like business, is all about give and take. When it comes to alliances, give and ye shall receive. Take and you'll only get taken.

 TAKEAWAYS

Alliance Secrets

- No matter how talented someone might be, it is impossible for any single person to outperform a finely tuned, highly focused group of individuals committed to achieving a unified goal.
- Strong relationships equate to measurable, sustainable returns.
- Selflessness and camaraderie inevitably results in the creation of a win-win-win scenario.
- By surrounding yourself with those who dare to soar and encourage you to join them for the ride, the possibilities for reaching astronomical heights are vastly improved.
- Emulate the successful. Know yourself, identify perfect partners, nurture alliances, serve first, and consciously maintain relationships.
- Leverage the power of your Circle of Four.
- Smash the box. To attract name-brand players, you must play in the major leagues.
- "When you are clear, what you want will show up in your life, and only to the extent that you are clear." Janet Bray Attwood.

CHAPTER 22

ESTABLISHING CREDIBILITY

Within any industry, there are gatekeepers and gates. Gatekeepers are those who provide access to the gates. Gates represent barriers that must be traversed to move one's career or company forward. By way of example, let's look at the music industry. There are millions of aspiring musicians. Many have immense talent and are able to create incredible music others would love. Although they have skill, most lack the experience to cultivate a sustainable entertainment career as well as the necessary funds to professionally record their songs, contract with a manufacturer to produce thousands of CDs, secure widespread distribution, and properly market their music.

Therefore, would-be recording artists must play the game as defined by the establishment. Success or failure largely hinges on one's ability to manage each step of the defined process. A proven strategy is to partner with a well-versed, capable entity that understands the intricacies of the system. Therefore, the large majority of artists pursue record label representation due to the label's ability to effectively manage their career and provide access to the best producers, distributors, and publicists.

As a result, the labels ostensibly provide a free pass through the myriad gatekeepers and gates. While the artist's net profit is massively reduced, it's a small price to pay when a comparative analysis is reviewed. But, is it possible to streamline this system? Can you achieve similar results without jumping through the traditional hoops? Christian Pankhurst—winner of Britain's Next Top Coach— is living proof that it is. He transitioned from relative obscurity to becoming one of Europe's top personal development coaches in expedited fashion.

He's worked closely with Neale Donald Walsh, author of *Conversations With God*, created joint venture agreements with top Internet marketers such as Brendon Burchard, and has accomplished virtually every personal and business-related goal he identified. By no means has his road been paved with lollipops and gumdrops but, as you'll see, creating one's desired results in expedited fashion is absolutely possible.

Create Your Future

Although Christian is now living his ideal life, he first had to endure significant pain to create it. At age, 15, Christian and a friend were brutally beaten by 18 people outside a nightclub. The physical damage was extensive. The mental damage was astronomical. The experience caused him to fall into severe depression. His social skills withdrew and, in his words, he began to "settle for less." After years of depression, he chose to reclaim his life and reconnect with his former self—an optimistic, charismatic, and socially adept individual.

This led him on a journey of personal development. Choosing to honor his gift for healing, which he had buried to the nether regions of his soul after the attack, he became a chiropractor and started his own practice. Here, Christian began making startling discoveries. As he worked closely with patients who had severe physical problems, he noticed they also had deep-rooted emotional issues. He hypothesized that the two were directly connected. He refined his practice to address both physical and emotional concerns. It soon became clear that most patients' emotional trauma manifested as physical hindrances and, as he addressed their emotional burdens, significant physical progress was realized.

While he now had meaningful case studies to leverage, he recognized that being a Chiropractor would not provide the proper platform to share his discoveries with the world. In 2002, at the age of 23, Christian sold his practice and began to pursue a career in personal development. The problem? Christian had NO credibility in the field. He lacked traditional tools—connections, products, books, etc. Essentially, he had no way of either reaching the gatekeepers or passing through the gates. Of course, that didn't stop him.

> *Instead of waiting until after he'd written a book or established credibility, Christian chose an equally powerful option: work with those who are where you want to be.*

During his career transition, Christian put bread on the table by teaching martial arts classes. One of his students suggested he read the book, *Conversations With God* and provided him with a copy. Though he wasn't religious, he graciously accepted the book and began to read it. Profoundly affected by the book, Christian sought out the author. Though he wanted to send an email and ask for Neale's guidance, he realized the author likely received thousands of similar emails every day.

Therefore, Christian opted for another approach. He made it his mission to provide immense value to Mr. Walsh and eventually land on his radar. Without the author's knowledge, Christian embarked on a speaking tour to share the wisdom found within the pages of *Conversations With God*. To secure attendance for each event, he contacted local personal development professionals and invited both them, and their clients, to attend the presentation for free. Often, attendees would be so inspired by his presentation they would make a monetary donation to

Christian as a token of their appreciation. Though not living large, he made enough to scrape by.

Serendipity Or Reality?

Over time, word of his teachings spread and attendance grew, as did the buzz about Christian and his ability to connect with others. His life reached a pivotal point when attending a play during a visit to Arizona. Christian was seated next to a woman who inquired about the purpose of his visit to the area. He informed her of his upcoming presentation and asked if she had ever heard of the book, *Conversations With God*.

> *Her response? "Yes, I've read the book. My husband is the author."*

She was kind enough to arrange a meeting with him, and from that moment forward, Christian made it his goal to attend all of Neale's events. He never went out of his way to speak to him, but always made sure the author recognized his presence. Then at one of the author's facilitator training seminars, Christian seized his opportunity. Neale and several associates were taking students through his proprietary teachings while ascertaining their respective knowledge about *Conversations With God*. This allowed Walsh's team to verify if the student was ready to represent their company. When it was Christian's turn, he so impressed the author that Walsh made him his protégé.

Opportunity Is A Direct Byproduct Of Action

The universe works in strange and mysterious ways. Some might argue there is no correlation between cause and effect. Others believe everything happens for a reason and we each live within a predestined path. Still others affirm that the universe presents opportunity and look for the higher purpose in all events.

Regardless of personal beliefs, there is evidence to support that, once a conscious choice is made to take action, initiative is rewarded. Would Christian have been given the opportunity to sit next to Walsh's wife if he hadn't first taken action? Even if he had sat next to her, had he not embarked on his mission of spreading Walsh's gospel, would a simple conversation have produced the same remarkable results? It has been said that luck is a combination of preparedness and opportunity. Was it just dumb luck that Neale's wife sat next to him that evening? Possibly. It could also have been the direct result of conscious action and honoring the multitude of "coincidental" opportunities:

1. Accepting the book from his student.
2. Reading the book.
3. Taking action and embarking on his tour.
4. Going to Arizona and attending the play.
5. Speaking with the person next to him.

Christian could never have planned this series of events. Rather, possibilities are created when one is in motion. Without movement, death is inevitable, both figuratively and literally. And, without acceptance and an openness to explore each open door of opportunity before us, stagnation and frustration are inevitable byproducts. Christian's life has been defined by failing to abide by other's standards and guidelines…and, continuously taking action. Winning Britain's Top Coach was the result of six years of concerted effort. Had Christian not boldly followed his passion while uncovering his *WHAT*, his greater life potential would have remain buried under a 9-5 grind and unavailable to help so many others.

This victory could have easily represented the pinnacle of Christian's career. It would've been simple for him to rest on his laurels and ride the forthcoming wave as long as possible. Christian, however, subscribed to the notion that he was designated as Britain's *next* top coach and therefore, the game had just begun. Now free to expand more fully into who he inherently is, it was time to introduce as many people as possible to his personal development work, which he calls *Heart Intelligence.*

Finding Friends

To gain significant exposure quickly and without prohibitive upfront costs, modern-day marketers partner with—and compensate—individuals, corporations, and organizations for the sale of proprietary products to their contacts. The agreements are typically structured as joint ventures, alliances, or affiliate relationships and promotion is nearly always done via email to the partners' respective tribes. This approach is extraordinarily effective and beneficial to all involved, while adding value for customers. Without partners, market penetration is limited to that of one's personal database, so aligning with just a handful of well-connected parties can massively increase reach. Given Christian's newfound notoriety, attracting others to promote *Heart Intelligence* was not difficult.

Maintaining these valuable connections though, is a different story. Because partners vouch for the third party's product when they introduce it to their audience, the product damn well better be good. If any aspect of the process is less than stellar—deliverability quality, content, customer service, tangible benefits for purchasers, etc.—partners will drop out quicker than Usain Bolt running the 100 meters. One of the hardest things for entrepreneurs to do is to spend more time up front, refining their systems, and checking all angles. Most are impatient and want to set their idea in motion to see results manifest as quickly as possible. However, investing time before the product is released to ensure customer satisfaction is significantly better for short—and long term—success.

The key is to create a high-quality product that both provides immense value and converts. In other words, your partners' audience must be compelled to buy what you're selling. And, while established professionals make this process appear seamless, developing the right mix of message, media, content, and execution is anything but. In Christian's case, the product was ready. He simply needed to finalize his list of promotional partners. Allies typically fall into one of two categories:

- **Friends and Associates:** The easiest way to expand reach is to ask for the support of those closest to you—friends, family, and business associates. While not everyone will have large subscriber or contact lists, do not overlook the power of personal relationships. Oftentimes, those with a small, but dedicated, audience will outperform their larger list counterparts. Presuming your product and systems are ready, the worst-case scenario is they send an email on your behalf and no one responds. Best case, both of you profit.
- **Internet Marketers and Niche-Related Site Owners:** Promoting to a warm audience will always convert better than sending random emails. Think about it. If you built your mailing list on the premise of featuring superior dog-related products and, all of a sudden, you send an email that touts the amazing results of a new foot cream, while some may find direct benefit from your out-of-scope offering, most will scratch their heads (or maybe their feet) and question whether or not you have breached the unwritten code of honoring your subscribers' best interests.

Therefore, an effective strategy is to seek marketers and niche site owners whose audience can most directly benefit from your offering. While partnering with potentially competitive companies may seem counterintuitive, few have the ability to consistently release new products. As such, they have a warm database ready to review the next hot shiny object and can go months without something to sell. This is where you come in.

Odds are good that if you have a solid product their audience can benefit from, they'll help you promote it. Although well connected, influential leaders are not as easy to reach as friends, family, and associates, they are paramount to your success, and you can contribute to theirs. To find key industry players, start with Google. Check keywords related to your topic and reach out for those that appear on the first three pages. These sites are typically well established, receive large volumes of traffic, and have significant authority within their niche.

Additionally, resources such as ClickBank, YouTube, and iTunes are great places to find potential joint venture partners. Bottom line—reach out. Sometimes you'll grab a hand, other times you'll grab air. It's the nature of the business.

Bonus Power!

A proven conversion strategy is to offer high-value bonuses as an incentive to purchase. For example, when Christian was promoting Brendon Burchard's product, he offered his list complimentary coaching sessions. This not only adds value for those who purchase Brendon's product, it ties the rationale for promoting someone else's products together. This can be exceptionally powerful if one's bonus directly compliments, and supports, the third party's offering.

In 2011, the creators of *The Passion Test*, Chris and Janet Bray Attwood, introduced their list to The Authority Formula—an offering from Greg Habstritt. In their email, the Attwood's offered the bonus of either two VIP tickets to The Passionate Life Summit, or A Weekend of Bliss, if someone from their list purchased Greg's new product. Both have exceptional value and tie the Attwood's work back to Greg's offering. When recruiting partners, strongly encourage them to offer bonuses that compliment their core message and focus. A bonus-driven approach consistently increases conversion rates.

Get Started Today

Although the techniques described can prove successful for the experienced marketer, to a beginner, this may seem overwhelming. Avoid focusing on everything you feel you need to accomplish. Instead, create an outline—a step-by-step guide—and start with square one. The most important first step is to get clear on who you are and what value you can add to others. Once you're clear on your genre and message, sign up to receive emails from experts in your niche. Most will be pursuing the outlined strategies and you can gain a front-row seat to their methods.

When Christian sought to create his own products, he replicated the proven methods of established experts. Not so long ago, this would have been called plagiarism and you'd be fined for doing so. Today, emulating the actions of those you admire is called *modeling* and not following their lead can cost you precious time and money. If you want to get from New York to Los Angeles, you certainly can blaze your own trail, but you might as well take the freeway. Although you didn't build the road, the journey is uniquely yours.

Most experts expend enormous effort nailing the promotional blueprint. Pay attention to timing, language, and pricing. There's much you can learn from those who have perfected this process. Best of all, the education is free. Be willing to become a student and soon you'll be teaching the class.

⏻ TAKEAWAYS

Establishing Credibility

- No experience? No problem. Having a massive following or household name is not a prerequisite for success. Action and clarity about what you're compelled to do, is.
- Gatekeepers and gates are surmountable. The key is to first provide value to those you admire or want to work with, and *then* pursue your agenda.
- Failure happens. Get used to it. Those who try, inevitably fail. Those who never fail are people you shouldn't be hanging around anyway.
- To become a recognized expert in your field, align yourself to others who already are.
- You're never too young (or too old). Age, and its benefits or perceived hindrances, is a matter of perspective. Stop trying to impress people you don't really care about anyway.
- When the student is ready, the teacher will appear. Access to what you need will be granted when you're ready to receive.
- Joint ventures can provide phenomenal, low-cost exposure. Partner with those you know and experts in your niche to disseminate your message. Consistently create A-level, impactful products that over-deliver.
- Bonuses equate to conversion. High conversion rates are directly correlated to the value of the entire offer. Encourage joint venture partners to tie the offer together with free products and services from their area of expertise.
- Model those you admire. In the past, this was called plagiarism. Today, it is known as modeling and widely accepted.

CHAPTER 23

BEING THE PRODUCER

How would your life change if you suddenly had an extra five figures of income each month? For most people, it would make a substantial difference in both lifestyle and peace of mind. This may not be simple, but it can be easier than you think. Step one is committing to becoming a *producer*. A producer is someone who creates value and shares knowledge with others. In the process, a producer helps improve lives and earns continuous active and passive income.

Jeff Vacek is one of the world's leading producers. His online products generate six to seven figures annually. Jeff was born with an entrepreneurial fire—as a child, he asked his mom for *two* bikes so he could rent one to neighborhood kids. But he didn't exactly start out as a world-class marketer.

The Rise Of An Internet Empire

As with most entrepreneurs, Jeff has launched, or been instrumental in creating, numerous ventures over the years. From music and computer programming to multi-level marketing and real estate, he's cut his teeth more than once on the business grindstone. As a real estate investor, Jeff achieved moderate success on his own. Recognizing that he'd benefit from the guidance of an experienced teacher, he sought viable options. After discussing his plan with peers, Jeff was referred to a real estate expert who offered to mentor him for $6,000. At the time that was a lot of money for him to spend, but he chose to make the investment.

Jeff ended up learning about both real estate and the Internet, as the majority of his mentor's business was conducted online. Then, tragically, the expert's programmer died in an accident. Jeff had a computer background so his mentor asked him to step in. In exchange, his mentor promised to teach him everything he knew about profiting online and off. Jeff seized the opportunity. He was given the green light to order multiple training programs and attend various Internet marketing seminars. In a short period, Jeff absorbed an immense amount of knowledge.

After several years, the two parted ways. At this point, Jeff has seen repeatedly firsthand how the Internet could be used to market real estate-related products. He quickly got to work creating his own program. The subsequent product launch grossed over $100,000 and he hasn't looked back since. Jeff and his business partner, Ken, have since become one of the world's most dynamic Internet marketing duos. Here, they share their proven, replicable strategy for generating meaningful online revenue. Let's head into the Batcave.

Evolution Requires Adaptation

Internet customers today are very different from when Jeff and Ken started out. After being bombarded with pitches, customers are far more jaded, increasingly adverse to email solicitation, and loathe overt sales-oriented marketing. To effectively sell online, you must now "pull back the curtain" and allow customers to become familiar with you. Credibility and trust come from your cultivating a personal relationship with your audience.

For example, fewer emails are being opened as time goes on; the current rate is less than 18% of all emails sent. However, nearly 100% of all handwritten letters are opened. Why? Customers reward effort. With the intense competition online, it has never been more essential to stand out from the crowd. If you're not willing to put in the time necessary to earn customer loyalty, someone else will. To be successful, however, it's not necessary to create the next Internet or iPhone, nor do you need to create your own wheel. You simply need to paint it your own color.

It's All About The Product, Baby

Which comes first, the product or the list? Far too many would-be Internet marketers have huge mailing lists but inferior products, or have phenomenal products but no efficient way of getting the word out about them. Either situation is undesirable. While the, "If you build it, they will come," approach worked for Kevin Costner, real life is more complex. Creating and releasing brilliant products may eventually result in the creation of a massive list—if you can stay in business long enough. Then again, a big list in no way guarantees the creation of value-packed products.

Spending time pursuing those with large lists makes zero sense until you can add value to their business. Therefore, online success is largely the result of investing significant time and resources into creating game-changing products. Once developed, securing affiliates to help promote and sell your products is more than doable—especially if you're willing to pay large commissions.

Winning Over Customers And Affiliates

To attract customers, and partner with affiliates who'll help promote your products, follow these principles:

- **Have a solid understanding of your customers' needs.** When you identify your target audience's biggest problems, you'll be able to create products that solve them. Once you do so, you'll have customers for life.
- **Be clear about what your customers are willing to spend.** You can't expect meaningful rates of conversion if you develop champagne products for beer budgets. Test, poll, research similar products, and interact with potential customers to discover what they're willing, or even able, to spend on your product.

- **Deliver your product in the expected format.** Trying to sell a magazine to someone who wants to see a movie is an effort in futility. A videocassette won't sell to someone who has only a DVD player. Learn how your target customer wants to receive your content and then deliver it via the appropriate medium.

- **Higher prices lead to greater affiliate participation.** Whether your product costs $10 or $10,000, it'll require roughly the same amount of effort for an affiliate to promote it. As a result, most affiliates will choose to invest their time into selling high-priced products that provide substantial returns. Printed books and ebooks, while often providing wonderful content, are ill suited for commission-driven relationships as are most other products that sell for under $500. Today's successful partnerships involve the promotion of products priced between $500 and $4,995. Products above and below these price points continue to be sold, but they represent the two ends of the bell curve. Successful Internet marketers offer products at the center of the curve—and right now that sweet spot is roughly $2,500.

- **Higher commissions mean happy affiliates.** Selling a high-priced product isn't the whole story. You must also be generous on commissions paid. Today, 40%-50% commission rates are commonplace, as is the payment of an additional 10% for second-tier affiliates. Second-tier affiliates, also known as brokers, help recruit affiliates for a product launch. When a product is sold, a second-tier affiliate typically receives 10% of the purchase price. Naturally, this cuts into your net profits. However, industry leaders understand that 40%-50% is a price worth paying for instant massive exposure, immediate income, and adding thousands of hopefully satisfied customers to their sales funnel.

- **Continuity programs create long-term relationships.** While instant cash is always nice, long-term passive income is even better. Whether they consist of bi-weekly one-on-one coaching, monthly product shipments, quarterly VIP programs, or annual membership dues, continuity programs provide ongoing benefits for both you and your affiliates. Many of your customers might balk at paying $2,500 upfront for a product, but would readily agree to spend $250 a month for life-altering content. Over a year, the latter adds up to $3,000. That means if you can get 100 people to subscribe at $250 a month, you'll earn $300,000 in a year. Conversely, if resistance to paying a large amount upfront results in only 50 customers purchasing your product at $2,500, you'll end up making $125,000. Which would you rather have? Which scenario do you think affiliates prefer? Think long-term to see the big picture.

The Golden Rule

Developing products from scratch is *hard*. But even more difficult is creating products that fulfill audience needs, provide immense value, are of superior quality, and convert prospects to paying customers. Success requires satisfying all four criteria. For example, if a product provides immense value, is of superior quality, and converts, but it fails to fulfill customer needs, expect massive returns. Similarly, if a product fulfills customer needs, provides immense value, is of superior quality, but fails to convert, neither you nor your affiliates will be pleased. As with a table, if one of the four legs is missing, everything topples.

A key step in achieving solid conversion rates is the creation of an engaging headline. Here's an example of one Jeff recently used:

> REVEALED: How average people with no prior experience are building a $10,000 per month online information marketing machine in 90 days or less…and how you can do the exact same thing starting immediately!

Jeff's use of a buzzword—REVEALED—instantly captures attention. It's human nature to want to learn more. The headline touches on lifestyle ($10,000 per month), abilities required (no prior experience), and timeframe (90 days or less). While a bit lengthy, it's easy to see how this headline led to above-average conversion rates. Smart product creators *soft launch* their offerings to a hand-selected group of customers, their in-house list, and/or in partnership with affiliates using small lists prior to conducting the full release. This allows both you and the affiliates to test headlines, subject lines, software, and product delivery. It also gives you time to garner feedback, secure testimonials, and have tangible conversion metrics. If the numbers don't work, it's back to square one.

Larger affiliates are consistently inundated with participation requests. Remember *The Golden Rule*? "He who has the gold makes the rules." Today, he who has the list controls the game. To gain a position on the team, you must approach potential affiliates with data in hand. These metrics are of significantly more importance than your resume. With this in mind, let's review two powerful ways to secure early buy-in, receive feedback, and determine conversion rates:

- **Give the product away for free.** This is commonly known as a beta launch. Effective marketers will often grant behind-the-scenes access to a select group of customers to test a product, run through the offering, and obtain feedback. Some of these customers will also agree to provide written or video testimonials touting the product's benefits. Having such positive reviews in hand is a necessity before the official launch. If you don't have a list of appropriate customers for the beta, begin visiting forums where potential customers post pertinent answers and advice related to the product's topic. For example, one of the most popular forums for Internet marketers is The Warrior Forum (WarriorForum.com), where thousands of messages are posted daily. If you invest time and effort, you can identify the enthusiastic experts on your subject and approach them to review your product. Jeff's business partner Ken became active in various real estate-related forums and assembled a list of over 100 real estate investors. By including his website address in his signature, readers visited the site, joined his email list, and eventually agreed to review his upcoming product. This enabled him to compile valuable feedback and detailed metrics for a larger-scale release.

- **Hand-select two or three affiliates as soft launch partners.** In soft launch mode, each affiliate typically keeps 100% of the sales revenue so they're able to make a ton of cash if the product sells. Further, the affiliate's customers appreciate having first access to the new product, so the affiliate further benefits from the goodwill, and you're able to secure conversion metrics for both opt-ins and sales which can be used to recruit a large number of affiliates for the official launch. Everyone benefits.

Once metrics are in hand, headlines and taglines are solid, bugs are worked out, and the product is a proven winner, it's time to bring it to the masses.

Wrangling Affiliates

If you're coming out of the gate with no track record or high-caliber endorsements, securing affiliates can be difficult. However, most successful entrepreneurs traveled a similar treacherous road to get where they are today. Tony Robbins began by attending a Jim Rohn seminar and subsequently spreading his message to anyone who would listen. Sir Richard Branson began by selling one record at a time from a mail order catalog. Sam Zell convinced one landlord to let him manage his building. Mother Teresa provided comfort and care to one person in need.

None of these iconic figures started out successful or famous. But by taking one small baby step at a time while focusing on their ultimate goal, they each achieved greatness. Most affiliates want to be part of the next big thing. Existing gurus can release only a handful of products per year; plus customers often grow tired of hearing the same perspective from familiar faces. This means there is a genuine demand for new messengers and their ideas. Affiliates want to satisfy the public's craving for exciting products and achieving "Super Affiliate" status for selling an exceptionally high amount of product is viewed as a badge of honor. Translation: Don't be afraid to ask for what you want. Knock on doors, send emails and most of all, persevere. There are three proven strategies for securing affiliates:

- **Use Google.** Enter relevant keywords, and identify those who rank high in the search results; they're likely enjoying significant traffic. Click links, assemble contact information, nail down your pitch...and begin introducing yourself to the site owners. Do not, however, start with page one. Start with page three, then page two, and finally page one. Why? Page one typically represents the biggest players. By the time you work through pages three and two, you'll be ready for primetime. Not everyone will respond to your query...but some will.

- **Go to where the affiliates are.** The best place to find affiliates is ClickBank (ClickBank.com). The following resources are also well worth exploring:
  - ShareASale (ShareASale.com)
  - Commission Junction (CJ.com)
  - AffiliateWindow (AffiliateWindow.com)
  - Trade Doubler (TradeDoubler.com)
  - Affiliate Future (AffiliateFuture.com)
  - Affiliate Bot (AffiliateBot.com)
  - PayDotCom (PayDotCom.com)

  Each site has specific rules and regulations you must follow. Scour each to find the big players and ask them to become partners.

- **Make personal connections.** Unlike Homer Simpson who believes that, "If something's too hard to do, it's not worth doing," successful marketers understand that creating a thriving business takes a lot of effort. Gone are the days of sending mass emails and simply watching the cash roll in. Therefore, go to the trouble of personally meeting affiliates so you can connect names to faces, and vice versa. Conferences are a fantastic way to meet a number of influential people in a short amount of time. The world's best consistently gather at:
  - Blog World Expo (BlogWorldExpo.com)
  - Affiliate Summit (AffiliateSummit.com)
  - Mike Filsaime's Internet Marketers Cruise (MarketersCruise.com)

Powerful alliances have been formed at these events that led to multimillion-dollar product launches. People want to conduct business with those they know. The only way to establish rapport is to put in the necessary effort to create it. The secret of life is remembering that it starts over now…and now…and now. Recognize that you have complete control to create your world, and you will.

Hungry? It's Launch Time!

Solid product? Check! Conversion metrics? Check! Affiliates? Check! All that's left is bringing forth your creation to the world and praying that your months of hard work pay off. (Please note that I've consciously omitted the ton of back-end technical work that must be completed prior to opening the cart.)

Bottom line: This is infinitely doable. Jeff went from the unemployment line to driving his Ferrari on the streets of Houston in just a few short years. Achieving success often requires significantly more giving than receiving. Help first, learn second, promote third, and request fourth. Keep this equation in mind and your efforts will be rewarded many times over.

⏻ TAKEAWAYS

Being The Producer

- Become a producer to create value and share your knowledge with others.
- Evolution requires adaptation. Adjust to the fact that the Internet customer of today is more jaded and demanding than customers of only a few years ago.
- Put your unique spin on what's already been done. You don't have to create your own wheel...simply paint it your own color.
- Understand and honor affiliates.
- The revised Golden Rule: He who has the list controls the game.
- Metrics must be secured. Early buy-in, feedback, and establishing conversion rates are critical to lining up affiliates.
- Most affiliates profit only when they have someone else's product to sell, so don't be shy about approaching them with something new and exciting.
- Achieving success often requires significantly more giving than receiving. Help first, learn second, promote third, and request fourth.

CHAPTER 24

PUBLICITY POWER

I t's often said that, "Any publicity is good publicity." While the truth of this may be debatable, there's no disputing that receiving unpaid, positive media exposure can add meaningful revenue to your bottom line. No one knows this better than Steve Harrison.

Steve is a publicity expert who's been credited with helping Robert Kiyosaki (*Rich Dad, Poor Dad*), Jack Canfield & Mark Victor Hansen (*Chicken Soup for the Soul*), and numerous others, launch their book sales and careers into the stratosphere. Rather than a mere "15 minutes of fame," Steve teaches authors, bloggers, Internet marketers, and others how to remain in the spotlight for their entire careers.

The Beginning

When Steve was a young reporter for his local newspaper, he discovered that many who ordinarily wouldn't give him the time of day found ample openings in their schedule to be interviewed for an article. This made clear to him the power of media. After a stint as a door-to-door salesman—which he says was invaluable for honing his interpersonal and sales skills—Steve received an invitation to work with his brother Bill on his newly launched magazine, *Radio and Television Interview Report.*

Steve jumped at the opportunity. The magazine focused on connecting interesting guests with producers who needed them. Steve and Bill were involved with all aspects of creating the magazine, which helped them develop copywriting skills. Over time, Steve began to offer complimentary services. He spoke to groups who sought information about publicity and provided one-on-one coaching. It was during this period that the brothers came up with an interesting idea. Steve and Bill would often attend publicity-related events. Most of these conferences featured producers of well-known shows or writers from major publications. What struck them was that attendees would mob the presenters after their speech, hoping to impress them with their message and land a spot on their show or be considered as a source for upcoming articles.

They designed a publicity-driven event in which guests would pay to receive coaching on how to best craft their "pitch," and subsequently have direct access to producers who could provide immediate feedback on their topic and/or book them on the spot. The result? The National Publicity Summit was born. Today, the National Publicity Summit sells out twice a year, and has proven to be a highly successful venture for attendees, producers, and the Harrison's company, Bradley Communications. You can learn more at GetMajorPress.com/NPS18.

Steve and Bill built their organization from scratch, and now pride themselves on helping people achieve careers that maximize their potential and add value to others. It's this personal mission that moves Steve to share his expertise—and the strategies that follow.

Give People What They Need

One of the key mistakes business owners make is failing to ask customers for feedback. The single most important question you can ask your target audience is, "What products or services do you *need* to build your business?" Too often companies create what they think the market will *want.* Seldom do they take the time to ask what is actually *needed.*

> *There can be a huge difference between what you think customers want and what they really need.*

To spare yourself from significant pain, create what the market is telling you it needs. If you create products and services with built-in demand, you'll chuckle as you head to the bank with checks in hand, wondering why other companies don't use this straightforward yet highly effective strategy.

Leverage The Power Of Publicity

How much do you think it costs for a full-page advertisement in the *Wall Street Journal*? What about a 30-second commercial during the Super Bowl? How about five minutes of airtime on Rush Limbaugh's radio program? In each case, it's A LOT! Most businesses can't afford such advertising. But what if there was a way to receive tens of thousands of dollars of free exposure for your company? When executed well, publicity is not only free, it delivers phenomenal exposure over and over again.

While people have become skeptical of advertising, an invited guest is typically welcomed. This is one of the direct benefits of establishing yourself as an expert in your field—you're perceived as an authority who people can trust. If your presentation is executed properly, it will lead to increased sales. From guest blog posts and newspaper articles to appearing on radio and television, there are ample opportunities to spread your message.

> *Always choose topics of interest to your specific audience.*

Don't expect *Men's Fitness* to feature you in an upcoming article if you're offering tips on the best ways to cope with PMS. But if you can provide, "10 Tips for Turning Fat into Muscle While You Sleep," the magazine is likely to follow up. Steve recommends taking advantage of free resources for accessing the media. These allow you to explore postings from reporters, producers, writers, and others looking for experts to be guests on shows and contributors to articles. Here are three excellent examples of such sites:

- ReporterConnection.com: Reporter Connection is a free daily email service that connects busy journalists with experts available for media interviews.
- HelpAReporter.com: According to the site, "Help A Reporter Out is used daily by nearly 30,000 reporters and bloggers, over 100,000 news sources, and thousands of small businesses that want to tell their stories, promote their brands, and sell their products and services."
- PitchRate.com: According to their site, "PitchRate provides free and instant access to the media and makes it easy to connect with journalists in need of your expertise."

To succeed with publicity, understand the medium you're pitching, be clear about what producers are looking for in their guests, and have significant value to provide to their audience. If you keep these criteria in mind while pursuing opportunities, then in due time, as the Counting Crows famously sang, "When I look at the television, (I'll) see me staring right back at me."

Create The Hook

Robert Kiyosaki, now renowned in both the financial and publishing worlds, originally self-published *Rich Dad, Poor Dad*. To generate exposure for the book, he and his wife, Kim, enlisted the help of a publicity firm, but it did little aside from placing Robert on a few college radio stations. There were few sales, and thousands of copies sat collecting dust.

That all changed when they enlisted the help of Steve Harrison. The book contained immensely useful information, but no one knew about it. One of Steve's first objectives was to help Robert craft a powerful "hook" that would attract both readers and the media. As they discussed the content, Steve suddenly came up with the perfect approach to grab attention:

> *"Learn what the rich teach their kids about money that the poor and middle class do not!"*

As you can imagine, people were instantly intrigued. Who wouldn't want to learn inside tips and shortcuts from the successful? Most people aspire to create a better life for themselves and their family. The hook had immediate, widespread appeal. After Robert's first ad appeared in *Radio and Television Interview Report,* the magic began to happen. First small radio stations brought him on to talk. Then medium and larger radio stations caught wind of this new inspiring guest and asked him to be on their programs. Eventually local and national TV shows sought Robert's insight on current events.

However, publicity is only as effective as one's ability to move people to take action. That's why before each show Robert would ask for an opportunity to mention his book at the conclusion of the interview. More often than not, the host obliged. When it came time to discuss the book, the host would usually ask where it could be found. Robert's answer: *"Everywhere!"* The truth is his book was not in any distribution channels aside from the copies sitting in his garage. So when radio listeners went into their local bookstores expecting *Rich Dad, Poor Dad* to be on the shelves and it wasn't available, they'd ask the manager to order a copy for them. Typically, a manager would ask how they heard about the book. When they responded, "on the radio," the manager would order multiple copies.

Soon large retail stores began selling his book. As a result, despite significant budget constraints and the lack of a large publishing house, thousands of copies of *Rich Dad, Poor Dad* were sold. Before long the book was a #1 *New York Times* bestseller. The success of *Rich Dad, Poor Dad* is largely attributable to the effectiveness of one attention-grabbing hook—and Robert leveraging it brilliantly. Yes, some of the content is controversial, such as Robert's contention that, "a house is not an asset;" but without the hook-based publicity, *Rich Dad, Poor Dad* wouldn't have achieved the momentum needed to soar.

This strategy is applicable to any business—whether you're selling books, cars, information-based products, consulting services, or trinkets. Grab people's attention and lead them towards wanting to learn more. The most successful hooks bust myths, question reality, and cause people to think. Leading with, "Why Chicago is going to be cold this winter," is not going to garner much attention. However, "Why Chicagoans will have more sex this winter than residents of any other U.S. city," will.

The first statement is a no-brainer. "Duh!" might be a typical response, and won't result in a call from a producer. The second hook, though, piques people's interest. "I wonder why that's the case?" might be the initial reaction, and is likely to be followed by an email or phone call from a producer. Of course, you need to have an interesting story to pitch, and be able to tie it to your business and expertise.

> *A strong hook instantly grabs interest. A weak one is instantly forgotten.*

To create a substantive business, people must know you exist. You may not be comfortable taking an eye-popping or controversial position, but driving free traffic to your business via publicity is a small price to pay for such temporary discomfort.

Create Demand For Your Products And Services

Steve is a master at creating demand for his products and services. Most people aren't, because they focus on what the product is and what it does. Instead, they should be emphasizing the product's *benefits* to the audience. For example, let's assume a woman who runs a yoga studio is invited to be a guest on a radio show. She proceeds to explain a few techniques that can be done at home. Feedback on the interview is positive...but no one signs up to take classes. Now imagine that instead of talking about yoga, the owner talks about how the lives of listeners will be improved by yoga. First, she provides statistics to make audience members realize they have a problem that needs solving:

"Did you know that 1 in every 4 people over the age of 35 suffers from back pain? What about sciatica? Have you ever felt the excruciating pain that tweaking the sciatic nerve can cause? If you have, you're not alone. Nearly 22% of all adults have experienced this misery." Next, instead of providing descriptions of specific poses, she'll provide case studies of people who have completely changed their lives through practicing yoga. These examples will include several of her clients and speak directly to the statistics:

"John suffered for 20 years from debilitating lower back pain. He had difficulty tying his shoes, could barely get out of bed in the morning, and was addicted to pain medication. Within two months of our working together, he could not only tie his shoes, but was able to resume his love for golf and no longer needed pain pills to help him through the day."

This makes the conversation personal. Audience members naturally connect with both her and her clients; and many will want to hear more. The last component of creating demand is providing a solution that solves the problem. Audience members are primed to hear it because the presenter has:

- Agitated their concerns
- Provided supporting statistics
- Offered case studies that demonstrate what she can do

By the close of a successful interview, many people will have their wallets out awaiting purchase instructions. Far too many people take the reverse approach to closing sales and continue making the same mistakes. Don't be one of them. You now have the code. Use it to your full advantage.

Provide Content-Rich Free Material

Ultimately, Steve is in the business of building relationships. By providing significant value and consistently over-delivering, he's able to construct long-term, trust-driven relationships that benefit both his clients and his organization. One way he does this is by supplying value-packed free learning materials. Steve understands that not everyone can immediately afford to pay $10,000 for personal coaching, or $1,000 or more for a seminar. He therefore also offers a variety of free teleseminars and webinars that provide a wealth of helpful information.

To access Steve's free events, customers must provide their names and email addresses. This results in his having a large database of leads. Steve then works to earn trust and develop a relationship with each of these customers via email newsletters, transcripts, podcasts, tips, and more. When a client attains the financial means to purchase a seminar, learning product, or personal coaching service, Steve's existing relationship will lead the customer to think of him first.

Further, in each of Steve's free presentations he subtly introduces his audience to various offerings such as *Radio and Television Interview Report*, The National Publicity Summit, and his premiere coaching program, Quantum Leap. While free offerings are technically loss leaders, the metrics work. Steve has an excellent ROI, and continually tweaks his cost/benefit analysis to increase overall returns.

Consistently Deliver

Steve prides himself on always providing pertinent, high-value tools, strategies, and shortcuts that answer key questions and can be immediately implemented. His staff receives frequent training on how to work most effectively with clients and tirelessly pursues excellence in everything they do. Some say you're only as good as your last victory. Steve believes you're only as good as your current victory. He not only teaches his clients how to prosper, but encourages them to soar well beyond his own level of success.

 TAKEAWAYS

Publicity Power

- With rare exception, any publicity is good publicity.
- Too often companies create what they think customers will want. Take the time to find out what your target audience actually **needs**.
- Become an expert. When you're perceived as an authority figure, people will be inclined to trust you. If you then present your message effectively, you'll enjoy increased sales.
- The most successful books have a provocative hook. Challenge accepted wisdom and cause people to think.
- To create demand for your product, provide statistics that agitate your audience's pain; present your product as the way to solve the problem; and provide case studies of people who've changed their lives as a result of using your product.
- Develop long-term and lucrative relationships with customers. Accomplish this by first providing content-rich free learning materials to cultivate prospects. Then, when a customer is ready to buy from you, be ready to deliver high quality products and services.

CHAPTER 25

VIRTUAL VELOCITY

Entrepreneurs have it rough. Whoever said business owners are living the dream obviously didn't witness the constant wrangling to create a profitable entity. First, there's ideation followed by market research, raising capital, and then hopefully, execution. Oh, and did I mention actual operation? Within each of these stages, there are multiple tasks that must be accomplished. At nearly every step of the process, things can go painfully awry. For example, when marketing to one's target audience, activities might include building a website, posting on forums to gain credibility, launching a social media initiative, blogging, contacting the media, direct mail, email newsletters, etc. Each element has hundreds of moving parts.

There's little disputing the entrepreneur's to-do list is as large as Charlie Sheen's ego. Although it's possible to effectively complete many of these tasks without assistance, doing so consumes an enormous amount of time. No matter how good one might be at time management, there are only 24 hours in a day. Once an hour has been spent, it can never be reclaimed. Of course, the apparent solution is to simply hire others to complete these tasks. While ideal, this is not always possible. Many entrepreneurs operate on a shoestring budget and paying someone to execute what are perceived as menial tasks makes zero sense. Others have trouble with (what's that word? ah, yes...) delegation and lord knows only the owner could possibly complete the activity correctly.

> *Trying to do everything by yourself will lead to certain things being done exceptionally well, but others...not so much.*

Fortunately, there's a modern-day solution to this age-old conundrum: *virtual assistants.* Virtual assistants can be invaluable for small business owners. They can help with literally any aspect of business—from accounting and secretarial work, to web design and research—without being in the same room or even the same country. Often, a virtual assistant can complete their assignments while you sleep. Pam Ivey is a leading 'virtual assistant' expert. Her company provides coaching, training, and mentoring in effective and profitable outsourcing strategies to business owners around the globe.

A strong advocate for freeing business owners from their self-imposed, control-driven shackles, Pam believes an effective leader should concentrate on what they do best and enjoy most. Everything else can be outsourced, ignored, or completed by a capable employee. The formula for building substantial wealth and passive income requires attaining balance, allowing others to help grow your business, and focusing on generating new ideas while cultivating sales. Interestingly, by allowing others to complete tasks you'd normally devote time to, additional income and freedom can be realized.

Establishing a system for managing virtual, or in-person, assistants must be viewed as an investment. Whereas there may be a slight drop in immediate income, over the long haul, massive dividends will be realized. The end result is flexibility—something every entrepreneur desperately needs. With Pam's help, a viable structure for increasing profits, carving out free time, and realizing peace and contentment is infinitely possible. Let's cross the border into Canada and learn more about how Pam reached her current level of success. Grab your passport, eh?

Beachside Daiquiris

Pam was born with the entrepreneurial spirit in her blood, as her father had always owned his own businesses as a carpenter, drywall and acoustic specialist and auto mechanic. As a young adult, she started her own business, Special Effects, and specialized in faux finishes and decorative painting. In all of Ontario, only two other companies provided similar services. Before long, she had a waiting list of clients. As fate would have it, Pam developed an allergic reaction to the alkyd paint and was forced to sell the business—thankfully, for a tidy profit.

She opted to join her then-husband's family business in electrical wholesale, commercial, and retail lighting and assumed responsibility for marketing and management of the showroom. But, as things sometimes go, divorce forced her to return to a 9-5 office grind some years later. Pam's job-for-survival provided little fulfillment and she began to look for something better. As she researched many possibilities, including magazine publisher and franchise ownership, Pam came across the term *virtual assistant.*

She tested the waters and very quickly realized the massive potential for helping entrepreneurs become exponentially more effective through outsourcing. So began her company Visual Persuasions Canada, which later became My Creative Assistant. Pam initially offered her services to "anyone with a heartbeat and a wallet," but quickly learned her marketing spoke to no one. Once she narrowed her focus, business took off. From these experiences she became clear on two important concepts:

- Serve an underserved market.
- Attempting to do everything by yourself results in working over-hard and over-long, while the return is unlikely to be commensurate with your efforts.

Pam enjoyed being the boss, but she came to recognize that nearly every waking moment was spent working. The fantasy of money pouring in while she sipped Daiquiris on the beach had not come to fruition. She knew she needed help, and chose to walk the talk by hiring virtual assistants to handle securing speaking gigs, copywriting, and general administration tasks. Today, Pam is a tireless champion of the virtual assistant industry, and is considered a thought-leader in outsourcing and online marketing who inspires countless business owners, virtual assistants, and other professionals to achieve greater heights.

We're fortunate to have one of the world's leading experts be our tour guide through this game-changing terrain.

What Is A Virtual Assistant?

As the name implies, a virtual assistant is someone who, for an hourly fee, helps with various aspects of business. There are three classifications to choose from:

- **Generalist:** A person who can complete rote tasks, such as data entry or forum posts.
- **Technical:** A person who can build websites, landing pages, handle product launches, etc.
- **Specialist:** A person who can handle management tasks and/ or specialized functions, such as accounting, human resources, training, etc.

Prices vary depending on skill. On the low end, overseas assistants can be hired for as little as $2.50 per hour. Native English speakers with high-qualifications or specialized skills can range from $20 to upwards of $100 per hour. Unlike a salaried employee, however, this represents the net cost for hiring. As with an independent contractor, substantial savings are realized given that state and federal taxes, bonuses, medical coverage, communication, and/or transportation expenses do not have to be paid for a virtual assistant.

And, while there is a known correlation between price and quality, one is often surprised at how good a $2.50/hour employee can actually be. With clear direction, they are more than capable of handling numerous tasks, especially data entry, networking (simply provide a form letter) and research.

When To Use A Virtual Assistant

Can *now* be any clearer? As business owners, it is certainly tempting to do everything. As discussed, for most, money is tight and paying even $100/week for a virtual assistant can seem overwhelming. After all, not only are you paying funds you could readily use yourself, you're also constantly managing someone else. Who needs it?

On the surface, both are legitimate concerns. However, the pain is temporary. It's important to realize that there will never be a perfect time to hire and train someone to complete tasks that have become second nature. Therefore, it's better to bite the bullet now. The sooner you call in the cavalry, the faster you can reap the benefits.

How To Best Leverage A Virtual Assistant

Hiring someone to execute monotonous and repetitive tasks is the perfect way to enter the world of virtual assistants. For first-time users, identifying exactly what to outsource and what to keep in-house, can be confusing. Pam recommends beginning your utilization of virtual assistants for the following activities:

- **Technology:** Business owners should concentrate on growth. Period. This requires focusing on front-end elements, such as ideation, management, marketing and promotion. Back-end details such as programming, bill paying, web design, and database management are ideal activities for a virtual assistant to handle. Each activity can be tied to specific performance milestones. This is an imperative element of the outsourcing equation.
- **Email Management:** As your business develops, your inbox will grow with it. Having a virtual assistant handle email can be a fantastic idea. Of course, there are numerous emails you'll need to handle personally. However, it's fairly simple

for a VA to sort through your inbox, answer frequently asked questions via template response messages you provide, delete spam, and categorize/flag emails that require your attention. After completion, you can then address what's necessary. According to a March 2011 Inc.com article by Courtney Rubin, which features findings from Fonality and web research firm Webtorials, the average employee spends more than half their day on "email and necessary, yet unproductive tasks, including routine communications and filtering incoming information and correspondence." Any further questions about where your time goes and why a VA might be a good idea?

- **Customer Service:** Though a bit labor intensive, training virtual assistants to handle customer service can be a worthwhile endeavor. As business blossoms, providing customers with the opportunity to have their questions answered at virtually any time becomes mandatory. This is clearly one area where you don't want to cut costs as poor customer service can have dramatic, negative implications. Creating scripts and providing responses to FAQs will be a necessary—but valuable—investment of time. That said, reasonably priced VA options are available. And, while you may hesitate to turn the reigns over to someone else, keep in mind that medium and large corporations have used telemarketing firms to handle inbound inquiries and customer service-related issues for decades. It's time for small business owners to join the ranks.

- **Bookkeeping:** Keeping the books current, paying invoices, reconciling statements, and billing customers is a tedious, yet essential requirement of every business. Further, there's maintaining records, submitting quarterly and annual reports, and filing state and federal income tax returns. None of this is fun…all of it is mandatory. These necessary evils are often outsourced to high-priced accountants or bookkeeping services to handle. Some of these activities should certainly be reviewed by a licensed professional, but a virtual assistant can handle much of the work involved for a fraction of the cost. This in turn, provides freedom for you to focus on more pressing concerns.

As your comfort level grows with allowing others to complete everyday activities, you can add further responsibilities. Eventually, this may include cultivating sales, human resources, and literally any element of operating a business. Step one is getting started. From there, anything is possible.

Hiring Your First Virtual Assistant

Before hiring your first virtual assistant, it is important to spell out your expectations. Too often people hire assistants and provide only vague guidance. Disappointment in performance becomes almost inevitable. The fact is, no one can read minds. Many entrepreneurs who complain the people they hire "just don't get it" are actually lazy communicators who don't bother to supply enough information and clear instructions.

> *Failing to clearly communicate your needs and expectations is a recipe for failure.*

The solution is clarity. Define exact tasks and specific outcomes. For example, if you'd like research to be conducted, make clear the information you need, the amount required, and the date by which the task must be completed. This is especially important when hiring an overseas VA. Cultural differences can lead to tasks being done as is customary in their country. This may not meet your standards. If you provide detailed instructions, you leave less to chance.

Once you decide to outsource a task, your next step is deciding what traits you want in an assistant. For instance, if you've chosen to outsource a repetitive task such as data entry, a less expensive assistant is a reasonable option. But if you require frequent communication and top-quality work for, say, a landing page with copy, hiring a more expensive, and preferably local, VA is a better choice. Pam highly recommends checking references from current and past clients, and engaging your first virtual assistant for 10 hours per month. This accomplishes two objectives:

- It allows you to determine if the virtual assistant is a good match for your needs.
- It allows you to review a sample of his or her work without spending a fortune.

A capable VA should be to accomplish a significant amount of work within this window. Most are trained to focus on completing specific tasks in expedited fashion and, unlike a typical U.S. office worker, are able to avoid distractions. It's also worth noting that paying hourly is not the only choice. Many assistants will agree to receive payment by the job, flat monthly fee, or on a flat fee plus commission basis (pay-for-performance). A defined salary encourages the assistant to work faster since compensation remains constant regardless of the number of hours invested. Whatever the arrangement, you'll likely find hiring an assistant useful and cost-effective. Your final step is to understand how to best ensure performance from your out-of-sight partner.

Managing Your Virtual Assistant

As with managing any assistant, attention to detail is required. Pam offers four proven strategies for making sure your VA is not only completing assigned tasks as directed, but also doing so in a timely manner:

- **Create a cloud-based workgroup.** Cloud systems allow employees across the world to access to the same worksheets, calendar, and timeline for project completion. Requiring your assistant to consistently update documents empowers you to stay current on work completed.

- **Set weekly meetings to talk face-to-face.** While communicating via email is acceptable, video conferencing is preferred. The medium allows you to forge a closer connection with your assistant and develop a relationship that moves beyond the impersonal nature of email. Too often people develop "overly strong fingers," saying things via a keyboard that they'd never say when looking you in the eye (even if it's via a camera lens). A minimum of two half-hour meetings should be held each week. Skype and Oovoo are two proven tools that make communicating face-to-face simple.

- **Set, and maintain, a specific schedule for project completion.** Holding to a specific schedule ensures that tasks are being completed in timely fashion and allows for monitoring of day-to-day activities. A virtual time clock provides an easy-to-use mechanism for tracking hours. While not a perfect system, it enables you to compare results versus hours paid. Virtual Time Clock at RedCort.com/timeclock is one of the best. Staying ahead of potential issues is an important component of working effectively with an assistant. Consistent updates allow you to keep an eye on progress.

- **Periodically throw a split-finger fastball.** Every now and again ask your assistant to complete a unique task—ideally one that requires additional information from you such as a hidden domain or password-protected account. After providing details, at some point in the near future, redirect the domain or change the password. If the assistant is really busting his rump on your behalf, he'll immediately contact you to say he can no longer gain access. If more than a day or two passes, odds are good he's not fully engaged with the project.

As with any employee, attention and encouragement are required in order to bring out a VA's very best. A virtual assistant must be treated as an integral part of your team. If you deal with your VA fairly and express appreciation for good work, that assistant can become a tremendously valuable resource. If not, don't be shocked if you suddenly stop receiving replies to your emails.

Virtual Value

Creating a thriving endeavor is a daunting task…there's no doubt about it. However, by remaining open to non-traditional opportunities, you provide yourself a reasonable chance to achieve an enviable level of success. Hiring a virtual assistant, though growing in popularity, has yet to be accepted by the mainstream. But, that's okay—effective leaders always play the game at a different speed and encourage others to catch-up.

So the next time you find yourself bogged down *yet again* with a repetitive task, ask yourself, "Could this be outsourced?" Quite often the answer will be yes. Ultimately, if you're willing to recognize there may be an easier way to accomplish your objectives, you greatly increase your chances of creating a profitable entity. Just remember, the world is not against you—it's simply waiting for you to ask for help.

⏻ TAKEAWAYS

Virtual Velocity

- No matter how good one might be at time management, there are only 24 hours in a day. Once an hour has been spent, it can never be reclaimed.
- An effective leader should concentrate on what they do best and enjoy most. Everything else can be outsourced, ignored, or completed by a capable employee.
- There are three types of virtual assistants: Generalist, Technical, and Expert.
- When getting started, Pam recommends utilizing virtual assistants for Technology, Email Management, Customer Service, and/or Bookkeeping.
- Before hiring your first virtual assistant, it is mandatory to define expectations.
- Engage your first virtual assistant for 10 hours per month to confirm compatibility.
- Leverage Pam's four proven strategies for making sure your VA is not only completing their assigned tasks, but also doing so in a timely manner.

EPILOGUE

This book has been a true labor of love and I learned more during this process than in almost 20 years of operating multiple businesses online. My hope is you found the information to be incredibly useful and have identified myriad ideas to immediately apply to your business.

As you know, however, technology changes in the blink of an eye and resting on your laurels for even a brief period can leave you in the dust of your competition forever playing catch-up. It is crucial to stay current on trends, tools, and strategies and take proactive measures to dominate your niche.

I encourage you to visit InternetProphets.com and join our mailing list. Each month, we offer *free* teleseminars, webinars, and poignant content from the world's leading Internet and mobile experts—valuable information you won't find anywhere else.

Internet Prophets will also host periodic live and Internet-based events, providing you with the unique opportunity to learn directly from industry trendsetters. For more information about upcoming events, please visit InternetProphets.com and join our VIP mailing list. Doing so will provide you with priority notification of upcoming conferences, the first opportunity to reserve seating—in-person or virtual—and access to exclusive material only available to *Internet Prophets* subscribers.

As a **BONUS** thank you for reading *Internet Prophets*, you can receive 50% off the ticket price for all of our live events. Discount details can be found at InternetProphets.com.

Hopefully, we'll have a chance to meet in person. Until then, live bold and *prophet*!

— **Steve**

FEATURED INTERNET PROPHETS

Janet Bray Attwood

Janet Bray Attwood is co-author of *The New York Times* bestseller *The Passion Test—The Effortless Path To Discovering Your Life Purpose*, and co-author of *From Sad to Glad: 7 Steps to Facing Change with Love and Power.*

Janet has given presentations to thousands of people at premier events such as Engage Today with the Dalai Lama and Sir Richard Branson, T. Harv Eker's Wealth and Wisdom Conference, Jack Canfield's Success Programs, Mark Victor Hansen and Robert Allen's Enlightened Millionaire conferences, and the International Festival of Yoga in Rishikesh India.

As co-founder of Enlightened Alliances, Janet, along with her business partner Chris Attwood, played a significant role in the success of T. Harv Ekers *Secrets of the Millionaire Mind* and Rhonda Byrne's *The Secret.*

Janet's alliance building skills and innovative approaches to marketing are legendary.

For more information, please visit http://tinyurl.com/janetipl.

Christopher (Kit) Codik

Christopher (Kit) Codik is the co-founder and CEO of Liquor.com, the premier digital media brand and platform focused on spirits and cocktail culture.

A Princeton graduate, veteran entrepreneur, and business development expert, Kit has served in numerous executive roles for companies such as Finacity (which he co-founded), Della.com, eVolution Global Partners, Infant Advantage, and The Gap.

For more information, please visit Liquor.com.

Dean DeLisle

Dean DeLisle is the founder of Forward Progress, a Chicago-based firm which provides integrated marketing solutions using his proven coaching and consulting methodology for driving business growth.

Dean is a social media expert committed to delivering the "lowest cost per lead," and "efficiently converting leads into sales." Dean helps companies establish a powerful online and media presence. His company has trained over 50,000 people in 35 countries.

For more information, please visit ForwardProgress.net.

Mike Filsaime

Mike Filsaime began his storied Internet marketing career in 2002. His advanced strategies are regarded among the world's best, and his revolutionary product Butterfly Marketing grossed over $1 million in five days when released as a home-study course.

As creator of numerous products, including PayDotCom.com and EvergreenBusinessSystem.com as well as serving as host of the famous Internet Marketers Cruise, Mike stands at the forefront of the online industry.

For more information, please visit http://tinyurl.com/filsaime.ipl

Pat Flynn

Pat is a professional blogger from San Diego, California.

Graduating in 2005 with a Bachelor's in Architecture, Pat was hired by a well-known architectural firm. In 2008, he was laid off. Though Pat didn't know it at the time, it was the best thing that could have happened.

Since then, thanks to blogging, being mentored, and a ton of hard work, Pat has been able to reinvent how he earns a living and, as a result, how he lives his life. Pat's website SmartPassiveIncome.com currently ranks in the top 5,500 of all sites worldwide, and he enjoys substantial passive income every day.

For more information, please visit SmartPassiveIncome.com.

Kathleen Gage

Kathleen Gage is a highly regarded Internet marketing advisor who works with socially conscious entrepreneurs, speakers, authors, and consultants ready to turn their knowledge into money-making products and services.

In addition to being a popular keynote speaker, Kathleen is a bestselling author. Her signature series *Street Smarts Marketing and Promotions*, is a favorite of thousands of clients around the globe.

For more information, please visit http://tinyurl.com/gageipl.

Steve Harrison

Steve Harrison is the co-owner of Bradley Communications Corp., a company dedicated to helping authors and experts gain publicity. Since 1986, Steve's firm has been responsible for booking over 10,000 authors and speakers on radio and television.

Steve's clients have appeared on *Oprah, The Today Show, Good Morning America*, FOX News, CNN, and many other top national programs and networks. Steve is the publisher of *Reporter Connection* and *Radio-Television Interview Report,* and the creator of the National Publicity Summit, which allows authors and experts to meet one-on-one with influential producers and journalists. Steve consistently seeks to provide high-value products and services that lead to massive exposure.

For more information, please visit GetMajorPress.com/NPS18 and GetMajorPress.com/QL15.

Dan Hollings

Dan Hollings is an online, offline, and mobile marketing strategist. Thousands of businesses worldwide have used Dan's proven blueprints and techniques, and/or attended his popular training programs.

Dan's client list includes talk show hosts, *New York Times* bestselling authors, universities, and businesses. Dan is probably best known for his role in the mega-successful Internet launch strategy for *The Secret* book and movie.

For more information, please visit http://tinyurl.com/hollings.

Pam Ivey

Pam Ivey is a principal of The Online Business Navigator, a coaching and consulting firm which partners with solopreneurs and small business owners to help them maximize their innate talents while building a lucrative business that's easy and fun to run.

Pam is also the owner of the Canadian Virtual Assistant Network (CVAN), co-founder of the REVA Institute and the Coaches, Authors, Speakers Professional Assistants Association (CASPAA), and founder of REA University, VA Training Academy and Webpreneur U.

In addition, Pam is the co-author of *The Business of Being Virtual*, and was a nominee for the 2010 and 2011 RBC Canadian Woman Entrepreneur of the Year.

A tireless crusader for leveraging the power of virtual assistants, she is known for her ingenuity, marketing skills, and business acumen.

For more information, please visit http://tinyurl.com/iveyipl.

Mike Koenigs

Mike Koenigs is a self-proclaimed geek, surfer, and didgeridoo player. He is best known, however, as the creator of Traffic Geyser, which distributes over one million videos per week.

Mike's other top products include Main Street Marketing Machines, which grossed over $9 million and Main Street Marketing Fusion, which grossed over $7 million. Mike also holds the world record for online direct to camera sales, earning over $3 million in a single day during an online webcast.

Mike has served as a producer, marketer, and consultant for numerous Fortune 500 companies, as well as for *New York Times* bestselling authors Deepak Chopra, Debbie Ford, and Tony Robbins.

For more information, please visit http:// tinyurl.com/koenigsipl.

John Kremer

John Kremer is an internationally renowned marketing expert. The strategies in his book *1001 Ways to Market Your Books* have been acknowledged by Jack Canfield and Mark Victor Hansen as helping launch the phenomenal success of their *Chicken Soup for the Soul* series.

A prolific author and Internet marketing strategist, John is a sought-after presenter, coach, and teacher.

For more information, please visit BookMarket.com.

Armand Morin

Armand Morin is an Internet marketing industry expert who has built a multimillion-dollar international company that does business in more than 100 countries. Armand has created some of the Internet marketing community's most popular software.

He is an international speaker and trainer, and has shared the stage with such celebrities as Donald Trump, Sir Richard Branson, and Jay Conrad Levinson. With his straight-to-the-point teaching style, Armand has the ability to transform a business in under 90 minutes.

Even though Armand is a self-proclaimed geek, he delivers his teachings to non-techies in plain English so customers can understand and learn from him. Armand sincerely believes that "Success Leaves Traces®", and has dedicated much of his online career to helping make it easy to market a business successfully online.

For more information, please visit http://tinyurl.com/morinipl.

Mike Muhney

Mike Muhney is the CEO and co-founder of VIPorbit, a software company focused on Mobile Contact Management solutions initially designed for the iPhone and iPad.

Perhaps best known as the co-founder and co-inventor of ACT!—the product that created the contact management category globally and has been used by more than 10 million customers since its release—he is also the co-author of *Who's in Your ORBIT? Beyond Facebook…Creating Relationships That Matter.*

For more information, please visit VIPorbit.com.

Marc Ostrofsky

Marc Ostrofsky is *The New York Times* bestselling author of *Get Rich Click! The Ultimate Guide to Making Money on the Internet*.

Marc is a professional speaker, consultant, venture capitalist, and serial entrepreneur. Known as a "technology wildcatter," his sale of the Business.com domain for $7.5 million landed him in *The Guinness Book of World Records* for the most expensive domain name ever sold.

Marc's Internet firms gross over $80 million annually. He has been quoted in over 1,000 media outlets, including ABC's *The View, 20/20*, and CNN. His firms have won numerous business awards, including the *Inc.* 500 and Ernst & Young's "Entrepreneur of the Year" Award.

For more information, please visit GetRichClick.com.

Christian Pankhurst

Christian Pankhurst is a coach, speaker, seminar leader, and author. He is a leading expert in a variety of fields including intimacy building, addiction recovery, emotional awareness, male sexuality, couple dynamics, conflict resolution, stress management, and heart-centered communication.

In October 2009, Christian won the Britain's Next Top Coach award, receiving 52% of the votes from 91 different countries. The prize was a media production package worth £100,000, which inspired his love for video and led to the creation of his industry-leading online interactive coaching experiences.

Today Christian is a sought-after teacher and he travels extensively sharing his huge heart, clarity, and wisdom.

For more information, please visit ChristianPankhurst.com/olsher.

David Riklan

David Riklan is the president and founder of Self Improvement Online, Inc., the leading provider of self-improvement and personal growth information on the Internet.

David's company was founded in 1998 and now maintains four websites on self-improvement and natural health:

- SelfGrowth.com
- SelfImprovementNewsletters.com
- SelfGrowthMarketing.com
- NaturalHealthWeb.com

SelfGrowth.com attracts over 1.2 million visitors per month, and David's six email newsletters reach over 950,000 weekly subscribers on the topics of self-improvement, natural health, personal growth, relationships, home business, sales skills, and brain improvement.

His first book, *Self Improvement: The Top 101 Experts Who Help Us Improve Our Lives*, has been praised by leading experts as the "encyclopedia of self-improvement."

For more information, please visit SelfGrowth.com.

Leslie Rohde

Leslie Rohde has been an Internet marketer since 1998. Today he continues to operate a number of profitable ecommerce websites, but is best known for his groundbreaking innovations in search marketing with the first explanation of link reputation in 2002, the invention of PageRank sculpting in 2003, and the release of the first search spider simulator in 2004.

Due to these and later innovations, Leslie has an international following, has mentored and trained thousands of successful entrepreneurs, and his teachings and tools are actively promoted by a who's who of search engine marketing experts.

For more information, please visit LeslieRohde.com.

Riel Roussopoulos

Riel Roussopoulos is a passionate technology pundit who speaks regularly on Internet-related topics.

With a keen focus on overall business objectives, Riel is able to apply technological solutions that help businesses streamline their operations, attract more prospects, engage more leads, and convert more sales.

His company, Scan 2, provides complete end-to-end mobile marketing and QR code solutions.

For more information, please visit http://tinyurl.com/scan2ipl.

Callan Rush

Callan Rush is the founder and CEO of Leader to Luminary Training, Inc. and a motivation and marketing maven.

Callan was the first woman to lead from the stage for the largest personal development company in the world, and is a top-notch trainer with over 15 years of experience in the speaking, training, and educational seminar industries.

An expert in sales and marketing and a genius in program design and facilitation, Callan delights audiences with her unique blend of humor, wisdom, honesty, and complete generosity of self and spirit.

For more information, please visit MagnetizeYourAudience.com/SteveOlsher.

Jennifer Sheahan

Jennifer Sheahan is president of FBAdsLab, and one of a growing number of people successfully balancing a thriving business with a busy family life.

Well-versed in the nuances of pay-per-click advertising, Jennifer has modified her strategies for use on Facebook's massive platform and helps others master its complexities. Originally from Chicago, Jennifer now lives with her family in Melbourne, Australia.

For more information, please visit http://tinyurl.com/fbadslab.

Yanik Silver

Yanik Silver is a serial Internet entrepreneur who has successfully bootstrapped eight different product and service ideas into million dollar companies.

Yanik is the author of the book *Moonlighting on the Internet*, and co-author or publisher of the bestselling marketing tools Instant Sales Letters and 34 Rules for Maverick Entrepreneurs. Yanik is also the founder of Maverick Business Adventures.

A highly sought-after speaker, Yanik is one of the leading voices for leveraging the power of the 'Net.

For more information, please visit MaverickBusinessAdventures.com.

Kristin Thompson

Kristin Thompson is the founder of SpeakServeGrow.com, and creator of the highly acclaimed programs Presentation Memory Power and Command Any Room.

Kristin left a successful media sales career to be a mom. She learned to leverage her expertise and create a full-time income working part–time, enjoying the elusive $10,000 month, week, and day.

Kristin now teaches others how to turn their message into a rush of new customers and cash. She helps her clients double their sales, double their closing ratio, launch their speaking careers, and live the life of their dreams.

For more information, please visit http://tinyurl.com/thompsonipl.

Jeff Vacek

Jeff Vacek is a former IT professional and author of *The New Masters of Online Marketing*.

Dubbed as "one of the major underground players" in Internet marketing, Jeff, along with his business partner Ken Preuss, host Blueprint to Financial Freedom, a life-altering seminar that teaches their proven formula for generating consistent online income.

For more information, please visit <u>InstantMarketingTips.com/Prophets</u>.

Christopher Van Buren

Christopher Van Buren is the CEO of LaunchMoxie, a service for authors, experts, trainers, and coaches that eliminates the stress of online launch campaigns and maximizes results. He's been mixing technology, publishing, and online marketing for over 20 years.

Christopher is a published author of 15 books, runs several popular websites in the health, beauty, and travel markets, and has worked for eight years as a literary agent. He's represented over 200 books in the areas of technology, personal development, body-mind-spirit, travel, and cooking.

For more information, please visit <u>http://tinyurl.com/vanburenipl</u>.

Jason Van Orden

Jason Van Orden and his business partner Jeremy Frandsen have an uncanny grasp for Internet marketing and online media strategy. Sought-after Internet media consultants, they teach others how to use the Internet to magnetically attract droves of new customers, boost sales, and turn fledgling businesses into market leaders.

Their show *Internet Business Mastery* has been the #1 podcast about Internet business and marketing since 2005, garnering over one million downloads and listeners from more than 100 countries.

Jason is also the author of *Promoting Your Podcast*, an Amazon.com bestseller.

For more information, please visit http://tinyurl.com/vanordenipl.

ABOUT THE AUTHOR

Steve Olsher is America's Reinvention Expert and has taught thousands how to **NICHETIZE!**™ by identifying and monetizing their *WHAT*— that is, the ONE thing they were born to do.

His singular approach for realizing permanent, positive change blends proprietary methods with ancient wisdom and revolutionary lessons from modern thought leaders and forms a proven system for ultimate achievement in business and life.

Steve is the author of USA Book News' Self-Help Book of the Year, *Journey To You: A Step-by-Step Guide to Becoming Who You Were Born to Be* and has appeared on ABC TV, FOX TV, CNBC.com, and more than 200 radio shows including national programs hosted by Lou Dobbs, Jim Bohannon, and Mancow Muller. He is also the co-star of the groundbreaking film *The Keeper of the Keys* with Jack Canfield, John Gray, and Marci Shimoff.

Steve is a successful entrepreneur who's applied his business acumen and communication skills to a wide range of endeavors. He has worked as a radio and nightclub DJ (Mr. Bold); owned his own alcohol-free nightclub at the age of 20 (The Funky Pickle!); launched the first wine and spirits store on CompuServe's Electronic Mall in 1993; launched one of the Internet's first fully-functional eCommerce websites in 1995 (LiquorbyWire.com); founded Bold Development, one of Chicago's largest boutique real estate development companies; co-founded San

Francisco-based Liquor.com; founded and runs The Reinvention Workshop; and founded and hosts Reinvention Radio.

Steve has earned the rank of brown belt in Brazilian Jiu-Jitsu, training under the late Carlson Gracie, Sr. All of his varied, real-world experiences have contributed to the concepts found in this book.

Steve lives in Chicago with his wife Lena and their three sons Bobby, Isaiah and Xavier—who remind him every day why his motto (and forearm tattoo) is "Let Love Rule." Meet him and receive free *NICHETIZE!*™ training at SteveOlsher.com.

CPSIA information can be obtained
at www.ICGtesting.com
Printed in the USA
FSOW01n0204230415
6631FS